Realist Perspectives on Management and Organisations
Edited by Stephen Ackroyd and Steve Fleetwood

Also published by Routledge

Routledge studies in critical realism
Edited by Margaret Archer, Roy Bhaskar, Andrew
Collier, Tony Lawson and Alan Norrie

1 Marxism and Realism
A Materialistic Application of Realism in the Social Sciences
Sean Creaven

2 Beyond Relativism
Raymond Boudon, Cognitive Rationality and Critical Realism
Cynthia Lins Hamlin

Explaining Society

Explaining Society is a clear, jargon-free introduction to the practice and theory of critical realism in the social sciences. This is the first ever book to comprehensively present critical realism and its methodological implications for social science.

The first part of the book introduces the reader to the basic components of the ontology and epistemology of critical realism, including the radical critique of empiricism and relativism; the theory of a stratified reality that consists of structures and mechanisms on different strata; the concepts of abstraction and causality; and the hermeneutic conditions of social science. The second part is a thorough examination of methodological guidelines for an explanatory social science based on critical realism. Main themes are concept formation; generalization; scientific inferences; models for explanatory social science; the relations between intensive and extensive research designs; and the relations between social science and practice.

This book will be immensely valuable for students and researchers in social science, sociology and philosophy in that it connects the philosophy of science, methodology, theory and empirical research. It provides an innovative picture of what society and social science are, and discusses various methods used to study and explain social phenomena.

Berth Danermark is Professor of Sociology in the Department of Social Science and Department of Caring Sciences, Örebro University, Sweden. His research interest is in the field of disability studies and he is one of the leaders of the Swedish Institute of Disability Research. **Mats Ekström** is Professor of Sociology in the Department of Communication and Media Studies, Örebro University, Sweden. He has published numerous books and articles on methodology, journalism, media and politics, and discourse analysis. **Liselotte Jakobsen** is Senior Researcher in Sociology and Gender Science at Karlstad University, Sweden. Her research centres on the analysis of everyday life, and she has published her results in *Life Mode, Gender and Risk*. **Jan Ch. Karlsson** is Professor of Sociology in the Department of Working Life Science, Karlstad University, Sweden. His publications are concerned with the concept of work, modern work organization, class and gender in everyday life, and critical realism and methodology in the social sciences.

Critical realism: interventions
Edited by Margaret Archer, Roy Bhaskar, Andrew Collier, Tony Lawson and Alan Norrie

Critical realism is one of the most influential new developments in the philosophy of science and in the social sciences, providing a powerful alternative to positivism and postmodernism. This series will explore the critical realist position in philosophy and across the social sciences.

Critical Realism
Essential readings
Edited by Margaret Archer, Roy Bhaskar, Andrew Collier, Tony Lawson and Alan Norrie

The Possibility of Naturalism 3rd edition
A Philosophical Critique of the Contemporary Human Sciences
Roy Bhaskar

Being and Worth
Andrew Collier

Quantum Theory and the Flight from Realism
Philosophical Responses to Quantum Mechanics
Christopher Norris

From East to West
Odyssey of a Soul
Roy Bhaskar

Realism and Racism
Concepts of Race in Sociological Research
Bob Carter

Rational Choice Theory
Resisting Colonisation
Edited by Margaret Archer and Jonathan Q. Tritter

Explaining Society
Critical Realism in the Social Sciences
Berth Danermark, Mats Ekström, Liselotte Jakobsen and Jan Ch. Karlsson

Critical Realism and Marxism
Edited by Andrew Brown, Steve Fleetwood and John Michael Roberts

Critical Realism in Economics
Edited by Steve Fleetwood

Explaining Society

Critical realism in the social sciences

**Berth Danermark,
Mats Ekström,
Liselotte Jakobsen
and Jan Ch. Karlsson**

London and New York

First published in Swedish language 1997
by Studentlitteratur, P.O. Box 141, SE-221 00, Lund, Sweden

Published in English language 2002
by Routledge
11 New Fetter Lane, London EC4P 4EE

Simultaneously published in the USA and Canada
by Routledge
29 West 35th Street, New York, NY 10001

Routledge is an imprint of the Taylor & Francis Group

© 2002 Berth Danermark, Mats Ekström, Liselotte Jakobsen, Jan Ch.
Karlsson and Studentlitteratur, Sweden, 1997

Typeset in Baskerville by Taylor & Francis Books Ltd
Printed and bound in Great Britain by The Cromwell Press, Trowbridge,
Wiltshire

British Library Cataloguing in Publication Data
A catalogue record for this book is available from the British Library

Library of Congress Cataloging in Publication Data
Explaining society: critical realism in the social sciences / Berth
Danermark ... [et al.].
p. cm. – (Critical realism – interventions series)
Includes bibliographical references and index.
1. Sociology – Methodology. 2. Social sciences – Methodology. 3. Critical
realism. I. Danermark, Berth. II. Critical realism – interventions.

HM585 .E85 2001
300~.1–dc21   2001019482

ISBN 0–415–22182–X (hbk)
ISBN 0–415–22183–8 (pbk)

Contents

Illustrations

Figures

Tables

Acknowledgements

The authors and publishers would like to thank the following for granting permission to reproduce material in this work: Daidalos for use of the table 'Deduction, induction and abduction – the formal structures of inference' (Table 3); Christine Roman for use of the figure 'Illustration of parts of the research process' (Figure 4); Open University Press for use of 'The positivistic circle' (Figure 5); Blackwell Publishers for use of 'Research map' (Figure 7); Verso Books for use of 'The transformational model of the connection between social structure and agency' (Figure 8); Cambridge University Press for use of 'Analytical cycles in the interplay between social structure and agency' (Figure 9).

Every effort has been made to contact copyright holders for their permission to reprint material in this book. The publishers would be grateful to hear from any copyright holder who is not here acknowledged and will undertake to rectify any errors or omissions in future editions of this book.

The authors are grateful to Lars Jämterud for his generous help with the translation.

1   Introduction

Our concern in this book is twofold. The main concern is to discuss some methodological implications of a critical realist approach to social science. However, this cannot be done without an introduction to the basic ideas in this approach. We therefore devote the first part of the book to introducing some of the most elementary elements of critical realism. But we would like to emphasize that in this book, although we take our point of departure from a specific philosophical perspective, we do not try to either develop or offer new interpretations of this perspective. What we try to do is to address some of its fundamental ontological and epistemological claims, and show how these by necessity have implications for investigating social phenomena.

Critical realism is not a homogeneous movement in social science. There are many different perspectives and developments. For instance, some authors discuss it from a philosophical angle, while others try to ground an analysis of current social phenomena in the approach. As will be obvious to the reader of this book, we try to avoid the current philosophical discussion revolving around critical realism; this is not within the scope of the book. So the more advanced philosophical reader will find nothing new regarding these issues. Instead the reader will find that we argue that the methodological implications of the basic ideas of critical realism make a difference in regard to issues such as generalization, scientific inferences, explanations, the role of theory, and so forth.

Our main arguments in this book can be summarized in the following way: critical realism helps us to develop and more sharply argue for, first, that science should have generalizing claims. Second, the explanation of social phenomena by revealing the causal mechanisms which produce them is the fundamental task of research. Third, in this explanatory endeavour abduction and retroduction are two very important tools. The latter is closely related to critical realism, and is a method for finding the prerequisites or the basic conditions for the existence of the phenomenon studied. Fourth, the role of theory is decisive for research. However, few would dispute this claim. In this book we emphasize that it is a claim which should be taken more seriously than is often the case, in the sense that theory should guide research and not be subordinate to specific methodological rules of how research should be conducted. Fifth, research involves a wide range of methodological tools, and we have to use many of these tools in a concrete research project. In other words, there is often a need to mix methods. However, we argue that this mix cannot be done without taking the ontological and epistemological dimensions into account. We call this perspective a 'critical methodological pluralism'. Sixth, there is a need to overrule the categorizing of methods in quantitative and qualitative terms. Instead we argue that in research we can apply either an intensive design or an extensive design (sometimes using both). Seventh, and last, the nature of society as an open system makes it impossible to make predictions as can be done in natural science. But, based on an analysis of causal mechanisms, it is possible to conduct a well-informed discussion about the potential consequences of mechanisms working in different settings. These seven claims are developed in Part II.

Since this book is an introduction to critical realism and an outline of its consequences for doing research in social science, our target readers are undergraduate or postgraduate students, but we also address researchers in the social sciences. Due to the introductory character of the book, we do not dwell upon the complexities that the questions addressed in the book will trigger. There are many issues we have to leave aside, and we refer to the substantial body of literature which has grown out of critical realism over the last decades. However, this does not mean that we are trying to avoid the complexity of the issues we discuss in the book. We hope that we have been able to achieve a balance between the task of simplifying and the need to do justice to the complexity of the social world and the work of investigating it.

Some unhappy dualisms

There is often an intense debate within social science about approaches and methodologies. Positivism is contrasted with hermeneutics, quantitative method with qualitative method, universalism with particularism – just to mention a few examples of such polarization. This dualistic perspective has to a large extent marked the debate. We might simplify it by calling it the 'either–or' approach. In this book we maintain that scientists are abandoning this approach in favour of one characterized by 'both–and' in many of the important issues that challenge social science today. We, too, shall advocate this viewpoint. It does not mean, however, that we see it as a simple mixture, drawing in an eclectic way upon various elements, without thoroughly reflecting upon the fundamental epistemological foundations on which they rest. We will instead present an attempt to create something new out of a number of different – sometimes irreconcilable – perspectives. This new perspective preserves the knowledge and insights from previous positions, but offers a distinct alternative.

In the methodology of social science the either–or perspective has been prevalent for a long time. This is particularly obvious in methodology disputes where there has been a clash between the proponents of the quantitative and the qualitative methodologies. However, it is perhaps in this area that a both–and perspective has gained most ground in recent years. Further, social science practice has often been characterized by either a theoretical or an empirical attitude.

Such division jeopardizes the sometimes difficult but necessary work on linking empirical research with theorizing. It may result in empirical descriptions lacking in theory. A third field in social science characterized by the either–or perspective is the gap between the philosophy of science and social science practice. During the latter half of the twentieth century, developments in the philosophy of science have provided insights which could noticeably influence social science research if they were allowed to have an impact. Unfortunately these insights have far too often lived their own lives, separated from social science. In this book we shall argue for a both–and perspective in these three areas, a both–and perspective building on a philosophy of science that demonstrates how a new standpoint, which draws partly on previous perspectives, is possible – that of critical realism.

Let us dwell briefly on these three dichotomies, since they are of vital importance for the theme of this book. We start with the last mentioned, that between a more philosophical discussion about the base of social science, metatheory, on the one hand, and social science research practice on the other. Metatheories deal with ontological and epistemological issues, that is, questions about the nature of reality and how we gain knowledge about it. The metatheoretical discussions that have influenced social science have to a large extent been about the role of theories in research practice. The question has been discussed ever since the social sciences were established as independent disciplines at the end of the nineteenth century. At that time a debate developed within the scientific world, where proponents of two basic viewpoints challenged each other: on the one hand those who advocated a social and human science which should – after the pattern of the natural sciences – try to ascertain general laws by applying and developing abstract theoretical models: a nomothetic approach. On the other hand, their critics who held that social science should describe empirical reality in all its complexity and diversity: an idiographic approach. If research is to be successful, such underlying assumptions must be highlighted and problematized. A consistent stance on these issues will improve the conditions for scientific progress. The history of science shows that theoretical and methodological development is closely connected to metatheoretical development.

Another and perhaps more serious division is evidenced by the fact that the theoretical part of scientific work is sometimes discussed separately from the more practical part, the empirical and methodological aspects. However, method and theory cannot be treated as two separate entities of social science. There are at least two reasons for this. First, theorizing is an inherent and absolutely vital part of the research method itself. Social scientific workmanship is basically about analysing and developing the theoretical language, about developing theoretical starting points for empirical analyses, and about linking, in various ways, theory with empirical research. Second, our objects of study are always theoretically defined. The theory-governed definition of the object determines which methods are suitable and which are unsuitable. These two unfortunate dichotomies should thus be surpassed, and we claim that the following tripartite regulatory relationship should prevail in social science: Ontology → Methodology → Social theories and practical research.

A third unfortunate division is that between quantitative and qualitative methods. A common reaction we meet in our tutoring is how surprised the students are about the lack of connection between what we teach about social science methods and how practical research work is often carried out. In many of the scientific theses that our students read, different methods are combined; the fruitfulness of such an approach is also more and more frequently emphasized in the literature. The arguments for it may vary, as we shall see later, but common to them all is an increasingly positive attitude towards use of a combination of quantitative and qualitative methods. However, it is still a common situation that education is conducted in a manner that does not allow students to learn what a fruitful combination, firmly established in a metatheoretical position, can mean. There is a certain discrepancy between, on the one hand, what is said to be interesting and fruitful, and how more and more research work is actually done in this way, and on the other hand, how the teaching itself is too often organized.

This book stems from the conviction that it is important, even crucial, for social science research systematically to reflect on these problems and allow the positions one takes to permeate the research practice. Metatheory should therefore be a central feature in all planning of social science study, and should not be introduced *ad hoc*, since there is otherwise a great risk of the work being conducted in an unsystematic and inconsequent manner. In other words there should always be a clear connection between the ontological and epistemological starting points and the practical research work. It is against this background that we have written this book on methodology – a book about the relation between metatheoretical questions and the methods of concrete research.

The emergence of critical realism

One of the reasons for the development of the perspective which we nowadays label critical realism is the critique of the positivist approach which has dominated many of the social sciences since the 1930s. Critical realism is increasingly being associated with the British philosopher Roy Bhaskar (b. 1944). This is very appropriate, as he is the scientist who has given critical realism a coherent philosophical language and has developed parts of the philosophic tradition. At the time he presented the first thorough description, *A Realist Theory of Science* (1978), he was strongly influenced by his teacher, Rom Harré, who in his book *The Principles of Scientific Thinking* (1970) had laid the foundations with his comprehensive criticism of positivism. Harré argued that there had to be underlying generative mechanisms were it to be at all possible to analyse the world in terms of cause and effect. The philosopher of science who at an early stage presented ideas very much like those that Bhaskar and others later advocated is Mario Bunge from Argentina (see e.g. Bunge 1979). Bunge argues, for instance,

(i)   that reality is arranged in levels;
(ii) that something qualitatively new can emerge from a lower level (emergence);
(iii) he points out the distinction between a real world and a conceptual one, between our descriptions of it and the factual reality; and
(iv) he criticizes empiricism for its reduction of reality to the observable.[1]

During the past fifteen years much has been written in the Anglo-Saxon world on critical realism. In this book we have primarily drawn on the works of Roy Bhaskar (e.g. 1978, 1989a, 1989b, 1993, 1994), Margaret S. Archer (1995), Andrew Collier (1994), Tony Lawson (1997), Peter Manicas (1987), William Outhwaite (1987) and Andrew Sayer (1992, 2000). Collier especially provides an exhaustive and partly critical presentation of (parts of) critical realism. There are also many examples of social scientists whose writings – without explicitly taking their starting point in critical realism – are partly consistent with its line of thinking: Anthony Giddens, Jürgen Habermas and Pierre Bourdieu are some of them.

So, what are the fundamental traits of critical realism? The question cannot be exhaustively answered here. We shall discuss the issue more thoroughly in the next two chapters. What we will do now is relate some of the fundamental notions in critical realism to other ways of understanding reality, thereby attempting to gain an insight on, first, what questions critical realism is trying to answer, and second, how these answers differ from other attempts to answer the same questions. We hope this will allow the 'distinctive character' of realism to become visible.

Within philosophy, critical realism involves a switch from epistemology to ontology, and within ontology a switch from events to mechanisms. This is the core of critical realism, and it indicates a metatheory with far-reaching consequences for scientific work. What Bhaskar wants to emphasize here is that the fundamental question in the philosophy of science is: 'what properties do societies and people possess that might make them possible objects for knowledge?' (1978: 13). This ontological question must be the starting point for a philosophy of reality – not the epistemological question of how knowledge is possible, which in the past has most often been the case. In short, the point of departure in critical realism is that the world is structured, differentiated, stratified and changing.

The conclusive part is also central. To switch from events to mechanisms means switching the attention to what produces the events – not just to the events themselves. Reality is here assumed to consist of several domains (to which we will return in Chapter 2). One of these is that of mechanisms. These mechanisms sometimes generate an event. When they are experienced they become an empirical fact. If we are to attain knowledge about underlying causal mechanisms we must focus on these mechanisms, not only on the empirically observable events.

Another key point in this context is that critical realism provides an answer to the serious dichotomy of realism versus anti-realism, where the fundamental question is whether there exists a world independently of human consciousness. The answer which critical realism provides us with is that there exists both an external world independently of human consciousness, and at the same time a dimension which includes our socially determined knowledge about reality.

Critical realism versus foundationalism and anti-foundationalism

In order better to understand the distinctive character of critical realism and how it can go from an either–or perspective to a significantly new both–and perspective in many of the fundamental ontological, epistemological and methodological issues, we shall briefly outline two currently dominating perspectives, foundationalism and anti-foundationalism.

Ever since the beginning of structured thought in what is now called science, philosophers have wrestled with the question of how we attain absolute knowledge. Shall we rely on sense experience or on mental ability to reflect? Both the formulations of the problem and the answers have varied. A central figure in this context is Descartes (1596–1650), who reacted strongly against what he saw as the great problem of society, the sceptical attitude. This attitude, deeply rooted in sixteenth-century humanism, only led to confusion and conflicts, according to Descartes. We must remember that Descartes' thinking was formed during a very turbulent period in Europe. There was enormous political, social and religious disorder. Among other things, he witnessed the terrible consequences of the Thirty Years War. Toulmin (1992) maintains that this had a decisive influence on Descartes, when he started his project of seeking a foundation on which to build a theory of knowledge which could be embraced by everybody. After Descartes had tried doubting everything, all that remained and was unquestionable was the insight that he was thinking and thus existed – *cogito ergo sum*. From this simple proposition Descartes then attempted to create a new epistemology. He started what became known as the epistemological project, and this project has ever since influenced the science of philosophy. The central question has been 'How can we gain absolute knowledge about reality?' The answers have varied. Descartes has been criticized from many different positions, and his attempt to build an epistemology on the original proposition, supplemented by the assumption of God's existence, is today regarded as belonging to the history of ideas. What has survived, however, is the notion that it is possible to gain universal knowledge through one universal language (that of mathematics) and one unitary method (that of physics).

Many new proposals have been discussed over the years. Among the more influential ones we may mention analytical philosophy and the logical positivists. They entered the stage as a group for the first time in 1930 in Oxford, and one of their proponents, Moritz Schlick, triumphantly declared that the future of philosophy would be very unlike its past, a past full of pitiful mistakes, futile contests and fruitless conflicts (Schlick 1930). However, within a few decades of this grand attempt to unify the sciences, the entire epistemological project was mistrusted. Many scholars even believe that there is a serious crisis for the very notion that knowledge can be firmly established in any principles whatsoever, principles which should make us absolutely sure about knowing what we think we know. We shall not expound the causes of this crisis here. Suffice it to say that there were both internal and external scientific causes. Examples of the former are the critiques of Kuhn and of Feyerabend, and an example of the latter is the political critique which argues that many of the human disasters of the twentieth century sprang from the leading ideas in modern society, in which the epistemological project played a large part. Many believed that both the death camps of World War II and Stalin's Gulags could be put down to this account.

We do not have to take a definite position here to the question whether this is really the case. What is important is to realize that the idea of a foundation for knowledge is in crisis. The characteristic feature of the epistemological dilemma is that an empirically grounded scientific theory with universal claims is opposed to relativism. Anti-realism, and hence an anti-foundationalism, has for many become the alternative to positivism and its naive realism.

Foundationalism

In the first decades of the twentieth century a perspective developed among a group of philosophers from Vienna. Inspired by philosophers like Bertrand Russell, his colleague George Edward Moore and the 'early' Ludwig Wittgenstein, they constituted a group of scientists known as the logical positivists. A central feature of this new movement was its empirical foundation. The struggle against the 'unscientific' metaphysics was given priority. It became important to clearly define what science was. Science should only be based on what is empirically experienced, in the terms of critical realism, within the empirical domain. The method was experimenting in the mode of the natural sciences. The logical language of symbols was the new unitary language. The Methodology with a capital M was Carl Hempel's 'deductive-nomological' or 'covering law' model, where all explanations are based on empirical correlation (this will be further elaborated in Chapter 5).

However, this fundamental confinement to what was regarded as science was soon undermined, and during the past few decades empiricism has either been abandoned or watered down to a trivial position. Manicas (1987: 243) lists eleven important events which have contributed to this, for example the abandonment of the verifiability of theory of meaning and the dissolution of the idea that scientific theories are axiomatic systems formulable in the extensional logic of *Principia Mathematica*; the dissolution of the analytic/synthetic distinction and the idea that verification/confirmation/falsification is rule-determined and grounded in theory-neutral 'basic sentences'. Further, the critique of Humean causality, i.e. the reduction of the concept of causality to universal correlation, has played a major role.

Outhwaite, Collins and many other social scientists also maintain that the most interesting contributions to social science have come from researchers who have not applied logical positivism, with its strict demarcation of what should be regarded as science. Durkheim was far away from this metatheory in his studies

of the importance of religion, for instance. Weber's analysis of the spirit of capitalism and the Protestant ethic, and Marx's analysis of capitalist society, as well
as Parsons' analysis of the age in which he lived, also differ completely from the
scientific ideal of logical positivism.

The Vienna Circle was an attempt to elucidate what was science and what
was not, at a time when this line of demarcation was not at all distinct. Thoughts
that we nowadays label New Age were flourishing.

Even if such an attempt was understandable and necessary, its philosophical
expression in terms of logical positivism is, according to the critical realist view,
impaired by a fundamental error: reality is reduced to what can be perceived by
our senses. Ontology is reduced to epistemology. In other words, in this perspective reality becomes 'flat'. Should one single feature of critical realism be
highlighted, it is the criticism of that reduction of reality which does not take
into account deep structure with its underlying mechanisms, and thus restricts
our understanding of the world.

Anti-foundationalism

Criticism of Western culture's trust in reason, and the perverted way in which it
was so often expressed, has been articulated by, among others, the pioneers of
the Frankfurt School, Theodor Adorno and Max Horkheimer. More and more
social scientists and philosophers (especially in France) expanded this critique
into a more fundamental criticism of modern science and technology. The entire
spectrum of social science classics – from Comte to Weber – was criticized for its
epistemology, for its universalism and its totalitarian claims, and for its trust in
rationalism. The notion that reality can be captured in theories objectively
reflecting reality was criticized from a Nietzsche-inspired 'perspectivism'. By
perspectivism Friedrich Nietzsche meant that we always observe something from
a certain perspective. He rejected the concept that we can observe anything from
a 'God's-eye perspective'. We cannot rise above ourselves and look at reality such
as it really is; all observation is made from a certain point. Our perspectives are
always situated some place. He also disputed that knowledge is free from individual interests. He emphasized that the act of knowing is rooted in our affective
constitution, or, in a better known phrase, that logos is entwined with eros (see
Owen 1995: 32–3). Possibly the most important point of perspectivism is, therefore, that knowledge is not separated from a concrete situation or from particular
individuals; that is to say, knowledge is local and contextual. Nietzsche even
claims that interests do not merely exist for us to take into consideration, but that
they are the very condition for and meaning of science. Hence there is no such
thing as universal scientific laws.

The scientist who has come more and more to the forefront of this type of
criticism is the American philosopher Richard Rorty. He writes that philosophers, after 2,500 years' assiduous pursuit, have still not been able to agree on
what universal laws govern reality – let alone how to confirm any such laws.
Since no such universalisms are known, he concludes that no foundation exists

on which to base the arguments (Rorty 1980). To Rorty, the search for such a foundation, an ahistorical universal base, is metaphysics. He is also very critical of the correspondence theory. To enable us to discuss how closely our knowledge corresponds to objective reality it is necessary to have a universal language – and this does not exist. Rorty's epistemological thesis is consequently that there are no transcendental perspectives from which we can assess our knowledge of phenomena and the phenomenon itself. To attempt to uncover universal laws is to invent theories. To Rorty, then, a concern with theories and theorizing in the traditional sense is a meaningless preoccupation. Theories are expected to represent something 'out there', and we have nothing to say about the 'out there'. He strongly denies the idea that some descriptions are closer to reality than others. Therefore, truth can only be truth to 'us', never to 'them'. Rorty's answer to the crisis of positivism, or in other words, the dead-end of the epistemological project, is thus a radical denial of our ability to say anything about reality in terms of what is true and what is false. We are prisoners of our own language, of our 'language games', says Rorty; he also believes that we do not have the tools to decide whether a Newtonian language game is better than an Aristotelian one, and writes 'a decision about which language game to play is arbitrary' (Rorty 1989: 6).[2] Thus Rorty replaces an epistemological fundamentalism with a contextual fundamentalism. The logical consequence of this position is an anti-theoretic relativism.

Instead, Rorty emphasizes that knowledge must be seen in relation to its usefulness for a given purpose, not to its veracity (which is an inadequate concept to him). The validity of some particular knowledge should not be tested theoretically, but normatively and practically. No description is superior to any other with respect to capturing the intrinsic nature of something. Descriptions are superior to one another only with respect to their ability to satisfy various human needs and purposes.

From a critical realist perspective, one might argue that he strongly disapproves of the notion that there exist underlying causal mechanisms of which we can obtain knowledge. Moreover, he also gives science too modest (and false) a role. Science is reduced to the discursive level – or in the terminology of critical realism, the transitive dimension. The intransitive dimension of science – the actual, existing reality – vanishes from sight. The insight that the transitive dimension is socially defined and that we cannot go beyond our language frames leads Rorty to a radical rejection of all possibilities of establishing how the transitive and intransitive dimensions are related to each other. In the example of Aristotle and Newton it is not a question of language, from the perspective of critical realism, or a 'jargon', as Rorty calls it, but a question of different theories about a reality independent of us. The clash between Aristotle and Newton is not a clash between jargons but between theories. Charles Taylor, for instance, finds that Rorty misinterprets shifts of paradigms to mean pragmatically determined shifts (in jargon), when in fact it is about a shift of rationally and scientifically tested theories. When a theory does not stand an empirical and theoretical test it is abandoned – but, as Kuhn has shown, not without agony. As a rule it is possible to say something about the quality of one theory or another. Critical realism claims that it is possible to gain knowledge of actually existing structures and generative mechanisms, albeit not in terms of a mirror image – in this respect Rorty is correct in his criticism of the naive realists – but certainly in terms of theories, which are more or less truthlike.

In the light of what we have said about the two perspectives above, we may sum up some of the fundamental traits of critical realism in the following words: 'critical realism claims to be able to combine and reconcile ontological realism, epistemological relativism and judgemental rationality' (Archer *et al.* 1998: xi). The first part of this statement implies that there exists a reality which is stratified, differentiated, structured and changing. The second part tells us that our knowledge about this reality is always fallible but, as the last characteristic suggests, there are some theoretical and methodological tools we can use in order to discriminate among theories regarding their ability to inform us about the external reality. In this book we shall attempt to show how this is possible without involving methaphysics, nor referring to a foundation of absolute knowledge.

Outline of the book

Critical realism could be said to contain two aspects – a general, philosophical aspect and a more social scientific aspect. On the whole that is how this book is structured, although the two parts blend together. In Part I, Chapters 2 and 3 are concerned with more general philosophy. Part II focuses on the role of theory and methodology and the role of science in society. The book concludes with a summary of critical realism. At the end of the book is a short glossary where we briefly explain some of the concepts addressed in the book, as they are often only explained when they are first introduced.

Chapter 2 deals with the most fundamental and decisive questions, on which we have to decide in research: the ontological question of how reality is constructed, and the epistemological question of our chances of acquiring knowledge about it. We argue that there is a reality, independent of our knowledge of it, but also that this reality is not something immediately fixed and empirically accessible. Furthermore, reality contains a dimension, not immediately observable, where we find the mechanisms which produce the empirically observable events. Our knowledge of reality is also something that is always conceptually mediated and thus more or less truth-like. Conceptualization thus stands out as being a central scientific activity, but as a consequence of the qualities of reality, it takes place under different premises within the social and natural sciences.

Chapter 3 further elaborates the significance of these epistemological starting points. We will discuss how scientific conceptualization is done and argue that the core of conceptualization is abstraction through structural analysis, which also permits a realist causal analysis. We will examine more closely the relation between the abstract and the concrete, and between structure and causality. On this basis, and in relation to the significance of scientific explanations, we discuss

the issue of causality and scientific laws. We describe the critical realist understanding of reality as constructed by different strata, where each stratum holds its
own emergent powers. For this reason we can establish that it is not only conceptualization that has different premises within different sciences. The scientists
perform their research within different strata of reality, implying more or less
open and closed systems, for the studies. This in turn affects what kind of knowledge that it is at all possible to obtain regarding different objects. It is primarily
the nature of the object under study which determines what research methods
one may use.

Chapter 4 deals with three central themes in social science methodology:
generality, scientific inference and models for scientific explanations. The
purpose of the chapter is to present guiding strategies for a research practice
based on critical realist ontology and epistemology. A common notion regarding
generalization – the empirical inductive generalization – is supplemented with a
generalization built on an understanding of what are called transfactual conditions and basic structures. Furthermore, the chapter deals with four modes of
inference, or thought operations: induction, deduction, abduction and retroduction. They are all seen as being complementary, but retroduction is the vital
contribution of critical realism to social scientific methodology. In the last part of
the chapter, a model is introduced to serve as a guide for an explanatory social
science.

Chapter 5 discusses the role of theories and of conceptualization in scientific
practice. What is a theory? What are the important considerations when
dealing with conceptualization? How should one relate theory to empirical
observations? These are questions to which we claim to provide some of the
answers in this chapter. In this context, we present two very influential
approaches within social science: grounded theory and middle-range theory.
These theories represent two radically different ways of relating theorizing to
empirical studies. Both the strengths and weaknesses of the theories are
discussed. We argue that both approaches are based on an ontology that tends
to reduce reality to the empirically observable. Theories about fundamental
structures are pushed into the background by superficial empirical categorizations and the testing of empirical hypotheses. In this chapter we emphasize that
the development and application of abstract theories about fundamental social
structures and mechanisms form an indispensable part of an explanatory social
science.

In Chapter 6, a model for critical methodological pluralism is introduced.
Here we argue that the traditional division between quantitative and qualitative
methods is often based on erroneous notions of the empirical and objective on
one side, and the idealistic and subjective nature of reality on the other. The
solution is not a simple merging of the two methods in a research process; one
must bear in mind that they are developed on the basis of two different metatheories. Based on Sayer (1994), we contend that a more fruitful division is that
between an intensive and an extensive approach, in a practical research process
which should contain both approaches.

In Chapter 7, we argue that a theoretically guided social science is indeed relevant for social practitioners. We are sceptical of the notion that social scientists are able to provide that which many people ask for, namely predictions concerning how society will develop, how people will act in a certain situation, etc. However, we do claim that knowledge about structures, mechanisms and tendencies is highly fruitful, although it requires a somewhat different balance in the collaboration between researchers and practitioners than is often the case today. Furthermore, we point to the fact that social scientific explanations in themselves often contain criticism of their research object – although this is not always expressed explicitly. At the same time, we warn against too easily drawing conclusions on these grounds.

Moreover, a central question for all social science is discussed – albeit very briefly – and this is the relationship between social structures and people's actions (agency). A critical realist perspective emphasizes that both social structures and agency exist in society, but that they are two completely separate phenomena with qualitatively different characteristics. Here structures are viewed as laying down conditions for people's lives, while agency provides the effective causes for what happens in society – only human beings can act.

To conclude, we would like to draw the reader's attention to the fact that we seldom explicitly discuss the increasingly extensive literature that can be characterized as post-empiricist. In some of these books critical realism is discussed, sometimes in agreement, sometimes not. Some authors express immanent criticism, others are sceptical of the fundamental assumptions we find in critical realism about the nature of reality. Neither do we deal with, at any great length, the vast flora of secondary literature discussing many of the questions we bring to the fore in this book. We have chosen mainly to build our presentation and argument on literature explicitly based on critical realism.

Part I

Introduction to critical realism

2   Science, reality and concepts

The introductory part of this book will deal with the basic requirements of science and research: philosophies of science – or metatheoretical conditions – and their methodological consequences. We will especially dwell upon similarities and differences between the natural and social sciences, and eventually arrive at a set of methodological principles for social science analyses. We shall start by discussing the most central issue in science: the relation between science, reality and concepts.

Let us first of all remark that the all-important significance of concepts and conceptualization in all production of knowledge is generally a downplayed field in books on methodology. It is hardly one of the aspects that researchers are requested to give particular consideration to in connection with a research project. Nevertheless every scientific (and everyday) attempt to understand and explain the world starts from our concepts of it. In every research project (as well as in many political, artistic and other endeavours) one important aspect of its aim is to influence – revise, modify, improve or revolutionize – our present concepts of reality. The radical implications of this may not always be apparent to the researcher herself; not even when, as is often the case, the outspoken aim of her research is to develop new concepts.

However, critical realism indicates that the relation between the real world and the concepts we form of it is the focus of the research process. In this chapter we shall describe why and how this is so. We start by looking at the relation between knowledge and the object of knowledge. This brings us to the statement that reality has an *objective existence* but that our knowledge of it is conceptually mediated: facts are theory-*dependent* but they are not theory-*determined*. This in turn means that all knowledge in fact is fallible and open to adjustment. But – not all knowledge by far is *equally* fallible.

We further find that science primarily is one *practical activity* among others, which causes us to take a closer look at the relationship between practice, meaning, concepts and language. The nature of this relationship is such that language, and consequently conceptualization, stands out as one of our most important instruments for scientific research.

We will then discuss similarities and dissimilarities between the objects of the natural and social sciences. Facts are conceptually mediated in natural as well as in social science, but there are still big differences. Whereas the objects of the natural science researcher are naturally produced but socially defined, the objects of the social scientist are both socially produced and socially defined. This means that the objects of natural science as such are uninterested in the acquiring of knowledge and the results of research; they are passive and unchangeable in relation to the definitions of the researcher. Social science, on the other hand, is carried out on hermeneutic premises. The objects of the social scientist include other people. They are interested and active participants in the search for knowledge where social science research is just one form among others. They make their own definitions and form their own concepts, which then constitute the social world studied and must be integrated with the concepts formed within social science. At the same time everyday concepts often compete with the scientists' concepts. Furthermore, the great capacity of people to change themselves in connection with new experiences and new knowledge generates continual changes in the studied social phenomena themselves. All this taken together means that conceptualization in social science takes place under very different conditions than conceptualization in natural science.

In this chapter we shall develop this perspective and see what it entails for the choice of research design and research methods in a wider sense. In accordance with what we have just said above, our notion is that if there are any differences between scientific knowledge and other kinds of knowledge, one decisive difference is that science not only reflects by means of its concepts, that is, employs the concepts as if their meanings were given, but it also consciously and systematically reflects upon them (Sayer 1992: 24). Conceptualization is a crucial activity in social science, and we will argue that it should take its starting point in a critical realist ontology and epistemology.

Knowledge and objects of knowledge

What exactly is 'knowledge'? What makes certain kinds of knowledge scientific compared to other kinds of knowledge? The predominant understanding of the concept of 'science' has for a long time been the notion of an activity steadily accumulating general and objective knowledge of its object, that is existence and reality, by means of systematic and neutral empirical observations. As an overall strategy this procedure has been relatively unproblematic. The 'art' of science involves developing and acquiring more and more sophisticated techniques of observation, as it is the ingenuity and stringency of these techniques that guarantee the specific 'scientific quality', the *truth* of the research results. This scientific paradigm, which in its pure form may be called an empiricist/objectivist ideal, is still very influential in practical research activity; it also corresponds rather well with our everyday understanding of how we attain knowledge and 'how we can know'.

Criticism of this ideal of science, this 'naive objectivism', has called attention in particular to the complex relation between language/concepts and reality. It has shown in a convincing way, that there exists a mutual dependence between the scientific concepts – the theories – and the 'neutral' empirical 'facts' assumed to verify or falsify the theories (in the same way as there is a mutual dependence between everyday concepts and the factual knowledge we try to obtain from our environment). As a matter of fact, all knowledge is necessarily socially determined conceptual constructions. Facts – the empirical observations, scientific data – are seldom objective or neutral in any definite sense. To be at all understandable they always comprise earlier, more or less hidden, everyday and/or scientific conceptualizations. That is, facts are theory-dependent or theory-laden (Popper 1963; Kuhn 1970).

These kinds of claim, which it has not been possible to refute, have in their turn stood out as death-blows to all expectations of an objective and true knowledge. If reality cannot be understood by anything but constantly varying forms of pre-understandings, if our different ways of seeing irretrievably determine *what* it is we see, what then remains of the scientific project? How do we choose between competing explanations and decide which one is 'the best' or 'the truest'? The criticism of objectivism has led to a swinging of the pendulum in the opposite direction, and to an increasing emergence of various forms of idealistic and/or cognitive relativist standpoints. In their more radical forms they seem to imply that we cannot uphold the existence of any reality at all outside language and its constant change of meaning, or at least that all knowledge is infinitely relative and so it is totally meaningless to search for general knowledge and general truth (see e.g. Rorty 1980). This also implies that, strictly speaking, we cannot compare and evaluate knowledge other than perhaps in very limited contexts.

It has been justly remarked that this standpoint is a self-contradiction ('the inward collapse of relativism'). If no general truths can exist, then the relativist statements cannot make such claims either. The researchers who adopt this position, what do they think they are doing when they carry out their research? If we were to take this kind of relativism seriously, the consequence would be that we would have to regard all scientific argumentation as completely meaningless.

Yet the criticism of 'naive objectivism' need not lead to such conclusions. Critical realism bears this criticism in mind at the same time as it tries to maintain the positive claims to a useful and liberating knowledge, which was the basic motivation for the Enlightenment project and for modern science. Realism maintains that reality *exists* independently of our knowledge of it. And even if this knowledge is always fallible, yet all knowledge is not equally fallible. It is true that facts are theory-dependent, but this is not to say that they are theory-determined.

What this means will be further discussed in the following chapters. It is obvious, however, that the crucial question for social science methodology concerns the relationship between science and reality.

What must reality be like to make the existence of science possible?

What then is the relationship between science and reality, between science and its objects? Even a cursory reflection on this relationship seems to presuppose that we are able to know at least something about reality. Assumptions of the intrinsic nature of reality, of 'what exists' and of the 'essence of things', are ontological questions and must necessarily form the foundation for every other assumption we make. Assumptions of the nature of knowledge, of how we acquire knowledge and of how we 'can know that we know', are epistemological questions, which tend to be intertwined with the ontological questions in a complicated manner. If we assume that our concepts of reality are 'theory-laden', that our understanding is filtered through our own and other people's previous and varied experiences and prejudgings, where are we to find a reasonably 'fixed point' from where to depart when we want to establish the nature of reality? How can we maintain that there is a reality beyond and independent of our concepts about it? No one can step out of their conceptual world and see if reality 'really exists' or what it 'essentially is', free of conceptual prejudging. And even if we could, we would not understand very much.

In everyday practice, the most obvious proof of the autonomous existence of reality is the fact that we can make mistakes. To attempt to 'define one's own reality' and live accordingly may turn out to be very impractical. As to the physical world, this is quickly realized, whether we wish to be able to fly, walk on water or through closed doors. But the conditions are the same regarding the social reality. Anyone who, for example, wants to lead a 'free life' without hampering social norms, constraints and duties, will soon find themselves in counterproductive circumstances, perhaps in jail. Most people have also experienced that even the best of intentions may have unforeseen and even very undesirable consequences. Reality simply does not react in accordance with our expectations, but on the contrary with considerable autonomy. How are we to understand such experiences?

The critical realist solution to the problem of the relationship between science and reality is to take one's starting point in practice, something we really know exists – namely science. 'Science' is once again understood as practical research work rather than scientific knowledge, which is the result of the practical research work. The fundamental ontological question will then be (Bhaskar 1978): *What must reality be like to make the existence of science possible?* This question can then be broken down into sub-questions about what actually is characteristic of this activity, science in practice: What do researchers actually do? What are they looking for? What properties of reality are prerequisite to enable this practice to serve any purpose at all?

If we begin with the question of what researchers actually do when they research, it turns out that *the experiment* stands out as the central procedure in practical research work in general. Let us therefore begin by taking a closer look at an example of an experiment. In the following section we will deal mostly with natural science, since the most fundamental conditions for science are the same for natural and social sciences. Further, it is essential to understand these common starting points in order to understand in what way, and why, there are at the same time distinct differences between natural science and social science.

An experiment

After seventeen years, Otto Loewi dreamt the solution and scratched it down on a piece of paper on his bedside table. But in the morning the note turned out to be unreadable. Next night the dream came back, but now Loewi woke up and immediately went down to his laboratory and carried out the experiment, the outcome of which would later render him a Nobel prize.

Before Loewi made his experiment it was generally believed that nerve control of body functions worked directly in the form of electric impulses. But this explanation was problematic, since one and the same impulse had a different effect on different organs. Certain drugs were also known to have the same effects. In a discussion with a friend, Loewi came to think that these substances were perhaps also to be found in the nerve terminals; in that case the electric impulse would start a chemical reaction, which would in turn affect the muscle. However, he could not think of any way to arrange an experiment and put the idea to the test.

This was in 1903, and seventeen years later, as mentioned above, he dreamt the solution. Once he had reached his laboratory in the middle of the night, he took two frogs' hearts, one with all the nerves intact and the other without any nerves. He put the first heart into a salt solution and stimulated the vagus nerve, which has a retarding effect, and the number of heartbeats was reduced. If his hypothesis was correct, the chemical substance should now have been released and be present in the solution, which should be able to affect the other heart, even if this heart had no nerves at all. It is easy to imagine the excitement Loewi felt applying the salt solution to the second heart. Would its heartbeats be reduced or not? It is also easy to imagine the joy of discovery that Loewi felt when its pace was reduced, as if the vagus nerve it no longer possessed had been stimulated. He could now conclude that the chemical substance operated through the muscle. He then varied the experiment by stimulating, in a new salt solution, the nerve that has an accelerating effect. When he put down the heart without nerves in this salt solution its pace, too, increased. A seventeen-year-old idea had at last reached the experimental stage and had resulted in a great scientific discovery.

In this way Loewi made it clear that the active mechanism is chemical substances started by a nerve impulse, which then works on the muscle. The events preceding Loewi's experiment are often referred to in discussions about the role of the unconscious in the creative process (see e.g. Koestler 1975: 204ff, from where this description is taken and simplified). However, our interest now is the experiment itself. What did Loewi actually do? And why was it so difficult to find out how to perform the experiment?

The three domains of reality

The experiment can be described as an active intervention in reality. By manipulating a certain series of events Loewi intervened in – got himself mixed up in – 'the course of nature'. The purpose of the experiment was to 'discover', 'detect', 'reveal', 'search out', etc., something about reality that was not yet known, something that could not be observed without great effort. The need to perform experiments demonstrates that it is impossible just to register passively and record how things happen in reality. Manipulation of the spontaneous events is necessary. And given this systematic manipulation, reality reacts and supplies researchers with results (provided that the experiment, as in Loewi's case, was performed skilfully enough – but then it took him seventeen years to find out how to accomplish it). However, the point is that researchers have to *produce their results*, and the results they get build up scientific theories and are included in our total conceptualization of reality.

From the existence of this scientific practice we can conclude that, first, there exists a reality independent of our concepts and knowledge of it. Second, this reality and the way it behaves are in important respects not accessible to immediate observation. If 'everything that is' were in the open, if reality were transparent, there would be no need for science; indeed no science would exist other than as mere data collection. Consequently, one property of reality is that it is not transparent. It has powers and mechanisms which we cannot observe but which we can experience *indirectly* by their ability to cause – to make things happen in the world.

We would like to emphasize that in this assumption there is no particularly remarkable or complicated meaning hidden. The insight that reality possesses a deep dimension, which is not directly observable, is not only a prerequisite for the existence of science (whether it explicitly acknowledges it or not); it is also a pretty self-evident part of everyday knowledge. We come across this insight in the form of common expressions such as 'something is going on below the surface' or the remark 'there must be something else behind this', when we are analysing everyday events of various kinds. However, it is actually this insight that makes up the very foundation of critical realism's philosophy of science. The rest of this book will deal with the methodological consequences of taking this understanding of reality seriously.

Bhaskar (1978: 56) provides us with the following 'ontological map'. A distinction can be made between three ontological domains: the empirical, the actual and the real. The empirical domain consists of what we experience, directly or indirectly. It is separated from the actual domain where events happen whether we experience them or not. What happens in the world is not the same as that which is observed. But this domain is in its turn separated from the real domain. In this domain there is also that which can produce events in the world, that which metaphorically can be called mechanisms.

The empirical domain, which in scientific contexts contains our 'data' or 'facts', is always theory-impregnated or theory-laden. All our data arise in connection with some theory, and thus we do not experience the events in any direct way – which is what the empiricist research tradition claims. Data are always mediated by our theoretical conceptions. The rather common expression 'the empirical world' is thus fundamentally misleading. It represents what Bhaskar (1978: 36) calls 'the epistemic fallacy', because it reduces the three domains to a single one; it reduces what is to what we can know about it. Scientific work is instead to *investigate and identify relationships and non-relationships, respectively, between what we experience, what actually happens, and the underlying mechanisms that produce the events in the world.*

This was what Loewi did. His experiment was based upon the notion that reality is *differentiated*: it consists of objects with qualitatively different powers and mechanisms, which can far from always be observed just like that. (We shall later see that reality is also 'structured' and 'stratified'.) Loewi was looking for the mechanism behind the nerves' control of bodily functions, but this was impossible to experience within the domain of spontaneous events, that is, by simply observing the various ways in which bodies function. He had to produce a special pattern of events (we will discuss such patterns of events in terms of 'closed systems') in order to experience the mechanism in a way other than had been done before. And this was not because the mechanism had changed; on the contrary, it was an absolute condition for the whole thing to work out, that the mechanism was there and functioned independent of all experiments. The chemical substance was there and was active even before anyone knew that it existed, even when it was still believed that the electric impulse acted directly on the muscle.

Loewi finally discovered what a pattern of events would look like if the mechanism he was looking for really existed – namely that in addition, the second frog's heartbeats would be reduced in the first experiment and increased in the second one. From this we can see that the object is separated from the pattern of events. If events had been the object of science – for instance, that something occurs with some degree of regularity – Loewi would not have had to stand there in the middle of the night.

From the analysis of experimental activity in (natural) science we can consequently say that its objects exist independently of human activity; that they are separated from the pattern of events arising; and that experiences are separated from events. Otherwise experiments would have been unnecessary. Now they are not: 'an experiment is necessary precisely to the extent that the pattern of events forthcoming under experimental conditions would not be forthcoming without it' (Bhaskar 1978: 33).

The observation of the third domain of reality, the deep dimension where generative mechanisms are to be found, is thus what distinguishes critical realism from other forms of realism (that is to say philosophical positions holding that things have an objective existence). As we shall see, this is true of social reality as well as of nature.

The transitive and intransitive objects of science

We have now argued that science as such is a proof of the existence and nature of reality. However, this argument might be seriously opposed, since scientists themselves disagree on these issues. Realist science standpoints have one characteristic in common: they claim that reality and things have an objective existence; but they disagree on the nature of reality and therefore also on how to attain knowledge of reality. In opposition to empiricist notions, critical realism maintains, as we have seen, that a scientific method necessarily involves observation of events, but due to the deep dimension of reality it cannot be reduced to observation of phenomena at the empirical level. To acquire usable knowledge it is essential that we know the mechanisms that produce the empirical events, and these are seldom directly visible. The knowledge we do attain is, however, always fallible, and its usefulness varies under different conditions. (We will later discuss the important question of how to validate and evaluate scientific results.)

Relativist and idealist views, on the other hand, in different ways doubt that there can be any more or less valid knowledge. Sometimes there is also a rejection of the idea that an objective reality should at all exist. In pure idealist philosophy, for instance in some parts of so-called discourse theory, it sometimes seems as if there is no reality outside language and conceptions. Or, as Hindess and Hirst (1977: 20) point out: 'Objects of discourse do not exist. The entities discourse refers to are constituted in it and by it'. Flax (1990: 32) formulates this postmodern position: 'In fact Man is a social, historical, or linguistic artifact. ... Man is forever caught in the web of fictive meaning, in chains of signification, in which the subject is merely another position in language.'

But at the same time, as we have earlier pointed out, such statements also claim to be true, to make statements about some sort of objective condition. Thus they do not only oppose realist conceptions of the world; they also constitute paradoxes in themselves.

How do we handle such situations in science? It is possible to do this within the perspective offered by critical realism, by avoiding the epistemic fallacy. If we refrain from reducing questions about what is to questions about how we can know, it follows that science deals with something that is independent of science itself, and that science is fallible at any time. This means that we pay attention to the fact that science has two dimensions: an *intransitive* and a *transitive* dimension.

Loewi produced a result in his experiment; he interfered with and changed a natural course of events. But he did not produce the mechanism that he discovered through the experiment. Even if he had never had this dream or carried out his experiment – or if it had been an unsatisfactory experiment or he had drawn the wrong conclusions – the mechanism would still have been there, independently of Loewi or any other human being. This dimension of reality that Loewi studied when he discovered the mechanism is the *intransitive* object of science. There is no direct relation between science and its intransitive object; an ontological gap is always present.

Science itself, or the scientific results, always consists of a set of theories of this independent reality. These theories – not reality – constitute the 'raw material' (Collier 1994: 51) that science uses in the practical work, and science continually tries to transform the theories into a deeper knowledge of reality.[1] Theories thus are the *transitive* objects of science; they constitute the dimension that indirectly connects science with reality. But all knowledge is fallible; science may be wrong at any moment when it makes statements of its object, and so theories in science can only be regarded as the best truth about reality we have for the moment. It is no ultimate knowledge. New scientific studies may show that the knowledge was false. Theories can always be surpassed by new theories.

Scientific activity is in this way a working process in the same sense as there are other working processes. It has the characteristics of production, that is transformation of raw material (existing theories) into temporarily readymade products (new but still fallible theories). The means of production are, among other things, specialist knowledge. Loewi, in our example, did not carry out his experiment in an intellectual vacuum. He had many years of study and professional experience behind him. He had acquainted himself with the work of other scientists, he had acquired a conceptual frame of reasoning and he had performed an endless number of experiments before – he had a large fund of previous scientific knowledge to draw on. As is often the case, special equipment was also needed. In Loewi's case it was a laboratory. Science, therefore, is practical work where scientific results always build on previous science, which can be surpassed by continued scientific research, and so on, all the time with the aim of deepening knowledge – the transitive object – about reality – the intransitive object of science.

Bhaskar calls the existence of these two dimensions the 'central paradox of science'. He means that it implies

> that men in their social activity produce knowledge which is a social product much like any other, which is no more independent of its production and the men who produce it than motor cars, armchairs or books, which has its own craftsmen, technicians, publicists, standards and skills and which is no less subject to change than any other commodity. This is one side of 'knowledge'. The other is that knowledge is 'of' things which are not produced by men at all: the specific gravity of mercury, the process of electrolysis, the mechanism of light propagation. None of these 'objects of knowledge' depend upon human activity. If men ceased to exist sound would continue to travel and heavy bodies fall to the earth in exactly the same way, though ex hypothesi there would be no-one to know it.
>
> (Bhaskar 1978: 21)

The above quotation refers to the natural sciences, and there are essential differences between the objects of natural and social science – social phenomena, for example, cannot exist without some form of human activity. But as we shall see, the principle of the reasoning is applicable to social science problems also. The main point is that the transitive objects of science, the theories about reality, like any other knowledge are social products, whose formation and contents are under the influence of many different social mechanisms. Beside the state of the art within science, which on all occasions must be the raw material of research, science is also produced by mechanisms outside the knowledge-seeking process as such, in the economical, political and cultural conditions, etc., of our time. Studies of the history of science and the sociology of knowledge have demonstrated this beyond all doubt (e.g. Kuhn 1970; Feyerabend 1993).

Such insight tends to bring about cognitive relativism. However, this does not follow by necessity. What follows is only that we understand a little more how scientific theories can take such different positions on the reality they comment on. They may even adopt the position that no science or knowledge of reality is possible. Or that any knowledge is equally valid – or invalid – as any other. Or, for that matter, that reality only exists in and through our concepts of it. None of this can change the fact that theories deal with *something* that is independent of the theories themselves. It seems reasonable, in all these cases, to call this something 'reality' or 'the world' – the intransitive object of science. Collier has this formulation:

> Rival scientific theories necessarily have different transitive objects, or they would not be different; but they are not about different worlds – otherwise how could they be rivals? They would not be scientific theories at all if they were not aimed at deepening our knowledge of the intransitive object of science.
>
> (Collier 1994: 51)

Science as practice

It is common both within and without scientific circles to consider science as something that has to do primarily with observation and/or contemplation. But as we stated earlier, science – and the acquiring of knowledge on the whole – is neither mere observation nor mere contemplation in relation to reality. Sayer (1992: 13) denotes such understanding of science 'the intellectualist fallacy' or 'prejudice'. Science is primarily a concrete, practical, social activity among others, aiming in one way or other at influencing – transforming, improving, modifying, manipulating – the reality of which it is itself a part. This goes for the world that natural scientists study as well as for human society.

The existence of scientific experiments, but also everyday experience, continually indicates that the connection between the real world and our knowledge of it is fundamentally a question of *practical relevance*. When the world in different ways makes our wishes, ambitions or expectations come to naught, we feel that we need to know something else or more about how the world functions, more about the reasons why our expectations are not fulfilled or why our actions have unwanted consequences. If we understood this better, we could try to take measures in order to be more successful. Knowledge, including that of science, can be seen as one instrument among others to help us deal with reality in a practical way.

From this follows that the validity of the knowledge/concepts we have is primarily a question of how well the knowledge functions in practice. And since all knowledge, from what we know, is fallible and open to correction – we cannot claim to be able to present an absolute truth – it will also become clear that all knowledge is nevertheless not equally fallible. As long as we assume that reality exists independently of our knowledge of it, it follows that knowledge is always more or less like the truth of this reality.

It is very important to have a clear understanding of what the above statement means. Especially since we are constantly observing how the practical relevance of knowledge varies in different contexts. What is usable knowledge to an MD of a multinational company is probably of very little use to a farmer in Ethiopia. And a Swedish woman with small children and a part-time job in health care would probably be better helped by some other knowledge, too. Hence a criterion of the practical usefulness of knowledge must not be confused with a general criterion of truth. The practical relation between knowledge and reality must not be interpreted to mean that knowledge is true as soon as it is useful to someone (the position known as instrumentalism). That a specific knowledge is useful in particular contexts tells us nothing about what is actually possible or impossible, either in these contexts or in others. This is still totally dependent on properties, powers and mechanisms in reality, which exists and is what it is, independently of what we think we know about it for the moment. The usefulness of knowledge will therefore always be a question of how well our concepts capture the generative mechanisms in the objects we study. 'Knowledge is useful where it is "practically-adequate" to the world' (Sayer 1992: 70).

Critical realism's emphasis on the relation between knowledge and practical relevance has therefore nothing to do with either cognitive relativism or instrumentalism (but it pays attention to important observations which have been made from these two perspectives). On the contrary, the insight that the practical usefulness of knowledge varies, is in agreement with the more general assumption about the objective existence and nature of reality. The practical relevance varies in this way, because characteristic of reality is that it is *differentiated, structured and stratified* – it is composed of many different levels and forms of practice. We have already dealt with the differentiation of reality when we described the three ontological domains. This means that reality consists of objects with powers and mechanisms, differing in quality, which are often not directly observable within the empirical domain. What it means more precisely that reality is structured and stratified will be discussed at greater length in the next chapter. But we will briefly mention something here: among other things it comprises the obvious fact that practical activities of people in the natural and material world are of various kinds. The matter we handle as such, like the purpose of the activity, requires many different kinds of knowledge. What we need to know if we are to build a house, for instance, differs from the knowledge we need if we are to perform a laboratory experiment, lay out a spice garden, take care of a baby or write a scientific paper – provided, of course, that we want to be reasonably successful in our business.

It is, however, not only properties in the natural world that make the relevance of knowledge varied. Just as important is the nature of the social world. When individuals intervene or in other ways relate to their environment, they do it as members of a social world – a society. Societies are structures of social relations where people occupy different positions, not least concerning access to the resources for interaction with their surroundings. (Relations of power and dominance seem to be constitutive qualities in most societies we know of.) Socially caused differences in starting positions with respect to resources and power, as well as cultural, ideological and other differences, make interests, problems and needs, among other things the needs of knowledge, very divergent. In many cases people will find themselves in conflict, so that one can figuratively, and sometimes even literally, speak of one man's loss being another man's gain. To this may be added that reality is changing in time as well as space. New social conditions and circumstances may make some kinds of knowledge irrelevant and/or require other kinds.

While it is evident that reality exists and is what it is, independently of our knowledge of it, it is also evident that the kind of knowledge that is produced depends on what problems we have and what questions we ask in relation to the world around us. And this is to a large extent an issue of social positions and specific experiences drawing up borders, which cannot easily be crossed. In science, too, and despite our efforts, we tend to see only some aspects of reality and are blind to others. We should therefore not think that just any person – and this includes scientists – can produce just any knowledge at just any time and under just any conditions – it is not possible to see just anything from just any viewpoint. Among other things, the emergence of feminist theory has made this very obvious (see e.g. Smith 1987).

These circumstances should be carefully considered. Without any doubt it is increased consciousness about such circumstances that has, among other things, given a boost to cognitive relativist standpoints in social science. But it would be a strange reaction if increased insight and knowledge of the nature of reality should lead to the conclusion that science is impossible. And that is not necessary. The adequate conclusion must be that these insights should form the foundation for research practice. However, the consequence is that many other questions arise instead, with regard to some well-established and highly regarded criteria of scientific status, because they have been formulated in other contexts, with another understanding of reality. This, for instance, is the case regarding the prevalent significance of the central demand that scientific knowledge should enable generalizations. Such criteria must therefore be reconsidered. We shall later discuss these problems exhaustively.

Now we shall dwell a little more on the meaning of science as a practice. And let us establish the fact that observation of, reflection on and contemplation of the phenomena and problems of existence are essential features in scientific practice. But since science basically is a practical social activity among others, science, too, is subject to the conditions of social practice in general. Regarding method, one condition, then, is of primary importance: questions of method are primarily practical questions (Sayer 1992: 3–4)! The methods must suit the object of investigation as well as the purpose of it. Method, object and purpose must be considered simultaneously and in relation to each other, and must also inform all other choices in the set-up of the investigation, including techniques of data collection and analysis. There is no specific knowledge or sophisticated technique that can guarantee by itself that results will be reliable, valid and relevant, if practical logic in the relations between object, purpose and method is not taken into consideration. How we understand our object depends, however, on our ontological and epistemological assumptions.

Science also shares with all other social products the basic conditions that it is produced in a context of *work* (material intervention) and *communicative interaction* with other people, with whom we share certain resources, not least a common language (Sayer 1992: 17ff). It is crucial for the relevance of knowledge to be aware of the methodological implications that follow from these premises.

The relation between practice, meaning, concept and language

It is the task of science to provide knowledge of reality, but as we have already observed, reality is not anything given. To the contrary, it is the deep dimension of reality, not immediately observable, the level of generative mechanisms, that forces us to seek knowledge rather than just accumulate experiences and facts. It seems rather obvious that the result of our search is influenced by the methods and tools we use, how we arrange experiments or how carefully we measure, among other things. It is generally less obvious that one of the most important tools in the search for knowledge of reality is language.

Let us first state that spoken and written language are certainly not the only ways in which we communicate with each other in this world. Meaning is communicated daily, to a large extent also by means of traditions, rites, rules, gestures, specific actions, etc. Human language, however, is a distinct feature in human societies, and anyway it has a very important role for conveying and exchanging meaning in the social world. At the same time language as such has specific qualities and ways of functioning, with far-reaching implications (cf. Sayer 1992: 17–22).

Language may appear to be a neutral and relatively uncomplicated medium for communication between people. Language is a form of practical convention. There is a set of common words and concepts, as well as rules for the combination and application of them, and mostly we use language as if words and concepts were labels with a meaning given to them beforehand. This, however, overlooks the fact that meaning is never definite or fixed, and also that there is an inherent relation between practice, meaning, concept and language.

Words and concepts are not names of anything already existing out there in the real world with set qualities. There are no 'facts' in the common sense of the word. It is characteristic of experiences and facts – knowledge – that they do not 'speak for themselves'. Knowledge has a meaning – hence it 'speaks'. And inversely: when we listen to statements we find meaningless, we find that they do not 'tell' us anything. This is not because nobody speaks, and it need not imply that we do not understand the words. What is missing in such cases is more likely a common frame of reference in the form of previously conceptualized and communicated experiences, which could make the words meaningful.

Meaning arises because it is innate in human practice that it is *conscious and intentional*. As human beings we always have at least some notion of aims and means for our daily toil, that is, we give it some sort of meaning. One might also express it as making concepts about existence. Human practice is at the same time always a sort of intervention in the material world, since we depend on it for our survival. This goes for the manager, the farmer and the mother, as well as for the researcher and everybody else (even if human practice and existential meaning under no circumstances can be reduced to this material dimension). As human beings we also register the results of our endeavours in relation to our goals. We reflect on them, and by means of language we can communicate, discuss and compare our experiences with those of others. As a consequence we may perhaps also change various things in our own practice and so make new experiences, which are in their turn communicated, and so on. The varying results of the practices will, in social interaction and through language, be continually conceptualized as meaningful knowledge of reality.

It is further characteristic that such knowledge has some kind of systematic nature. Particular words and terms – and sometimes also events, gestures, and so on – have their specific meaning in relation to each other and within the totality of the conceptual frameworks they at the same time constitute. That there may be differences in the significance of the same terms (not to mention gestures) is well known, and can sometimes be striking when people from different ethnic groups meet. But there are differences even within what is usually regarded as one and the same culture: life mode research on the Swedish population (Jakobsen and Karlsson 1993), for instance, has shown that common and everyday words like 'work', 'leisure time' and 'family' have a totally different meaning to people with different social life modes, people whose everyday life makes them experience the means and goals of existence in radically different ways. However, such differences remain largely unnoticed, since people have the words of the language in common.

Consequently neither objects nor conducts or activities of different kinds have any meaning whatsoever, in themselves. Meaning is created from the starting point in different practices and in the interactive communication between members in a community where language is the principal medium. But whereas language no doubt is a medium of communication, it is by no means an independent, passive or impartial medium. It does not convey any 'truths' about reality, and it does not reflect in a true way the different notions people have about existence. Often it is quite the opposite.

Since language is a convention (and must be, in order to fulfil its practical role), one of its qualities is that, at a certain level, it has so to speak 'a life of its own', which it lives independently of our intentions here and now:

We are accustomed to thinking of language as something which we, as users, speak with and through. But there is a sense in which the reverse applies too; I am not the sole author of this book: the structure of language and narrative forms, such as those of academic texts, of which I am only partially aware, speak through me. At one level we might say that this is analogous to any act of production, such as the construction of a house, for the nature of the materials, as well as the work of the builder, determine the properties of the result. But the effects of language are not fixed like those of bricks and steel. New interpretations are always possible; they can never be foreclosed.

(Sayer 1992: 20)

As far as academic texts are concerned, the writers of this book cannot but agree. The cited text, however, emphasizes the social nature of language: for us to be able to think and express ourselves, we need a language, a language already existing and independent of what we want to express here and now. Hence when we take on the language of our society, that is to say when we enter the linguistic world of meaning, we also enter an already interpreted world. At the beginning we are always confined to using the terms and concepts already existing in our language, and this is the case even when we wish to express the most personal things. If we want to express new knowledge or convey a new meaning to phenomena in the world we are forced to ask for intersubjective confirmation of it. We must have other people's – our fellow-subjects' – approval and permission if we are to be successful in our pursuit. The scientific community is a good example in this connection. Activities here aim directly at producing new knowledge, and the demand for intersubjectivity has been institutionalized in a number of rules and conditions about publication, discussion and criticism of research results – reports, seminars, the defending of theses, and so on. But the same is true for all attempts to convey new knowledge. The validity of what we say will always be subject to intersubjective judgement and decision.

How it all ends depends on many different things. That is because knowledge does not only have meaning but also – as was briefly mentioned above – *different meaning* to people with different practices developing/using the knowledge. Since reality is differentiated, structured and stratified, and involves many different and sometimes conflicting practices and interests, there also exist several parallel conceptual frameworks and different and sometimes competing interpretations. An essential aspect of social life is the very existence of conflicts and power struggles over whose concepts will be valid and who will consequently have the power to define reality – sometimes expressed in the well-known saying that 'History is written by the victor'. In this context we do not usually talk of different 'conceptual frameworks' but rather of different 'viewpoints'. This expression, however, conceals the fact that without any form of previous creation of meaning and conceptualization, what we 'view' would have no meaning at all. Therefore it is often not a question of different ways of seeing things, but that we see different things.

When we speak or convey meaning in some other way, we live and at the same time reproduce a reality, which is to a high degree already conceptualized and defined on the basis of other people's varied practices and experiences and the relative conditions of power and dominance between them. In this meaning reality can at every moment be seen, among other things, as an expression of the 'score in a match' (but with many more teams than two involved), and in this meaning it is also a social construction. It does not mean, however, that it exists only in people's minds. Social constructions are constructions of something.[2] They are constructions of a reality existing independently of what the constructions look like at the moment. These conditions, common for all knowledge formation, are the reason why we must carefully distinguish between the transitive and intransitive objects of science in research situations.

The function of language in the human, social world is thus far from being just a practical means of communication. The human social world as such is a world of concepts. What 'exists' to communicate about, what can be communicated, is largely determined by language, which, however, by no means simply reflects that which really exists. Still, we must always have our starting point in the concepts provided by our language world, and in that we are always also prisoners of the concepts; and there is no way to escape from this prison.

Consequently it is no use trying. Taking one's starting point in critical realism instead, one will find the solution, namely to become aware of and see the relation between language and reality, that is to see the intrinsic and mutual relation between concept/knowledge, the practices that we as human beings are involved in, and the world our practice is dealing with. It is because of this relationship that language is one of our most important instruments for exploring reality: that is why critical realism focuses on the importance of scientific conceptualization. For researchers it means they must be aware that facts are theory-laden. It also implies being aware of the different conditions at hand, when we as human beings study the natural world, as well as when we study our own human social world.

The objects of natural science and of social science, respectively

In accordance with what has been said above, all knowledge and understanding, all sets of concepts are currently subject to negotiation and change within the framework of social practice and social interaction. It is an everyday experience that concepts arise, disappear and are replaced by new ones. Some concepts have a short lifetime. They are almost like buzzwords, and for a short time exert a limited influence on existence. Other conceptual constructions are associated with greater changes in our ways of living and are stable over a longer period. This is true of, for example, the concept of 'childhood', which only started to develop at the beginning of the Modern era (Ariès 1973), and the concept of 'the unconscious', which from the beginning of the last century has more and more become part of everyday understanding. Other conceptual changes involve the entire worldview. This was the case in our part of the world when the earth was found to be spherical instead of flat, as was earlier believed, when it turned out that the earth was revolving round the sun and not the opposite, and when the Enlightenment gradually replaced the conception of the world as created by God with the theory of evolution and the idea of man as moulding his own existence. All these developments were in their turn logically connected with the emergence of the natural and social sciences as practices and concepts.

It is characteristic of cognitive shifts of a more or less radical kind that whereas they do not change the natural world of which they speak – that world exists and is what it is, independently of our knowledge of it – they are often connected with more or less dramatic changes in our way of living in this world – that is, society. The earth was round even before this was discovered, the solar system looked as it does now, also when everybody believed that the earth was its centre; and whether we believe that God or the Big Bang created the world, this does not affect how it was in fact created. But when the new conception of the world gradually began to dominate, this happened in interplay with the emergence of new social practices, which eventually changed the very society where they took place. There were more voyages of trade and exploration and they went further and further (while most people still believed the earth was flat, such ventures were impeded, among other things, by sailors afraid of sailing off the 'rim'), new continents were discovered, the Europeans began to colonize other continents, industrialization accelerated, and so on. The course of events was complex but taken together it meant that a foundation was laid for totally new and fundamentally different social class, gender and ethnic relations, and that a completely new society – 'modern society' – came into being.

The transformation of knowledge does not always lead to such revolutionizing changes, of course. The historical changes of the social world compared to changes of nature, however, display essential differences between the objects of natural science and social science respectively, differences that also set the conditions for which methods can be employed.

Let us first observe that the fundamental conditions are common to the natural and social sciences, and that they imply an intrinsic and mutual interaction between concept/knowledge, the practices that we as human beings are involved in, and the world that these practices deal with. Knowledge as such, independently of what it is about, is likewise always a social product. This means that in both the natural and the social sciences facts are dependent on theories. Facts are relative to the conceptions we initially form of the phenomena we are interested in, and the tools we develop on the basis of these conceptions to enable a study of the phenomena will have a decisive influence on what we are going to see.

Natural science 'facts', just like social science 'facts', are thus theoretically and/or ideologically conditioned. The important difference is that whereas the objects of natural science are indeed socially defined but still *naturally produced*, the objects of social science are both socially defined and *socially produced* (Sayer 1992: 26ff) – but they are nevertheless just as real. That is the core of critical realist ontology. Let us first expand on what this means, and then discuss the consequences it has for social science conceptualization.

In a natural science context the researcher's relation to the object of study is a simple subject/object relationship, thus only involving what has been called a 'single hermeneutic' (Giddens 1976; Sayer 1992: 35ff). The interpretation, or understanding, of natural phenomena is a one-sided concern of the researcher. The objects of natural research, like light or chemical substances, which interested Otto Loewi in our aforementioned example, are inherently indifferent and unin-terested in relation to the world in which they exist, including the doings of the researcher. Natural objects do not give existence itself, and the natural world of which they are a part, any meaning or significance; they have no special intentions for their existence, they do not put forward ideas and do not form any concepts competing with those of the researcher. Neither do they react on the formation of knowledge; they are passive and unaltered in relation to the definitions and conceptualizations of the researcher – they are and remain what they are.

This must not be understood as if nature were unaffected by the manipula-tions to which we expose it. Current experiences of environmental pollution and disasters have certainly proved the opposite. But it does not mean that natural science objects actively react, partake in and are affected by natural science's production of knowledge as such. One may rather see environmental problems as examples of nature's spontaneous reaction when we have treated the environment with deficient knowledge about the generative powers and mechanisms of the objects (and of course when we have treated it without consideration for the sake of profit). In recent years growing insight into global environmental problems has also created an ever-increasing interest in the rela-tion between environment, environmental problems and societies experiencing environmental problems and producing knowledge about them. In social science these issues constitute a new and expanding field of research (e.g. Beck 1992; Giddens 1990, 1991).

This kind of research involves totally different kinds of problems than those encountered in natural science research into the environment. The relationship between researchers and research objects is very different when the object is human society. While the study of the objects of nature only involves a simple hermeneutics, the study of social objects involves a 'double hermeneutics': the social scientist's task is to 'interpret other people's interpretations', since other people's notions and understandings are an inseparable part of the object of study.

In contrast with the natural scientist's object of study, the social scientist's object is a world, where inherently interested and committed co-subjects are most active, taking part in and relating to the social world they are a part of, but also partaking in and relating to the production of knowledge taking place there. As we have pointed out, the social world is at every moment a world that others have already interpreted and allocated meaning and significance to, and which they will continually interpret, and reinterpret, though often in different ways. Not least the environmental issues offer a recent example of this. There are many different opinions about new environmental problems, and differences exist both between and within various groups of so-called lay people, researchers and other experts.

Different schools in social science have maintained that since so-called everyday knowledge is often false, unreflecting, contradictory and anyhow subjective and unscientific, everyday notions and interpretations should, as far as possible, be left outside any scientific study of society. We wish to stress, however, that whether these varied notions and interpretations are founded on correct or false ideas and concepts of reality, they must be included among the objects of social science research. Human society is an inherently meaningful world, and people form their practices and direct their activities in accordance with the varied significance they allocate to their world. The contents of everyday knowledge constitute the immediate mechanisms behind the activities making up the social phenomena. As Sayer remarks about the social phenomenon of using money,

> we could observe the physical behaviour of handing over the little metal discs until the cows came home and we could use every statistical technique in the book to process our observational data, yet if we didn't know the meanings on which the use of money is dependent in the society under study, we would still not have any idea of what was actually happening, or what kind of 'action' it was.
>
> (Sayer 1992: 31)

Another and more common methodological attitude views everyday knowledge and its concepts as phenomena that indeed can and should be studied, analysed and explained; but as such they are of no use when it comes to scientific conceptualization. Everyday knowledge presents interesting and important information about the social phenomena under study (compare for instance studies of attitudes and opinions of various kinds), but the scientific formation of concepts of the phenomena is done on its own internal premises. Here critical realism goes a step further in claiming that everyday concepts must be included in the very manner we conduct research and form concepts. The concepts of reality that people, including researchers, have formed and are forming – 'science', 'everyday knowledge', 'common sense', and so on – are not only concepts 'about' or 'within' society. They are often *constitutive* for the social phenomena making up the field of research as such. The *concept dependency* of social phenomena is another factor which fundamentally distinguishes the objects of social science from those of natural science.

Social practices, like using money, and institutions, like banking, as well as the rules of the interest system or the convention that you repay money you have borrowed, are what they are by virtue of what they mean to the members of society. If they had a totally different meaning or no meaning at all, nobody would perform any actions related to them and they would simply cease to exist as phenomena; no activities would occur in society where we could identify the use of money as a causal mechanism. Such is not the case with the objects of nature. The mechanisms of nature exist and work independently of what meaning and significance we assign to them.

In the case of using money, and in many other cases, it is easy to see that the phenomenon would hardly cease to exist just like that. We realize that the use of money is related to an immense complex of other social phenomena in our society – goods and labour markets, ownership, wage labour, and so on, and when all is said and done the possibilities of individual human beings to secure their existence in this society. None of this would in its turn exist independently of the other things, or if nobody understood any of these phenomena. And *if* they did not exist it would at the same time mean that society, as we know it, would not exist in its current form either. Consequently some concepts are constitutive, not only for limited social phenomena but for the whole of the society where they occur. Perhaps we should add that 'social phenomena' also include what we think of as 'roles' and even to a large extent 'characters' and 'identities', for example 'salesman', 'buyer', 'consumer', 'entrepreneurial mentality' and 'labourer identity'.

The example of the use of money emphasizes the relational character of conceptualization and demonstrates two conditions of vital social scientific importance: first the relation to an existing structured social totality, and second, the relation between this totality and the material aspects of existence. At the same time this is the reason why critical realism, despite the emphasis on the importance of language and concepts, is a realist and not a relativist philosophy of science, as it is these relationships between concepts and reality that make up the transitive and the intransitive dimensions of science.

In the first case it is about the fundamental connection between the concepts and the social relations, which basically structure and constitute the social worlds that social science studies – that which cannot be excluded without also dissolving the very object of study. It is these social structures that constitute the deep dimension of social reality, where those mechanisms are located which ultimately generate the events in this reality, in society.

In the second case it is about these social structures always having a material dimension; they are made up of social *material practices* on which we, in different ways, are dependent for our survival as individuals and as a species. The concept dependency of social phenomena and societies may give the impression that social worlds are in fact a form of construction. Societies can also be transformed qualitatively (the generative mechanisms can be transformed into other mechanisms) in a way not known in the natural world. Societies have appeared and disappeared in the course of history, and in our own time too we can find examples of qualitatively different societies. Social mechanisms do not have the same stability as natural mechanisms. But any transformation of society implies transforming processes over a very long time. The structured and relational character of social practices in connection with their being fundamentally linked to the material world gives stability and durability to particular formations of society. The fact that social phenomena are concept-dependent should under no circumstances be seen as if the social world only exists as mental constructions in people's minds – we may make the same reflection as Bunge (1993: 209): 'Indeed, if the world were a figment of our imagination, we would people it with friends'. The social structures, that are reproduced or transformed when members of society act in accordance with their concepts of reality, are real. They contain powers and mechanisms which operate independently of the intentions of the actions here and now. In this capacity they constitute at every moment the intransitive object of social science, which scientific conceptualization, that is the transitive object of social science, is all about.

Therefore it is correct to say that the object of social science research is at the same time socially produced – and so in some sense constructed – and real. The critical role and function of concepts regarding social worlds – together with the actions they inform – these can be said to *mediate* the existence of these worlds – are, however, the reason why everyday concepts must be the very starting point, when we build the scientific systems of concepts, that is to say theories. The content of everyday knowledge is part of the 'raw material' that scientific knowledge must systematically include, if theories are to be valid. It is also one of the reasons why a contemplated analysis of concepts and concept formation is on the whole an essential activity in social science. Concepts are the very key to knowledge about society.

Another reason why conceptualization is so important has to do with another distinct characteristic of social worlds, mentioned above. Societies are *changeable* in a way that nature is not. As human beings, 'knowing' and reflecting subjects, we continually evaluate the experiences we are making, which may lead to changing our actions and practices in various respects. Since we have language, this can happen just by our partaking in and discussing other people's experiences and notions. Therefore even the social phenomena under study might themselves change through people's learning of and adapting to – or rejecting and opposing – knowledge continually being produced in society.

This also means that the social scientist cannot use the natural scientist's most important method: experiment, in the usual sense of the word. Nevertheless there has been a strong endeavour within social science to imitate such procedures, as far as possible (in Chapter 4 we will discuss what experimental design could be feasible within social science). Beside the ethical arguments one might bring against social experiments, it is hardly possible to create a social situation where one can systematically manipulate and control the influences from all conceivable social factors, in order to study the effects of one or a few of these factors. The creation of a social situation would rather result in the creation of another and often quite specific social situation, which the subjects of the experiment would react on and interact with. And so the original object of study would often be lost – 'social phenomena are likely to be irreversibly changed by them [experiments] in a way which does not happen with non-social phenomena, which learn nothing from being manipulated' (Sayer 1992: 29).

All this taken into consideration, the differences between the objects of social science and natural science imply that within the social sciences conceptualization will have a function which comes close to the function of experiment within the natural sciences. And yet conceptualization takes place under very different conditions.

The conditions of conceptualization within social science

Regarding nature, conceptualization represents a 'single hermeneutic', whereas social science conceptualization involves a 'double hermeneutic'. The natural scientist has the capacity to interpret and create the meaning of the objects one-sidedly. As for the social scientist, other people, who have themselves the same capacity for creating meaning as the scientist, have already interpreted the objects.

In other words, in the social sciences conceptualization is part both of the research process and the research object; in the natural sciences it is only part of the former. In opposition to social science traditions holding that other people's interpretations can and should be left outside the scientific study of society, we maintain that the ideas, notions and concepts of 'the others' must be included in the social scientist's study. We also maintain that they must be included in our manner of research. Social worlds are inherently meaningful. It is necessary to understand the meaning people assign to their actions in order to understand the actions. The actions in their turn mediate everyday social phenomena as well as deeper underlying structural relations, which are constitutive of the society under study.

These are the inevitable 'hermeneutic premises' (Collier 1994: 161) of social science. But if the purpose is the development of social science explanations, it is, however, not enough just to collect and repeat the interpretations and explanations that people themselves have of various social phenomena. Nevertheless such a procedure is not uncommon in different kinds of research. Of course it is enough if the aim is just to register views and notions existing in society and nothing else. Very often, though, what is to be explained here is mixed up with the explanation. But if the explanations of others were really the very explanation, there would be no need of social science. Then everything would lie in the open and we would only have to collect and register 'facts'. But as we have shown, reality encompasses a not directly observable deep dimension – the level of generative mechanisms – which justifies the existence of science. It is the business of science to 'dig deeper' than the immediate experience of events in the world is able to do – for instance the experience of the events that A has this view and B has another. We would normally find such reports rather unsatisfactory as answers to questions we ask regarding different social phenomena.

Still, everyday notions and concepts may be correct, as well as false. They can be delusions or misconceptions and they are often contradictory. Yet they are important. A false conception of a phenomenon may be just as important information to the researcher as correct information; it may be an essential aspect of the phenomenon itself that it can be understood in this wrong way. It is also important to see that even if a conception is wrong or false, it is nevertheless real

– it exists and it informs and motivates concrete actions and social phenomena. It is the job of the social scientist to 'read' these 'other', often quite varying but still informative, notions and concepts.

In this, however, in opposition to some interpretative social science approaches, we claim that an interpretation of the 'second order' does not constitute a social scientific explanation either. It is not enough just to build on various social agents' own descriptions and understandings of themselves and of existence. As we have already pointed out, social phenomena have a material dimension, and it is essential to explore how people's notions and concepts are related to social practices of various kinds. We have also stated that the presence of power and dominance relationship in society is of vital importance in this context. There is a mutual relationship between material practices and constructions of meaning, but

> Systems of domination invariably exploit both types of dependence. They are maintained not only through the appropriation, control and allocation of essential material requirements by the dominant class, race or gender, but also through the reproduction of particular systems of meanings which support them. ... The relevant constitutive meanings (e.g. concerning what it is to be a boss, master-race, untouchable, husband or wife) are certainly not neutral or indifferent to their associated practices and different groups have very different or even contradictory material stakes in their reproduction or transformation.
>
> (Sayer 1992: 35)

To have relevance, then, social science conceptualization must both be grounded in the contents of everyday knowledge and integrate the same, while everyday concepts at the same time must be surpassed and surveyed in a theoretical form at a more general level – otherwise no new knowledge has been added.

However, this entails certain problems. It goes for scientific concepts as well as for other concepts that we must look for an intersubjective confirmation of their validity. The concepts must be *negotiated* in the social world they claim to understand. Regarding scientific concepts, there is a situation of double negotiation: first, a negotiation within the scientific community where the scientist wants to have her conceptualization acknowledged, and second, a negotiation with the outside, the real world this conceptualization aims to explain. For even if science is a practice among others, and scientific knowledge a form of knowledge among others, it is still a defined practice and the knowledge is a defined knowledge. Scientific concepts have, and should have, a further characteristic than do everyday concepts – they should be examined, consistent and be at a higher level of integration. By this is meant that they should sum up essential and decisive traits in the phenomena explored; they should endeavour to speak of the mechanisms that produce courses of events and go beyond more superficial and accidental circumstances, including ideologically conditioned understandings of various kinds. Scientific, theoretical concepts are typically *abstract* concepts. The difference between scientific concepts and everyday concepts implies, however, that the researcher's two negotiation partners, the scientific community and the neighbouring society, tend to use extremely different evaluation and assessment criteria.

Furthermore, it is characteristic that it is often more difficult for everyday knowledge to accept and incorporate social science concepts than those of natural science. One significant reason for this is of course precisely the fact that social science concepts, like for instance 'socialization', 'social interaction', 'primary group' and many others, are inevitably far from the experiences that form the base for everyday knowledge. But this is hardly the complete explanation of the difference in acceptance of natural concepts on the one hand and social science concepts on the other. Natural science concepts, for instance 'quarks', 'super strings' or 'black holes', are indeed far from everyday experience but are usually accepted, albeit with varying degrees of interest or disinterest, even by non-scientists.

The difference is also due to the fact that natural science explores a basically value-neutral world, where the objects are neither good nor bad; they simply exist and are what they are. Social science, on the other hand, investigates an inherently value-charged world of social phenomena, positions, roles, identities and relations, whose meaning and significance always to some degree involve evaluations of good and evil, right and wrong, and so on. When social science brings into question and analyses everyday knowledge, it therefore risks not only getting into conflict with alternative experiences and concepts, but also with deeply felt values and ethical guidelines. And social science cannot avoid a critical attitude to everyday knowledge, for if we tried to 'understand popular consciousness, *as it is*, in examining what is normally unexamined, we cannot help but become aware of its illusions' (Sayer 1992: 39). This fact strongly contributes to the difficulty of social science concepts to become particularly popular in society. A further reason is that this type of concept, which 'digs deep down' into everyday knowledge, tends to get down to the socio-structural relations ultimately producing and reproducing the social phenomena under study. Thereby they also challenge vital power and dominance relationships and material interests. Critical social science concepts such as 'class' and 'patriarchy' are examples of this.

For the social sciences it is thus impossible, even if it has been regarded as an ideal by many practitioners, to adopt a completely value-neutral position in relation to one's object; a reflecting position, though, implies of course that the analysis comply with established scientific demands for comprehensive elucidation and consistency. The double hermeneutic, however, places the social sciences in a particular position compared to the natural sciences, a position in which the critical dimension is always present. Indeed, science is in all fundamental respects like any other knowledge, and it is far from being the only relevant form of knowledge. Likewise, the issue of *how* concepts and values of everyday knowledge are to be integrated in the scientific conceptualization is most important in every social analysis. But if 'science' signifies examined concepts, a conscious and systematic reflection *on* the concepts, this means among other things that social science knowledge will always be something else and something beyond more unreflecting everyday knowledge. The latter is naturally based on traditions and conventions and practical considerations 'here and now'. A social science that does not surpass this kind of conceptualization would simply be superfluous. However, the consequence is that there will inevitably be more or less of a competition between everyday knowledge – everyday concepts, common sense – on the one hand, and knowledge/concepts on the other.

The differences between the worlds that social and natural science study are of such a nature that this will necessarily influence the choice of methods to be used. It even has an effect on what kind of knowledge we can acquire. The particular qualities of social reality, which we have discussed here, are all of them aspects of the central difference between social and natural science, the difference that has contributed more than anything else to the doubt about social science being able to produce useful knowledge: whereas natural science is generally able to study its object in more or less *closed* systems, human and social phenomena always occur in *open* systems. This fact has far-reaching conse-quences. In the next chapter we shall examine the significance of this fact, and also discuss what kind of analyses are appropriate within social science.

Conclusion

In this chapter we have begun to present critical realist ontology and episte-mology. We have discussed some assumptions of the nature of reality and knowledge, which must form the foundation for the methodological considera-tions that guide the choice of concrete methods in practical research work.

We have focused on the central problem of science, that our knowledge of reality always is filtered through language and concepts that are relative and changeable in time and space. This has resulted in doubts about any possibilities of acquiring valid knowledge of reality, and sometimes even doubts about the objective existence of reality. From the critical realist position we claim, however, in opposition to cognitive relativist and idealist positions, that there is a reality independent of our knowledge of it, and that science, like all other practices, offers an opportunity to obtain more or less truthful knowledge of this reality. Against 'naive objectivism' and empiricism we maintain, on the other hand, that reality cannot be studied by neutral empirical observations alone. Characteristic of reality is the condition that there is an ontological gap between what we experience and understand, what really happens, and – most important – the deep dimension where the mechanisms are which produce the events. Scientific observations and theories are thus always concept-dependent but not concept-determined.

We have pointed out the importance of seeing science as a practical social activity, which is carried out under similar conditions to other forms of social practice. This means that questions on method are primarily practical questions, which must always be considered in relation to the character of the object of investigation and the purpose of the investigation. It further means that it is imperative to understand the relations between practice, meaning, concept and language. In this context we have also begun to discuss the decisive differences between the objects of natural and social science respectively. These differences, among other things, lead to the situation that whereas experiment is seen as the principal method of the natural sciences, the focus in social science practice is on conceptualization through conceptual abstraction. But conceptualization in the social sciences is done under totally different conditions than in the natural sciences, due to the hermeneutic premises.

In the next chapter we shall treat critical realist ontology and epistemology at greater length, and deepen our understanding of the specific conditions existing in social science research practice.

3 Conceptual abstraction and causality

In the previous chapter we dealt with the significance of conceptualization for knowledge production in general and social science in particular. We established that all knowledge is conceptually mediated and thus it is impossible to make neutral observations of 'facts' about reality. The observations are always theory-laden. This does not determine, however, what reality is like – it exists independently of our knowledge about it. It is decisive that we do not merely think *with* the concepts without reflection, but that we also think *about* them. This is because within the social sciences, what other people hold to be true, and their concepts of reality, are an integrated part of the object of science itself. If we are not aware of this, we suffer great risk of incorporating flawed ideas and ideological delusions into social science theory formation, thus legitimizing it as science at the same time as the understanding of reality remains distorted.

The methodological implication of this is that conceptualization stands out as the most central social scientific activity. In this chapter we shall begin to analyse the question of how concept formation should be constructed as an efficient social science research tool. We shall maintain that *conceptual abstraction* by means of structural analysis is the core function of social science conceptualization, and from this follows *realist causal analysis*. Here we will also deal with what it means to have a realist understanding of key concepts such as 'structure' and 'causality'. This in turn means that we deepen the description of critical realist ontology and epistemology. Of vital importance here is the understanding that critical realism has of the stratification of reality, of emergent powers, and of open and closed systems.

The basic methodological argument which follows is that the nature of the object of study determines what research methods are suitable and also what kind of knowledge it is at all possible to have of different phenomena in the world. This leads to different sciences doing research under different conditions. Furthermore, it is this very circumstance which is behind the success of the natural sciences, as compared to that of the social sciences. The possibilities for the social sciences to produce practically relevant knowledge is a question of having both our expectations of knowledge, as well as our methods, adapted to the specific character of social phenomena, to a higher extent than has so far been the case.

Conceptual abstraction

A very common, and important, way of conceptualization is through abstraction. Scientific activity is, to a large extent, abstraction, but the function and purpose of abstractions are seldom made the object of explicit analysis and discussion. Abstraction is, however, as Sayer (1992: 86) says, 'a powerful tool and hence also a dangerous one if carelessly used'.

What, then, is an abstraction? How does it work and why do we abstract? How can we distinguish between good and bad abstractions? In everyday thinking, 'the abstract' is not thought of very highly as useful knowledge. 'This line of argument is very abstract and has really very little to do with concrete reality' is a common objection raised in various situations, not least when theoretical explanations are given. Everyday knowledge tends to oppose the term 'abstract' and the term 'concrete', rather in the same way as 'theory' is opposed to 'practice'. The abstract, as well as the theoretical, is in various ways associated with notions of vagueness and distance in relation to reality. In fact it 'is' only in the minds of people, which is basically the same as saying that it is non-existent and that it need not have anything to do with reality at all. The concrete, on the other hand, is what 'exists'; it is tangible and real in contrast to the abstract, just as facts exist and are real in contrast to theory. This distinction often also involves ideas about what we cannot observe in contrast to that which is observable.

Now, this way of perceiving the distinction between abstract and concrete is not just something characteristic of everyday knowledge. Even in scientific contexts from time to time, there are pleas for making research less abstract and theoretical, and instead more concrete and more in touch with reality. The argument may sound sensible, and critics of 'abstract theory' often seem to have good grounds for their view. These grounds often imply that abstractions simplify or disregard the factual circumstances by not paying attention to the complexity of social life and the variations thereof. Thus knowledge is out of touch with reality, hence also irrelevant and of little use.[1]

This way of understanding the difference between abstract and concrete is, however, based on a misconception. Moreover, this misconception tends to influence the usefulness of knowledge very negatively. Given that all our knowledge is conceptually conveyed, including our observations of 'facts', the difference between the abstract and the concrete is not fundamentally a matter of involving different degrees of distance to reality. It is correct, however, that it is a matter of varying degrees of isolation and complexity respectively, but abstractions are not there in order to *cover* complexity and variation in life; they are there in order to *deal* with just that.

An abstract concept, or an abstraction, is something which is formed when we – albeit in thought – separate or isolate one particular aspect of a concrete object or phenomenon; and what we abstract from is all the other aspects possessed by concrete phenomena. Abstraction is necessary, because the domain of the actual – the events in the world – makes up such a tremendously diversified and heterogeneous dimension of reality. Concrete phenomena, like the weather, machinery, people and organizations, are constituted by a number of different elements and properties, powers and influences. If we seek to explain concrete objects and phenomena – for example how a thunderstorm is formed, the locomotive powers of living organisms or gender segregation on the labour market – then we must have a means of isolating the different mechanisms involved, which together produce these events. Here, conceptual abstraction is used as a kind of social science equivalent to the natural science experiment. Later (primarily in Chapter 4 in the discussion of retroduction) we will examine more closely how conceptual abstraction is used in the social science working process, but let us here also look at the reasons why these kinds of thought experiment have come to play such a crucial role in social science in particular.

In the previous chapter we saw that neither the social nor the natural reality is something fixed, flat or transparent. Reality consists of three domains: our experiences of events in the world, the events as such (of which we only experience a fraction) and the deep dimension where one finds the generative mechanisms producing the events in the world. Further, it is the business of science to establish the connections between the empirical, the actual and the real; to observe and identify the effect of underlying generative mechanisms. Within natural science this is done by manipulating natural courses of events through experiments. The task is to find an experimental design that will allow for the mechanism under study to be triggered and permit it to work without interference from other mechanisms (like the example of Loewi in the previous chapter, when he wanted to explain how it is possible for living objects to move).

As we have seen, however, such experiments are virtually impossible within social science. Apart from weighty ethical objections to social experiments, social agents – people – unlike natural science objects, are conscious, intentional, reflective and self-changing; we learn by being manipulated, and consciously or subconsciously we change our actions as a reaction to the experimental setting. It is simply not possible to create a social setting where one can isolate certain mechanisms and check that no other mechanisms are involved in the course of events. Thus when we wish to gain knowledge about generative powers and mechanisms in social worlds, one of the most splendid tools at our disposal is the isolation of certain aspects in thought – abstraction – rather than isolating them by manipulating events.

An abstract concept, then, should not at all be associated with 'vagueness' or 'unreality'; on the contrary it aims at, in a very precise way, isolating an essential aspect of a concrete course of events. Social science abstractions, such as 'class', 'gender', 'role' or 'norm', are not more vague or more unreal than natural science abstractions, such as 'air pressure', 'density', 'energy' or 'gravitation'. What unites all these phenomena is that they manifest themselves through their effects, but it is not possible to immediately observe or 'touch' what the concepts represent, that is, the generative mechanisms. Nevertheless, it should be observed that the difference between abstract and concrete is not always equivalent to the difference between the observable and the not observable. Some mechanisms are fully observable, for example when we are dealing with mechanical devices such as different kinds of machines and equipment.

There are, however, various ways of making conceptual abstractions, but not all are equally good. Since conceptualization means that we perceive differences – we differentiate between individual occurrences and phenomena – knowledge also must, for it to be practically relevant,

> grasp the differentiations of the world; we need a way of individuating objects, and of characterizing their attributes and relationships. To be adequate *for a specific purpose* it [knowledge] must 'abstract' from particular conditions, excluding those which have no significant effect in order to focus on those which do. Even where we are interested in wholes we must select and abstract their constituents.
>
> (Sayer 1992: 86; our italics)

How, then, do we set about it so that our conceptual abstractions really do express the distinctions and relations relevant to our research problem? In natural as well as social worlds, the object under study has certain properties and powers that seem necessary, so to say indispensable, for the object to exist at all and be what it is. This may refer to the photosynthesis in green plants, people's sociality, slaves' lack of freedom, or private ownership in the private capitalist production systems. Other properties, however, appear to be more contingent and of minor importance to the existence of the object; for example, if someone has a large circle of friends or not, or whether a slave receives good or bad treatment. Critical realist analysis is built around this understanding of *natural necessity*, and our abstractions should primarily aim at determining these necessary and constitutive properties in different objects, thus determining the nature of the object.

Here we must also make it clear that in this context, the term 'nature' does not contain any suppositions whatsoever, of any fixed, naturally produced and unchangeable essence of an object. Here, 'nature' in general terms refers to the type of an object, be it naturally or socially produced; to that which at a certain moment determines what a certain object is. The nature of the object may change, but then we will be dealing with a new object with other constitutive properties. The abstractions must, however, at any given point in time, separate the object's necessary properties from the contingent ones and show what it is in the object that makes it what it is and not something else. Abstractions should 'neither divide the indivisible nor lump together the divisible and the heterogeneous' (Sayer 1992: 88).

Abstraction, therefore, means that we make conceptual distinctions between occurrences and phenomena in the world. Further, practically relevant scientific knowledge presupposes that we make well-reasoned and systematic abstractions in relation to the problem we have addressed – that is to say that the abstractions determine the nature of the research object, its constituent properties. A significant part of this, 'theorizing', is about continually applying oneself to such activity. We continuously structure, re-structure and adjust abstractions with the purpose of avoiding irrelevant abstractions, which inevitably diminish the usefulness of the knowledge. There is a special kind of abstraction for this, which correctly applied is very useful, namely 'structural analysis'.

Structural analysis

How do we satisfy the principle that questions of method should primarily be related to the nature of the object under study and the purpose of the study? Since aims and approaches to a problem vary unlimitedly, while an object at any given point in time is what it is, we may qualify this methodological principle by observing that it is the nature of the object under study which is the 'fixed point' from where to start regarding choice of methods – it is the nature of the object that determines the possibilities we have for gaining knowledge about it.

We have further pointed out that the purpose of abstraction is to make it possible to separate that which is characteristic in an object from that which is more contingent. That is to say that the abstractions should lead back to those properties which determine what a certain object is – its nature. These determinative properties in their turn emanate from the object's specific set-up or 'structure'.

What, then, is the result of applying these principles to social science objects? What is the nature of society and of the social phenomena? It is possible, like Bhaskar, to make a

> methodological distinction between the *social sciences* ... and the *social psycho-logical sciences*. ... If the object of the former is *social structure*, that of the latter is *social interaction*. They may be linked by the study of *society* as such, identi-fied as the system of *relations* between the positions and practices agents reproduce or transform.
>
> (Bhaskar 1989b: 93)

Here, we are confronted with the crucial realization that the objects of social science are relational – they are what they are by virtue of the relations they enter into with other objects. In a concrete research project, however, this means that we will have several different types of relations to work with – types that are illustrated in Figure 1 (see on next page).

In social contexts we must first distinguish between relations that are respectively substantial and formal (see also Sayer 1992: 88ff). *Substantial* relations means there are real connections between the objects, *formal* that there are not, but nevertheless the objects somehow share a common characteristic – they are in some respect similar. An example of a substantial relation is that between landlord and tenant. They both cause each other's existence as a result of the relation existing between them. If we also suppose the landlord and the tenant are both thirty years old, that is an example of a formal relation. Those in the category '30–39 years' share age as a characteristic, but need not have any other

FORMAL

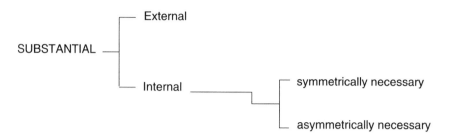

Figure 1 Different types of social relations

connection than that. The age category is just a formal relation and not a substantial one. In fact, an age category as such does not at all represent any social relation.

Further, when analysing specific social phenomena, among the substantial relations it is essential to separate between those which are internal and necessary, and those which are external and contingent, *for the phenomenon under study*. This is the reason why questions of method must be considered in relation to the nature of the object and the purpose of the study.

Bhaskar (1989a: 42) gives this definition: 'A relation R_{AB} may be defined as *internal* if and only if A would not be what it *essentially* is unless B is related to it in the way that it is. R_{AB} is *symmetrically internal* if the same applies also to B'. When the relations are internal, the objects condition one another. Then they can condition one another mutually, which signifies a symmetrically necessary relation. One such relation is that between landlord and tenant. Were that relation to disappear, the social phenomenon 'housing market' would also disappear; the two individuals would no longer be landlord and tenant respectively. They would still exist as individual human beings, but their earlier social positions would disappear.

Instances of external relations, however, and let us continue to use the landlord and tenant example, are such that landlords may be stingy or may mismanage their property; landlords may also be generous and undertake ambitious renovations, but they will still be landlords. Which of these situations is the case may still depend on substantial relations, but these relations are outside the relation landlord/tenant, they are external to the study of the social phenomenon 'housing market'. Whether a relation is necessary or contingent for a certain research object is thus not a logical question but one that can only be answered through a concrete study. And if we are not clear about which aspect or aspects of a phenomenon we are interested in, we suffer great risk that the abstract structural analysis will only result in confusion and chaotic concepts.

However, the relation may also be asymmetrically necessary. This means that the one object can exist without the other, but not vice-versa. Thus houses and flats can exist without the existence of landlords, but the opposite is not possible. It should also be observed that necessary relations do not have to be harmonious; on the contrary they often include one-sided dominance, such as the classic examples master/slave, capitalist/wage labourer and man/woman.

The relational character of social science objects further helps us clarify the meaning of the much used, but often ambiguously so, concept of 'structure'. In every concrete situation there is a complex combination of formal and substantial, external and internal relations. That is the reason one must make an abstract study, an analysis of the structures involved in the social phenomenon under study. We abstract, that is isolate, a particular aspect, a set of internally defined social relations: a particular structure. Thus a structure is defined as a *set of internally related objects*. We can then, should our investigation call for it, continue to isolate more internal social relations, more structures. This is in contrast to a concrete analysis, where various separate events are studied and explained through the activity of the structural mechanisms involved.

Let us immediately clarify, however, that the concept 'structure' does certainly not refer only to social structures. Structure refers to the inner composition making each object what it is and not something else, for example the biological structures separating an animal from a plant or one plant from another. And in relation to social phenomena, structures not only refer to macro conditions, despite the fact that much of social science literature gives that impression. We can analyse social structures at all levels and in any area: organization structures, small group structures, the social structures of the dyad or the triad, the structures of street life, communication structures, linguistic structures, personality structures, and so on. In many contexts, mechanisms on an overall macrostructural level are of great importance for producing the concrete social phenomena we are studying, but they need not be determining for the existence and essence of a certain social object. A social phenomenon, such as socialization, exists in all societies independently of specific social macrostructures. One can also talk about what socialization is in terms of taking the role of the other and identity creation, etc. (as theorized by G. H. Mead) regardless of the macrostructural circumstances in the society where it takes place. It is when we encounter concrete cases of socialization that we come across variations. Here, there are many other mechanisms involved, among them not least the macrostructural mechanisms of that specific society. The latter will greatly influence such questions as which roles may be involved in the role-taking, what identities can be created, and so on.

When we are interested in an object and wish to uncover its structure, this can in practice be done by asking a number of simple but basic questions (Sayer 1992: 91): 'What does the existence of this object (in this form) presuppose? Can it exist on its own as such? If not what else must be present? What is it *about* the object that causes it to do such and such?' A key question could be: *What cannot be removed without making the object cease to exist in its present form?*

These kinds of questions are both uncomplicated and effective, but nevertheless it is quite common within social science research that such questions are never asked at all. This in turn has to do with the fact that social science, just as everyday knowledge, sometimes has a tendency to disregard the relational character of social phenomena. This seems to be the case especially when it comes to the planning of concrete studies – one example being the fairly common studies where one in various ways tries to illuminate how social gender structure operates, but where the empirical observations solely include women or men.

It is thus of the utmost importance to observe that abstractions in the sense described above are just as real as the concrete – the structures do have a factual existence. The social relations – the structure – we seek are constitutive for the social phenomenon in which we are interested, they are what makes the phenomenon exist. It is not true that the abstract and the concrete should be in opposition to one another, which is often claimed. The abstract is to be under-stood as an 'extract' from reality, an extract consisting of the 'fundamental part', the 'essence' or the 'core' of a phenomenon, which is as real a phenomenon as any other.

In this context, yet another aspect is of crucial importance regarding methodology: we must keep the social structure apart from the people who at a given point in time occupy its different positions and specific practices (Sayer 1992: 92). Everyday thinking constantly tends to identify people with positions and consequently attribute to individual people the properties held by the positions, resulting in fatal consequences for the understanding of social life. Unfortunately, it is not uncommon that social science research acts in the same way. (Below we will describe two cases where this happens: reduction of the concrete to the abstract, and the expectation that abstract socio-structural categories should correspond to concrete empirical categories of people, respec-tively. These two courses of action are in many respects different, but they share the inability to separate between position and person.) Social science analysis must, however, if it is to be of practical relevance, reach beyond this kind of conceptualization.

Here we are reminded of the fundamental methodological requirement, that the methods must suit the object of our study and the purpose of the study. In this context it is very important to see that though abstractions are indispensable tools in the research process, they cannot replace empirical studies of the concrete conditions or render such studies superfluous. Rather, it is a question of being aware of the nature of the relation between the abstract and the concrete, to understand the scope and limitations of abstract and concrete research approaches respectively, and furthermore, to understand that most research processes require both approaches, though the emphasis is often on one or the other. Here, the inexperienced researcher could encounter many pitfalls. Sayer points to a number of problems: a common research method, which aims at dealing with the complexity of concrete phenomena, runs along the following lines: the researcher specifies her object in terms of 'ideal types' or 'ideal typical cases' which are then studied and compared with actual cases with the purpose of finding similarities and differences. Thus ideal types can sometimes resemble abstractions, but under no circumstances must they be mixed up with them. The difference is how ideal types and abstractions are formed, respectively. Generally, ideal types are formed without any deliberate considerations based on ontological circumstances. Therefore the problem is that 'the methodology pays no attention to the structure of the world and hence is unable to recognize that some elections are better than others according to their relationship to this structure' (Sayer 1992: 237).

That is to say: ideal types do not aim at grasping differentiations in the world and identifying objects in terms of their specific generative mechanisms.[2] As a rule, therefore, differences and similarities between the ideal type and the actual cases give us little information; we do not know what has produced them or how to assess them.

Another problem as regards abstract and concrete research, respectively, consists in researchers tending to (Sayer 1992: 238) 'over-extend them by expecting one type to do the job of the others'. Concerning abstract studies, this is quite often expressed in what Sayer calls 'pseudo-concrete research'. This kind of research makes the mistake of expecting theoretical abstractions to explain concrete phenomena directly, without empirical studies of what combinations of objects, what forces and mechanisms exist, and how they together contribute to the building up of the concrete phenomenon at hand. This mistake is a common one in, for example, Marxist analysis, which generally speaking tends to reduce people's *concrete* individual existence, activities and social relations to the two basic forms of existence used in the *abstract* concept of class: capitalist and worker (see for example Sève 1975, who tries to create a theory of personality based on Marxist historical materialism). Feminist analyses of patriarchy have shown similar tendencies to pseudo-concrete analysis, demonstrated through statements that rape is 'a conscious process of intimidation by which *all men* keep *all women* in a state of fear' (Brownmiller 1975). However, the error appears in many other research contexts, but in more or less incisive forms. This always stems from disregarding the fact that abstract categories – in the above examples 'class' and 'gender' – are not concrete individuals, events and processes. The abstract categories deal with those mechanisms that produce the concrete phenomena. And the latter are – as the critics of abstraction have quite correctly pointed out, but drawn the wrong conclusions from – complex and full of variations. Using our terminology, they are a result of the activity of many mechanisms. Instead of refraining from abstraction, we therefore often need several different theoretical abstractions in order to explain a certain concrete phenomenon. We may also need theoretical abstractions at several different levels. What abstractions are necessary is decided by the purpose of the study, but that can under no circumstances be decided without having empirical knowledge of the concrete conditions.

Misunderstanding of the relation between abstract and concrete in the above cases leads to (Sayer 1992: 238) a reduction of the concrete to the abstract. But the opposite is even more common, that abstract concepts are criticized for not working in a way which means they exhaust every single concrete particularity and variant, in advance. Such a reduction of the abstract to the concrete comes from the fact that an empiricist view of knowledge is predominant both in many scientific contexts and in everyday reasoning. This kind of understanding of reality and knowledge creates an expectation that abstract categories, such as class and gender, should correspond to people demonstrating unambiguous sets of characteristics, attributes and actions, which in a similar way divide them into and place them into empirical boxes. But abstract concepts are isolations of aspects of concrete phenomena and thus will never live up to such expectations. However, when they fail to do so, the conclusion often drawn is that the abstract category is 'non-existent' and that the concept should accordingly be rejected. Even if the consequence here is different compared to that of pseudo-concrete research, the misunderstanding is yet again due to the fact that one forgets that abstract concepts are not to be used as classifying or predicting concrete observations; they are tools to shed light on that which we observe, and provide explanations of what mechanisms lie behind its existence. The rejection of abstract concepts, therefore, means that often the researcher also discards her most powerful scientific tools.

As regards concrete research, the over-extension consists of 'the illegitimate extrapolation (or generalization) of specific findings about a particular (contingent) conjuncture of a system to the rest of the system, when in fact it may be unrepresentative' (Sayer 1992: 240). This kind of over-extension easily arises as a consequence of circumstances such as the impracticability of carrying out a concrete study of all aspects of an extensive and complex research area, such as the emergence of 'Modernity' or the relationship between technological development and work organization. In such cases abstractions to reach underlying generative mechanisms can be of great use and be a warrant of some generality for the results. As we shall see (in Chapter 4), however, the concept 'generality' based on critical realism means several different things.

Taken together, the argument above implies that it is crucial that abstraction is not made mechanically or by routine. We should not use conceptual abstractions casually if they, for example, are already well known and established within the scientific community. Although it often seems to be evident right from the outset of a research project that certain established abstractions really are relevant, this cannot simply be taken for granted. The abstractions are necessary to enable us to explain and understand concrete phenomena, but it is important to remember that in each research process the concrete phenomena must be the starting point of the abstraction process. Further, it is characteristic that we are dealing with precisely a *process*. Different phenomena or problems may need rethinking, before we decide what we can abstract from. And since a concrete phenomenon is a complex product made up of the activity of several mechanisms, it is often productive to use and combine different kinds of abstraction. However, this must be done in such a way that the abstractions do not contradict one another, and we must be aware of and understand their limitations and possible incompatibility.

When we wish to understand a concrete problem, this therefore involves a double movement (Sayer 1992: 87): *concrete → abstract, abstract → concrete*, and we wish to underline once more that the starting point is the concrete problem. Imagine that we are interested in the mechanisms behind people's highly varied everyday notions of what constitutes risk and security in life (Jakobsen and Karlsson 1999). Here, right from the outset, the abstraction 'social life mode' could appear to be relevant: we know that 'the good life' represents different things to different life modes; hence we may also consider it plausible that different things endanger or secure, respectively, this good life. We can therefore, for fairly good reasons, decide to undertake a study of the area, with life mode analysis as the point of departure. Here we have, right from the outset, described a process from the concrete to the abstract.

On the other hand, it is absolutely necessary to undertake a concrete study, partly to see whether the expected connection exists, partly to then see the nature of it. In performing such a study we concurrently move from the abstract to the concrete. When we then analyse our data – *inter alia* by continuously posing questions regarding what is essential for the existence of the object, etc. – it may become apparent that the life mode structures cannot provide a thorough explanation of the phenomena we come across. This in turn might mean there is a need to revise the life mode concept; it might also mean there are other structural mechanisms involved, and we must ask ourselves which.

If, for example, we find that particularly women with a housewife life mode tend to focus on family when they form associations around risk and security, then it would be fitting to suppose that the life mode concept could explain everyday notions of risk and security. However, if we find that a housewife suddenly and inexplicably turned ill when she was going through a period in which family life was threatened (Jakobsen and Karlsson 1993), and if we seek to explain what brought about that particular event, then the life mode theory would be just one of the theories we could use. It would not be legitimate for us to reduce this specific concrete event to what the abstraction 'life mode' is able to explain. Here we would need more theories. In this case it could be symbolic interactionism for the interpersonal relationship between the woman and her husband, together with some theory on psychosomatic illness (that is to say, what mechanisms are involved when a psychological condition produces physical manifestations).

Our reflection upon these different aspects of the problem, however, at the same time means that we once again move from the concrete to the abstract. In practical research this double movement – concrete → abstract, abstract → concrete – is often going on simultaneously and it has no given end. It only stops when we ourselves end the analysis.

To sum up, let us emphasize, however, that when we initiate this kind of process

> our concepts of concrete objects are likely to be superficial or chaotic. In
> order to understand their diverse determinations we must first abstract them

systematically. When each of the abstracted aspects has been examined it is possible to combine the abstractions so as to form concepts which grasp the concreteness of their objects.

(Sayer 1992: 87)

If, however, we seek to explain a concrete social phenomenon, it is not sufficient merely to refer to its constituent internal relations, and thus make a structural analysis. It is a feasible inception of social science research, but not its end. Social science explanation requires that we move on from structural analysis to causal analysis.

Causality

It is in the nature of abstractions that they are synchronous – simultaneous. They 'freeze the moment' and refer to 'here and now'. Consequently they cannot, other than at best indirectly, tell us anything about processes and change. If we wish to understand the dynamic dimension of reality (doubtless, knowledge would mostly be both dull and practically irrelevant if it did not contain this dimension) the abstract and the structural analyses must be supplemented by an analysis of the causal conditions – causal analysis.

Causal analysis deals with *explaining* why what happens actually does happen. Naturally, the purpose of explanation is not the only guiding principle of every scientific study. In certain contexts it may be highly satisfactory to primarily describe, count, survey or interpret the phenomena we are interested in. Nonetheless it is the very possibility of determining causal conditions, or causal relations, underlying various kinds of events (in other words explaining 'how the event came about'), which is and has been central to science. This is connected to the fact that science is a practical activity we make use of to orient ourselves in life. If we know what underlies a certain course of events we can also – this is the assumption – intervene and direct future courses of events and make them correspond better with our intentions and purposes in various ways. Alternatively, if we find that we cannot influence the course of events, we can still, by predicting it, better adjust accordingly. For example, we can run away from an earthquake, or an epidemic against which there is no vaccination. In any event we regard increased predictability as something which also increases our chances of controlling our existence.

As we shall see, such assumptions are in themselves considerably problematic. In this, however, the natural sciences have been very successful in some respects (one example being the achievements in the field of technology during the past few centuries), and this has been of major importance as regards the reputation and legitimacy of science, generally speaking. Within social science the story has been quite different. Here the examples of erroneous predictions are numerous (we refer to some of them in Chapter 7 concerning science and practice). This has strongly influenced the apprehensions one has about social science's ability to produce any useful knowledge whatsoever. In order to elucidate wherein this difference lies and narrow down the conditions for useful social scientific knowledge, we must start from the beginning and try to establish what the concept of 'cause' actually may imply.

What is a 'cause'?

Particularly when it comes to explaining, so that we can make tenable predictions about the future, it seems that what is required by the causal connections we need to establish has the character of universal regularities and 'eternal laws' or the like. And as regards the natural sciences, it is the identification of natural laws, such as the general law of gravity or the laws of chemical compounds, that constitutes what may be called the 'fundamental features' behind the achievements of these sciences. The social sciences, or at least a considerable part of them, have in many respects aimed at living up to the scientific ideal of the natural sciences, but with limited success. What is remarkable in this context is that despite considerable efforts to imitate natural science methods, the very core of natural science research has seldom been understood. Where social scientists oriented towards empirical research have concentrated on making neutral observations of empirical regularities, and other researchers criticize this as unfeasible since facts are theory-laden, none of them – at least not explicitly – has perceived the crucial point: natural science is not based on observation of directly observable events. Rather, it is the opposite.

In the previous chapter we dealt with the question of how reality must be constructed to make the existence of (natural) science (with experiments as the leading method) possible. We saw that this requires that reality is not immediately observable or transparent. There must exist a level of reality beneath the level of events and the level where we make our empirical observations, a deep dimension where those mechanisms are which make the events occur. This is what natural science research has taken as its point of departure, and it is also the reason why experiment plays such a central role in natural scientific practice.

Hence the predominant methods of empiricist social science, the study of empirical regularities or co-variation between standardized variables, cannot offer opinions on anything but only empirical regularities and statistical correlation; they cannot answer questions regarding causes. A classic example of this problem is the connection found between the presence of storks and the number of babies born in certain German villages. The correlation was strong and unambiguously showed that the more storks, the more babies were born. Had this conclusion not clashed with other, well-substantiated knowledge, it would have been quite 'scientifically correct' to at least pose the hypothesis, based on these data, that the stork brings babies, or at least that storks one way or the other cause human babies. As was now the case, one had to continue the study, and found an 'underlying variable' which could explain the existence of both storks and babies. That variable was 'countryside'. Storks are more common in the countryside than in the cities, owing to larger food supply, and over a long period of time nativity was higher in the countryside than in the cities due to a number of social and cultural differences. Here the connection proved to be a 'sham connection'. The point is, however, that a great number of scientific studies are designed in exactly the same way as the stork study. And when the results are not as absurd and there are no other factors contradicting the findings, it is very common that the finding of empirical regularities and co-variance is mixed with the discovery of causes and is used as a basis for predictions.

Statistical investigations of frequency, spread, co-variance, and so forth, can be extremely useful when applied in accordance with their capabilities. However, they cannot at all inform about causes, they cannot produce explanations (though this term is much used in this context). A cause is something totally different to statistical co-variance. To ask what has caused something is (Sayer 1992: 104) 'to ask what "makes it happen", what "produces", "generates", "creates" or "determines" it, or, more weakly, what "enables" or "leads to" it'. From a realist perspective it is not a matter of a relation between two events, separated and demarcated from each other. Causes are about objects or relations and their nature. It is a matter of what *causal powers* or *liabilities* there are in a certain object or relation. In more general terms it is a matter of how objects work, or a matter of their *mechanisms* (see also Sayer 1992: 103ff.). Thus water has the causal power to quench fire, living creatures have the power to reproduce, people the power to speak and think, and human beings also have 'work power' and 'love power' (Jónasdóttir 1994).

It is important to observe, however, that 'powers and liabilities' also include such properties as 'weakness' and 'vulnerability'. Water also has the intrinsic liability to evaporate, living creatures to die and human beings to be dependent upon other human beings in order to develop their specific powers and become humans. As regards society as such, then, a specific 'weakness' proves to be a difficulty: humans' individual power to work for their own quality of life always latently threatens the solidarity which ultimately is a prerequisite for our being humans. Similarly, the weakness of solidarity is that it may threaten people's individual existence and potential, since it is liable to group pressure and establishment of power- and dominance-relations.

The latter reflection indicates that causal powers can also be located in the social relationships or structures that people build. The landlord in our example does not primarily have the 'power' to claim rent based on his or her qualities as an individual. That power necessarily requires the landlord's relation to the tenant, and to other landlords and tenants as well as to laws protecting the landlord's ownership of the property, and so forth. In the same way, the investor's 'profit power' is not primarily based on personal qualities but on the social relation between capital and wage labour; men's social surplus value compared to that of women is not based on certain male and female characteristics respectively, but is rendered possible due to social and patriarchal gender relations.

Here, it is crucial to recognize that powers and liabilities exist whether they are exercised or endured or not. Water can quench fire irrespective of whether any one uses it thus. The owner of a property has the potential power to claim rent even if they have no tenants at that particular moment. People can work even when they are unemployed, and love whether or not they ever enter into a love relationship. On the other hand, the existence of causal powers is not an assumption about fixed, unchangeable, eternal essences. The object is indeed what it is by virtue of its intrinsic properties, its nature, but as we have already established, the nature of the object may change. If it does, the object's causal abilities also change. These are two sides of the same coin.

Treated thus, a causal statement does not deal with regularities between distinct objects and events (cause and effect), but with what an object is and the things it can do by virtue of its nature. This also entails that objects have the causal powers and liabilities they have, independently of any specific pattern of events. The mechanism is not only existent when A leads to B, but also when A does not lead to B; this is a cardinal point in critical realist causal analysis, and has far-reaching consequences for social scientific explanations.

The objects and their structures, powers, mechanisms and tendencies

Our line of argument thus far allows us to sum up: critical realism is based on the understanding of *natural necessity* in life. We will now more thoroughly investigate the four concepts making up this perspective: structures, powers, generative mechanisms and tendencies. The objects have the powers they have by virtue of their structures, and mechanisms exist and are what they are because of this structure; this is the nature of the object. There is an internal and *necessary* relation between the nature of an object and its causal powers and tendencies. This can also be expressed as follows (Collier 1994: 43): 'Things have the powers they do because of their structures. ... Structures cause powers to be exercised, given some input, some "efficient cause", e.g. the match lights when you strike it.' This in turn is an example of a mechanism having generated an event. A mechanism is that which can cause something in the world to happen, and in this respect mechanisms can be of many different kinds.

Where, then, do 'tendencies' fit into the context? We have established that a generative mechanism operates when it is being triggered. Unlike the internal and necessary relation between objects and their causal powers, however, the relation between causal powers or mechanisms and their effects is not determined but external and contingent. The fact that a generative mechanism only operates when it is being triggered indicates that it does not always operate – and that, if it is ever triggered, or when it is, the present conditions or circumstances determine whether it will operate. And if it does, the actual effect is also dependent on the conditions.

We must ask the reader to observe the radical significance a critical realist perspective has in this matter, compared with large sections of the established understanding of science. The reason for this external relation between causal mechanisms and their effects is that underlying the phenomena in the domain of the actual, there are many mechanisms concurrently active. The outcome of this – that is the events – is therefore a complex compound effect of influences drawn from different mechanisms, where some mechanisms reinforce one another, and others frustrate the manifestations of each other. Taken together this – that objects have powers whether exercised or not, mechanisms exist whether triggered or not and the effects of the mechanisms are contingent – means we can say that a certain object *tends* to act or behave in a certain way. Whether it will actually act or behave in this way, however, is a completely different matter. The match has the causal power to flare up if triggered, but for it to do so it is required that someone tries to light it, that it is not wet or otherwise damaged, that there is oxygen in the air, and so on. In most cases there are countless combinations of accidental circumstances (other objects having their own powers and mechanisms) which may influence whether a specific causal power will manifest itself or not.

The same principles apply for social objects, but the implications are somewhat different, since social structures cannot exist independently of people's actions. For the sake of simplicity, let us use the example of the organization and positions of wage labour, which in our society is a strong social structure with very tangible effects. The wage labour structure has the causal power to influence – to lay down the conditions for – the situation we as human beings in this society are in. Thereby, it makes us inclined to reason in certain set ways, and perform certain set actions: we want a job, we look for a job, we get an education, we go to work every working day, we spend a large part of our lives working, etc. And each time someone acts in this way, the mechanism which reproduces the wage labour structure is triggered, which in turn generates new actions of the same kind, and so on. Since social structures require human actions for their existence, the actions make up both triggering factors and effects of social structures' generative mechanisms, in this example the mechanisms of wage labour.

However, it is still a matter of us *tending* to carry out this kind of action. All people do not always carry them out; the mechanism is not always triggered, and it does not produce the same effects each time it is triggered. People's actions are never determined by a certain structure; they are merely conditioned. For various reasons, people can see, choose or be forced to choose alternative actions. Self-subsistence is one example where the wage labour mechanisms are not triggered at all. An example of a situation where wage labour mechanisms can be counteracted by other mechanisms is when someone takes care of small children in the home and therefore does not work for wages. And unemployment is an example of how wage labour mechanisms, under different circumstances, produce distinctly different actions. There is, at any given moment, an uncertainty as to the actual outcome of the activity of different mechanisms. There is always the possibility that we 'make a mistake', intentionally or unintentionally, compared with different structural 'imperatives'. But none of the aforementioned examples means that one may assume that the causal powers and mechanisms of wage labour have ceased to exist; it only means that at the moment they are not realized, or are not realized in a 'pure' form.

This also means that 'causal laws … must be analysed as tendencies' (Bhaskar 1978: 50). This is a completely different understanding of what a 'scientific law' means to the prevalent one. What is usually meant by 'scientific laws' is wellsubstantiated statements about universal empirical regularities of the following kind: 'if A, then B', and it is the regularity of the course of events in itself which is understood to be the causal connection. Yet we have ample, daily experiences of the fact that laws hardly ever work in that way. Aeroplanes and birds constantly break the laws of gravity. In those cases, however, we usually do not consider these laws to have been nullified; rather we draw the correct conclusion that the mechanisms of the law of gravity may temporarily be modified by other mechanisms (inherent in birds and aeroplanes).

An important aspect of this is a characteristic of tendencies which may seem peculiar:

> Two tendencies may counteract one another so that neither of them is put into effect. To want something is for a human being the same as having a tendency to act in a specific manner. And we all know that such tendencies may neutralize one another. Everyone has probably at one point been in a situation, where he, like Buridan's ass, has stood between two wisps of hay not knowing which one to choose. We may simultaneously be drawn in two opposite directions, the result being that we stay put; seen from outside it might look as if we were not influenced by anything. Tendencies can also be directed in the same direction and thus reinforce one another. However, their distinctive features are most clearly evident when they counteract one another.
>
> (Johansson 1984: 88–9, our translation)

Thus when we wish to explain phenomena in the world it is not sufficient to make empirical observations; these very rarely succeed in capturing the underlying mechanisms producing phenomena. However, it will not suffice to merely refer to the mechanisms of objects. We must also take into account their nonmanifest or non-realized modes of operation. Powers and mechanisms may be present and working without us being able to immediately perceive any connection between them and the effects they produce. 'It is the idea of continuing activity as distinct from that of enduring power', says Bhaskar (1978: 50), 'that the concept of tendency is designed to capture. In the concept of tendency, the concept of power is thus literally dynamized or set in motion.' Thus statements about tendencies are *transfactual*, that is, they say that objects are working independently of the factual outcome, separated from the factual events. Scientific laws are thus neither empirical statements (that is to say statements about experiences), nor statements about events; they are statements about independently existing and transfactual active objects' mechanisms or ways of working. The relation can be described as in Figure 2.

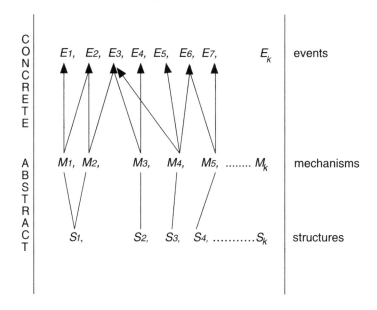

Figure 2 Structures, mechanisms and events
Source: Sayer 1992: 117

Figure 2 shows a set of events, mechanisms and structures as they exist in a complex and compound whole, for example human society. When the structural mechanisms are activated, they produce certain effects, depending on what other mechanisms they at the time happen to combine with. A particular mechanism can produce completely different actions at different times, and inversely the same event can have completely different causes.

It is therefore also the task of science to try, as far as possible, to reach beyond the purely empirical assertion of a certain phenomenon, to a description of what it was in the object that made it possible. We cannot be satisfied with just knowing that A is generally followed by B; a scientific explanation should also describe how this happens, what the process looks like where A produces B – if there is any real causal relationship at all between the events observed. Here we must pose transfactual questions; we must look beyond the factual event by postulating and identifying the generative mechanisms which made the event possible.

This type of questioning process thus works generally with structural and causal analysis involving both abstract and concrete studies. The knowledge we acquire in this way can always be the object of new studies; it may at a later stage be corroborated or falsified. Such is science's path to knowledge, in practice. The working procedure is actually quite common, and we find many examples of it in scientific literature. It is, however, seldom discussed explicitly in books on method.

Critical realist understanding of natural necessity, that is, the internal and necessary relation between structures, powers, mechanisms and tendencies, is applicable both within the natural and the social sciences. But the circumstance that the relation between causal powers or mechanisms is *contingent* has very particular and often neglected implications when human society is the object of knowledge.

A stratified world with emergent powers and mechanisms

When we analyse a concrete and complex object of any kind, it means we divide it into its components to be better able to explain and understand its constitution and way of working. Abstraction is one way of achieving this. Above, we also discussed the importance of making relevant abstractions, that is, abstractions which take the object's nature into consideration – its constituent structures, powers and mechanisms – and do not divide that which is necessarily related. Nor do we make categories of that which lacks internal connection.

There is, however, another and very common form of 'decomposition' which one must be cautious about (Sayer 1992: 118), namely such a *reduction* which means that a concrete compound phenomenon is decomposed into smaller and smaller components. The underlying idea is that the complexity and lack of clear cause-and-effect connections observable at the aggregate level will actually turn out to be an effect of a combination of quite simple and regularity-guided circumstances at the individual level. This approach is not least common within the social sciences, where questions regarding the relationship between society and individual are central. Sayer comments:

> Many researchers have been seduced by the simple idea that if only indi-
> viduals and their attitudes, etc., were understood, the macro patterns of
> society would become intelligible. But it is not always so straightforward.
> We would not try to explain the power of people to think by reference to
> the cells that constitute them, as if cells possessed this power too. ... Nor
> would we explain the power of water to extinguish fire by deriving it from
> the powers of its constituents, for oxygen and hydrogen are highly
> inflammable.
>
> (Sayer 1992: 118–19)

One of the reasons this kind of reduction is common is probably because in our empirical studies we are actually obliged to study social phenomena through the way in which they are expressed in individuals. The relation between the parts and the whole is, however, not of the kind required by reduction. The fact that the properties of the components included cannot in themselves explain their combined effect is a sign that reality contains not just one level of mechanisms below the 'surface' events; the world is not only differentiated and structured, it is also *stratified*. The mechanisms in their turn belong to different layers or strata of reality, and furthermore, these strata are hierarchically organized.

We will illustrate this in a simple way by imagining that we start from 'the bottom', finding physical mechanisms in one stratum, chemical mechanisms in another, biological in a third, and 'at the top' are the psychological and social strata. When moving 'upwards' through these strata, we find that each new stratum is formed by powers and mechanisms of the underlying strata. At the same time, this new stratum represents something entirely new, unique and qualitatively different, which cannot be reduced to underlying strata. When the properties of underlying strata have been combined, qualitatively new objects have come into existence, each with its own specific structures, forces, powers and mechanisms. The start of this new and unique occurrence is called *emergence*, and it is thus possible to say that an object has 'emergent powers'.

What reasons could there be for assuming that the world is of this stratified nature? Bhaskar (1978) again derives the arguments from the existence of the scientific practice: scientific experiments are not merely necessary, they are also possible. Let us for a brief moment return to the example of Loewi and his experiments in the previous chapter. We see that his experiments were based on precisely the supposition of a stratified world. As has been shown, Loewi wanted to explain a biological mechanism, namely living bodies' capacity to move. In other words, he was looking for the mechanism behind this biological mechanism. To find it he had to search at a more basic level; not at the biological level but at what might (in a simplified way) be called the physiological level. The mechanisms that explain a specific level – a specific stratum – of reality are themselves at a different level, at another stratum. Loewi based his experiment on this ontology – he looked for the mechanism behind a biological mechanism in chemistry. He subsequently succeeded in solving the problem he had set up.

Naturally it is possible to continue here and search for mechanisms in the underlying physical strata explaining the mechanisms of chemistry, and then continue with the aim of explaining the existence of these physical mechanisms, and so forth. This also corresponds to how the sciences have developed historically. It is characteristic for scientific practice that the search for explanations never ends. Bhaskar (1978: 168–9) gives an example: observable reactions within chemistry, such as $2Na + 2HCl = 2NaCl + H_2$, are explained by references to the theory of atomic numbers and valency and chemical compounds. The theory here points to the causal mechanisms, which cause – explain – the reactions:

> Once its reality has been established (which justifies our assuming that chemical bonding occurs and the laws of chemistry hold outside the laboratory) and the consequences of the theory have been fully explored, the next task consists of the discovery of the mechanisms responsible for chemical bonding and valency,

and so on. Hence the historical development of chemistry can be described as follows:

Stratum I	$2Na + 2HCl = 2NaCl + H_2$ explained by	
Stratum II	theory of atomic number and valency explained by	Mechanism 1
Stratum III	theory of electrons and atomic structure explained by	Mechanism 2
Stratum IV	(competing theories of sub-atomic structure)	(Mechanism 3)

Source: Bhaskar 1978: 169

As Collier observes, there is agreement between the realism inference that scientific practice proves reality is stratified, and the results science thus far has come up with regarding the evolution of life on earth:

> It appears that the material universe existed before there was organic life, and that living organisms can only exist as composed and surrounded by matter. In this sense, matter may be said to be more 'basic' than life; life in turn may be said to be more basic than rationality (in the sense that we are rational animals), and hence than human society and its history.
>
> (Collier 1994: 46)

However, the methodologically significant consequence of the stratification of reality not only lies in this, that we can isolate causal mechanisms 'downwards' through strata. What is really important in all this is the concept of 'emergence', the understanding of the new non-reducible properties and mechanisms that are added at each specific stratum. The existence of basic strata, whose laws in some sense explain the laws of 'shallower' strata, has led to, for example, speculations about a fully developed science of matter, which could explain everything, thus rendering other sciences redundant. But such 'materialistic reductionism' disregards the phenomenon of emergent powers. Even though mechanisms within more basic strata can explain some things regarding the mechanisms of less basic strata, they can never explain away these. In connection with this, we would also like to stress the crucial insight that it is just the mechanisms that are stratified, not the phenomena – events, creatures or things – as such:

> There is a common tendency, both in everyday discourse and in theory, to commit what has been called the fallacy of misplaced concreteness: to treat as if it were a kind of concrete thing or event or activity or institution what

is in fact a kind of mechanism. Thus it is commonly thought that only certain kinds of substance are 'chemicals', and that there aren't any in natural foodstuffs; that certain human needs are 'biological' while others are 'social'; that certain social institutions are 'economic', others 'political' and others 'ideological'. If these last terms, for instance, are treated instead as applying to mechanisms, all of which may govern any particular institution and codetermine its activities, a lot of mistakes can be avoided.

(Collier 1994: 47)

This also means that even if each stratum by necessity involves the mechanisms of the underlying ones, when it comes to concrete phenomena one can still never beforehand assume that the mechanisms of more basic strata will also prove to be the causally most effective ones. Actually, one cannot predict anything regarding the influence of different mechanisms. Concrete phenomena are complexly composed of powers and mechanisms, which affect, reinforce, weaken and sometimes neutralize the effects of one another. The question of which mechanisms are the most significant for the object under study can therefore only be decided from case to case, through empirical studies and in relation to the problem we address.

This perspective could also shed new light on the many inter-scientific debates on how different concrete phenomena should be explained. What is characteristic of these debates is that they all rest on the notion of single-factor explanations. What is most influential – heredity or environment? What brings about alcoholism – is it biochemically, psychologically or socially conditioned? How are gender-specific patterns of behaviour and values explained – are they biologically or socially determined? When dealing with social phenomena, there is generally in our culture a tendency to consider the social as being less 'real' than the natural. So-called sociobiologism, that is, reduction of the social to the biological, is a widespread phenomenon. This way of thinking has been regarded as particularly tempting in the area of gender differences. Let us look at a famous example of such an argument:

Behind the facade of modern city life there is the same old naked ape. Only the names have been changed: for 'hunting' read 'working', for 'hunting grounds' read 'place of business', for 'home base' read 'house', for 'pair-bond' read 'marriage', for 'mate' read 'wife', and so on. ... It is the biological nature of the beast that has moulded the social structure of civilisation, rather than the other way around.

(Morris 1994: 74–5)

It is quite easy to see that such a line of argument in no way contains any notions whatsoever about society as a stratum in its own right, whose structures are real and hold their own emergent powers and mechanisms. A more adequate position, from critical realism's point of view, is presented by Connell, when he, against lines of argument of the aforementioned kind, objects that doctrines of natural difference ... are fundamentally mistaken. This is not to contest the facts of reproductive biology, nor to deny their interest and importance for understanding human life. What I will challenge is the assumption that the biological make-up of our bodies is the 'basis', 'foundation', 'framework', 'essence' or 'mould' of the social relations of gender. This argument accepts that there is a strong relation between social practice and biology; indeed 'gender' would be inconceivable without it. I will propose that this relation has a very different character from that assumed by theorists of natural difference.

(Connell 1987: 67)

With critical realism as the starting point, we can say that this relation implies that mechanisms within different strata of reality cooperate to produce concrete events. In the case of gender differences, it is a matter of biological mechanisms producing people of two sexes, and social mechanisms producing societies where people, on the basis of different sexes, assume different positions in social gender relations. The biological mechanisms are thus not fundamental in relation to the social mechanisms in explaining *social* gender relations – rather they are simply mixed up in them. Neither type of mechanism can be reduced to the other; each is emergent at its own stratum. What mechanism or mechanisms we choose to concentrate upon is decided by what our study object is, and the purpose of our study. However, herein also lies the realization that a certain scientific theory can hardly claim to, on its own, give an exhaustive explanation of different concrete phenomena. Depending on the purpose of the study, several theoretical perspectives and approaches may be necessary. In the light of this, disputes between different scientific disciplines regarding the preferential right of explanation appear to be the effect of a lack of understanding of strata and emergence, which is also the reason for the tendency to come up with single-factor explanations. If, on the other hand, we accept that the world consists of strata, each of which has its own emergent powers, this permits completely new scientific possibilities. Interdisciplinary research approaches, not least, in this perspective look promising.

Within the individual disciplines, however, the following applies (Sayer 1992: 120): 'A fortunate consequence of the stratification of the world is that we don't have to work back through all the successive constitutive strata in order to understand objects in any specific stratum'. In many cases, the underlying strata can be taken for granted and our main concern is those mechanisms which constitute the stratum where our own research problem belongs; that is to say, we keep to that which is emergent within 'our own' stratum (at the same time we are conscious that there are mechanisms within other strata that also lay down conditions).

For example, within social science it is often not relevant to derive the problems we study primarily from the fact that people are made up of biological components, which in their turn are made up of chemical components, which in their turn are made up of physical components, and so on. This kind of reductionism overlooks precisely the phenomenon of stratification through emergence, and very easily leads to erroneous conclusions regarding causal powers and mechanisms. The social constitutes its own stratum, and hence society has other properties and powers than the individuals constituting it.

Sayer (1992: 119) explains emergence in terms of the difference between external and internal relations. When the relation between objects is only external (contingent) the nature of the objects is such that they are independent of each other and hence they do not modify one another's causal powers and mechanisms (however, they can of course influence the *effects* when the forces are exercised). On the other hand, if the relation is internal and necessary – in other words the objects depend upon one another for their existence, as is the case with social relations such as landlord/tenant – then emergent powers ensue, since precisely this combination of individuals in a decisive way determines the powers they exercise on one another. It would be of no avail trying to explain the existence of landlords and tenants with reference to people's biological, chemical and physical constituents. These are involved – in this case biological creatures' need for protection plays a part – but they cannot explain why certain people pay money to others in order to receive protection (neither can they explain 'money', or why the protection is of the kind it is, and so on). Social phenomena are produced by social mechanisms:

> Even though social structures exist only where people reproduce them, they have powers irreducible to those of individuals (you can't pay rent to yourself). Explanation of the actions of individuals often therefore requires not a micro (reductionist) regress to their inner constitution (though that may be relevant too) but a 'macro regress' to the social structures in which they are located.
>
> (Sayer 1992: 119)

However, critical realism not only objects to reductionism in the above sense – 'atomism'. There exists another kind of methodology, which paradoxically enough often is considered the opposite to reductionism, namely 'holism'. Holism is nonetheless reductionist, insofar as it asserts that the parts of a system can only be explained in terms of the whole they together constitute. Both these positions are reductionist in that they deny autonomous emergent powers in one or the other stratum:

> Indeed, if either is taken as a methodology with general validity, it will generate a regress reducing wholes to greater wholes of which they are parts, or parts to smaller parts of which they are composed, until we reach either One Big Whole … or a mass of literal atoms, differing only numerically and related only mechanically.
>
> (Collier 1994: 117)

One can agree with Collier that the critique of reductionism has mainly been directed towards atomism, in a way that the risks of holism have been obscured. The theory of emergence, however, allows for us to distinguish genuine wholes – for example social relations – which cannot be reduced to something else, at the same time as they are composed by parts which themselves are indivisible wholes – for example human beings. And the latter can in their turn be parts of greater wholes, such as society. Each level in this hierarchy of composition has its own specific mechanisms and emergent powers. This in turn means that it is possible to understand dysfunctions in these wholes, which yet are functional to their nature. The parts are certainly not mere functions of wholes, they also go their own way (Collier 1994: 117).

With reference to the discussion of strata and emergence, we would like to stress that there is not any definite, beforehand-given number of strata. Neither is there a definite answer to the question regarding how strata are organized. There is an ongoing debate regarding this. In particular, the issue of the psychological sciences in relation to the social sciences has been the object of discussion.

The question is which stratum ontologically presupposes the existence of the other – must societies exist in order for human beings to exist, or is it the other way round? It is certainly not a trivial question. It is a matter of which mechanisms can explain which – are societies the way they are because people are the way they are, or is it just the opposite? Or is it perhaps that society and human beings presuppose one another and hence must have emerged together? This discussion has every chance of being long-lived.

At the same time, this complex problem reflects the two dimensions of science, which were dealt with in Chapter 2: scientific theories – the transitive objects of science – are always about something which is independent of the theories themselves, namely the generative mechanisms of reality – the intransitive objects of science. Hence theories are at any given moment fallible; they may always be transcended by new theories. We would like to stress, however, that the debate here referred to is of no immediate significance for the lines of argument conducted here. What is of importance is the realization that strata and emergence exist.

It is characteristic of the higher strata of reality, to which the objects of the social sciences and the humanities belong, that they have the ability to react on and intervene in both in their own stratum and in underlying strata. Throughout history, people have interfered and changed 'the course of nature' in the same way as we are constantly manipulating ourselves and the social settings of which we form a part. Science itself is a good example of this ambition. The reason why this is at all possible is that mechanisms within different strata operate independently of their effects and of any specific course of events. At the same time, this is also the reason why problems have arisen regarding the scientific study of higher strata. How is it actually possible to do research into a complex and continuously self-changing world such as human society? Let us examine the background of the problem: how reality itself makes different conditions for natural and social science respectively, as a consequence of stratification and emergence.

Open and closed systems

We established earlier that 'science' is often strongly associated with the establishing of regularities and laws, and that the legitimacy and prestige of science is to a large extent traceable to the achievements of the natural sciences in this area. These kinds of knowledge have, above all, made it possible to predict and thus to a higher degree intervene, control and direct our existence in the world. The social sciences, on the other hand, in this respect have encountered considerable difficulties; there are a great number of examples of unsuccessful social prognoses. This has, among other things, led to the conclusion that the social sciences so far are undeveloped and 'immature' sciences. But more and more people have also drawn the even more discouraging conclusion that it is not at all possible to produce relevant knowledge about people and about society, in the sense of being general and predictive.

We would like to contend, however, that the problems primarily have to do with epistemological mistakes (which actually could be seen as giving some support to the view that the social sciences are immature; such mistakes must certainly have impeded the development of the social sciences). One such mistake has already been discussed: the oversight that the very core of (natural) science practice is the study of the level of mechanisms and not the observation of immediately observable phenomena at the level of events. Another mistake is made by overlooking that the objects' powers and mechanisms are in different strata of reality, which must certainly affect what knowledge we may have of them.

A central theme in our present line of argument has been that issues of method must always be considered related to the nature of the object under study and to the purpose of a particular study. The understanding of reality as stratified and emergent shows that the decisive difference between the worlds studied by natural and social sciences, respectively, could be defined as the difference between *open* and *closed* systems – or rather the difference in making it possible to close systems. The failure of the social sciences in defining regularities is not only ascribed to the omission of the generative mechanism level. Critical realism also poses the question of what reality must be like for it to *be possible* for phenomena such as regularities and laws to occur at all. The answer is that this entails 'closed systems'.

Generally speaking, a closed system is at hand when reality's generative mechanisms can operate in isolation and independently of other mechanisms – closed systems require non-change. Bhaskar (1978: ch. 2) specifies two criteria for closure:

1   There must not be any change or qualitative variation in the objects having the causal powers, if the mechanisms are to operate with consistency – as

qualitative change in the objects means that we will be dealing with other objects having different powers and mechanisms. This is the *internal condition for closure*.

2   The relation between the causal mechanisms and the mechanisms in their environment, which influence their mode of operation and their effects, must be constant for the outcome to be regular; this is the *external condition for closure*.

If both 1 and 2 are met, we are dealing with conditions where no new emergent powers and mechanisms develop, and these are the conditions necessary to make it possible to produce regularity.

The problem is, however, that a stratified reality is also an open reality. Nature as such does not produce closed systems; in all probability there is no such thing as a naturally closed system, even though certain natural phenomena, such as the solar system, may appear to be near to that definition. This points to the crucial factor: the issue of openness or closure is primarily a matter of gradation. The relation between a mechanism at a 'high' level and a mechanism at the underlying level means that the 'higher' mechanism is rooted in, and emergent from, the more basal one. This gives us the possibility to create closed conditions – in certain strata. Collier explains it thus:

> The 'lower' the strata in the hierarchy of rootedness and emergence, the closer we get to a closed system. For it is possible to isolate, for instance, a chemical process from the interruptions of organic processes, but it is not possible to isolate an organic process from the effects of chemical processes, since it is rooted in them. ... It is often possible to isolate a system from processes generated by 'higher' strata, but never possible to isolate one from those generated by 'lower' strata. Hence the further up the hierarchy we go, the more distant our approximations to closure become.
>
> (Collier 1994: 121)

This can also be expressed thus: the higher the strata, the more mechanisms and possible combinations of mechanisms and emergence. This is also a shared reason for the achievements of the natural sciences and the problems of the social sciences: the natural sciences deal with lower strata and can generally study their objects in more or less closed systems, whereas the social sciences are interested in strata where closure is not possible.

This is also illustrated by the importance of experiment for natural science practice. As we have seen, the aim of the experiment is to study reality's deep dimension, the causal mechanisms underlying the surface of events. And the experimental set-up as such aims at giving the researcher a way of ensuring that what she is studying is precisely a specific mechanism and not a different one, and that the way in which this mechanism operates is not influenced by other unknown mechanisms. That is to say, the set-up must satisfy the two criteria for closure. Experiment thus is an example of artificially closed systems.

As we have seen, however, experiments in the natural science sense of the word are not possible for social science. Here, the objects are distinguished by operating in open systems. On the one hand, people are capable of learning and self-change. People can adapt to new knowledge and change themselves to become in a true sense new people. This is, for example, the *raison d'être* of psychoanalysis, but it is also the pronounced purpose of several everyday activities such as teaching and education of various kinds. People can also change more as an unintentional result of new experiences. This obstructs the first condition for closure: that there must not be any change or qualitative variation in the objects.

In addition, people's behaviour and their actions constantly influence and change the set of objects and mechanisms in their environment with which they interact. More or less explicitly, people strive to change the situations and the settings of which they are part. And they are often successful, even though the changes often result in unintended consequences, in view of their initial intentions. Nevertheless, this obstructs the second condition for closure: that relations between the causal mechanisms we study, and the mechanisms in their environment, must be constant for the outcome to be regular.

Within higher strata, however, there are many examples of what we might call pseudo-closed systems. These could be seen as expressions of higher strata's causal powers to intervene in other strata with the purpose of achieving some kind of closure – that is to say regularity – thus achieving predictability and control. Any type of social organization, such as the judicial system, the organization of working life, family, the educational system or the health care system, are examples of such pseudo-closed systems – they are the result of a conscious striving to make society (and nature – nature's mechanisms are inevitably involved) more controllable in relation to people's different aims. The closure achieved, however, is always of a spurious kind, and far from the natural science experiment's artificial closure – change and renewal are part of human society's constituent characteristics.

The problems of predicting social events and processes are thus a consequence of the open systems applicable to the study of human society. Where regularities do not occur other than sporadically, it is not possible to make predictions with any high degree of certainty – there cannot be any social science laws of the kind 'if A, then B'. This also means that the view of a theory's predictability being the best test of its validity is not generally applicable. That view is not true in natural science, and certainly not in social science.

To begin with, explanation and predictability are not one and the same: if we can explain how something works it does not automatically follow that we can also predict how it will behave, and vice-versa. There are non-predictive explanations as well as non-explanatory predictions. We will use some examples from Sayer. The example of non-predictive explanation comes from geology, a natural science working with open systems. Geologists know the necessary conditions for petroleum to be formed. Hence they can say where petroleum might be found, but they cannot predict where petroleum actually is to be found – there is still a need for drilling in order to discover this. But that is not due to insufficient knowledge of the mechanisms that form petroleum – the mechanisms are well known – but there is a lack of empirical knowledge of the accidental conditions within which these mechanisms operate. It is not the causal explanation that is incomplete, but knowledge about the accidental conditions. And this is inevitable when we are operating with open systems (Sayer 1994: 131–2).

If, on the other hand, we have access to closed systems, it is possible to make models that give accurate predictions. Machinery and instruments of various kinds operate in closed systems – as long as they do not break down. It is precisely their predictability in this respect which makes them so useful. If output in this way is regularly related to input, any predictive formula, which fits the regularities, will do. A quantitatively closed system such as a barometer can be used to predict weather changes and vice-versa. But such predictions are not explanatory, as they tell us nothing about the mechanisms which have caused the results.

These examples demonstrate that abstractions are not to do with factual events, but are about what produces them; and concrete explanations require empirical knowledge to make it possible to describe how and under what circumstances exactly these mechanisms exist, and how they interact in exactly these circumstances. Or to use Sayer's words:

> Abstract theory analyses objects in terms of their constitutive structures, as parts of wider structures and in terms of their causal powers. Concrete research looks at what happens when these combine.
>
> (Sayer 1992: 116)

Thus a scientific explanation is based on both abstract and concrete research. Predictions, on the other hand, are about factual events and need not take into consideration what produces them. A prediction's reliability, however, varies with the grade of closed and open systems respectively, and fully closed systems neither exist in society nor in nature; furthermore, in society it is not possible to artificially create these. The general conclusion, based on the understanding of nature's stratification and emergent powers, is that our claims on knowledge and on methods must be adapted to the nature of the object we study if knowledge is to have practical relevance. Among other things, this means that social science explanations, in particular, cannot be predictive in the usual sense, such as when astronomers predict a solar eclipse or the return of Halley's Comet. Furthermore, it means that the criticism levelled against the social sciences for their lack of predictability is misguided; what could be criticized is when the social sciences claim that they *can* make predictions. We will return to the specific problems surrounding predictions in Chapter 7, but for the remainder of the book we will continually try to expound how social science explanation can still be practically relevant, despite the impossibility of making predictions.

Conclusion

We have now introduced critical realism's ontology and epistemology, as well as discussing the basic methodological consequences that follow from this.

We have demonstrated why conceptual abstraction stands out as a central activity for social science, and we have described how one should go about making good social science abstractions. Such abstractions are characterized by aiming at identifying the necessary, constituent properties of the study object, since these characteristics define what actions the object can produce, that is to say they identify the object's generative mechanisms. It has also been shown how structural analysis can be used to make abstractions, and how such an analysis also leads to relevant causal analysis. We analysed the critical realist causality concept and saw that scientific explanations are not to do with empirical covariance or statistical correlation: an explanation is about causes, and a cause is that which can make something happen in the world. In connection with this we saw what objects, structures, mechanisms and tendencies mean. This resulted in the crucial conclusion that while there is a necessary relationship between an object and its causal mechanisms, the relationship between the generative mechanisms and their effect is contingent. On the concrete level many mechanisms may be concurrently active, and they may just as well reinforce as neutralize each other's manifestations. This in turn leads to the situation that 'scientific laws' always have to be analysed as tendencies.

We have emphasized that it is the nature of the object under study that determines what research methods are applicable, and also what knowledge claims one may have. In this connection we have explained the significance of the world being not only differentiated and structured, but also stratified. The mechanisms belong in separate hierarchically arranged strata of reality, where each stratum is composed of mechanisms from underlying strata. At the same time, this composition results in the emergence of qualitatively new objects, having their own powers and mechanisms, which cannot be reduced to more basic strata. A consequence of this is, among other things, that while natural science can be carried on in artificially closed systems – experiments – where the activity of individual mechanisms can be isolated and studied without uncontrolled interference by other mechanisms, social science is always carried out in open systems: change is a constitutive characteristic of human societies.

This in turn results in the impossibility of making predictions in social science, and is the reason why it is crucial for the practical relevance of social scientific knowledge that it is not used in that fashion.

Part II
Methodological implications

4 Generalization, scientific inference and models for an explanatory social science

In Part I of this book critical realism is presented primarily as a metatheory containing a specific ontology and epistemology. Together these chapters show that critical realism apprehends the object of social science in a manner quite different from both positivism, hermeneutics and postmodernism.

But what significance does this have for the methodology of social science? This is the all-embracing question we shall discuss in the second part of the book. When we talk about methodology, it is about the borderline between on the one hand the philosophy of science, and on the other hand the critical methods or working procedures used in specific studies. A recurrent argument in this book is that we cannot commit ourselves to a particular research method; we cannot decide which method is the most appropriate without taking in to consideration the properties of the object we wish to acquire knowledge about.

Critical realism does not claim to develop a new method for social science. On the contrary, it criticizes any ambition to develop a specific method for scientific work. There is no such thing as the method of critical realism. On the other hand, critical realism offers guidelines for social science research and starting points for the evaluation of already established methods. What we discuss in this chapter is just such guidelines. The starting point is three fundamental methodological arguments. Besides this introduction, this chapter contains three sections, unfolding each of the three arguments:

1   All science should have generalizing claims. Methods for acquiring knowledge of the general and for examining the validity of generalizations are fundamental for all social science research. Generalizing may, however, mean different things.

2   Quite essential for scientific methods are various modes of inference. In a science based on critical realism, abduction and retroduction are two indispensable modes of inference besides induction and deduction. In this chapter these four modes of inference will be presented. We shall use the concept of inference in two different meanings: in the first place as the logical inferences treated in formal logic, in the second place as thought operations, i.e. different ways of reasoning and thinking in order to proceed from something to something else (cf. Habermas 1972: 113). To avoid

misunderstandings it is important to state that we use the word 'inference' in
these different ways.
3   An overall aim in social science research is to explain events and processes.
     To explain something implies (from the perspective of critical realism) first
     describing and conceptualizing the properties and causal mechanisms
     generating and enabling events, making things happen (see Chapter 3), and
     then describing how different mechanisms manifest themselves under
     specific conditions. This kind of investigation requires a methodological
     approach based on abduction and retroduction, and breaking with the so-
     called Popper–Hempel model of scientific explanations.

Thus the aim of this chapter is from these three points to present methodological
guidelines for a social science based on critical realism. What we will discuss with
reference to each of these three issues is at the same time linked to a common
problem central to modern science and the philosophy of science. The problem
we have in mind is the relationship between the individual/specific and the
universal/general. Common to different schools in the philosophy of science
(positivism, hermeneutics, Marxism, etc.), and to philosophers who have been
active in these schools, is the fact that they have emphasized this problem in their
discussions of the logical structure of science.

The whole of this chapter relates to this fundamental problem of science. In
the first section (cf. argument 1 above) we shall distinguish between two different
forms of generalization. It may seem controversial to assume, like we do, that all
science should have generalizing claims. In social science there have been
discussions over the years in which some have defended the generalizing ambitions of science, while others have emphasized the value of seeking more
thorough knowledge of unique cases. We find the origin of this division
(between the general and the unique) in the debates of the late nineteenth
century, when several prominent historians and philosophers pointed out that
human science is principally idiographic, in contrast to natural science, which is
nomothetic (Liedman 1994). An idiographic science draws attention to the individual and unique – a historical event is described with regard to the
combination of circumstances making the event unique, people are studied with
regard to unique biographies, and so on. Nomothetic science instead seeks the
general, the universal and that which conforms to law (*nomos* is the Greek word
for law). This division between idiographic human science and nomothetic
natural science caused tension within social science. Social science has been
influenced by both of these views, but it has always endeavoured to attain some
form of general knowledge. However, the relation between the specific and the
general has been treated in different ways in different schools of social science
(see e.g. Coniavitis 1984).[1]

In Chapter 3 we gave law a totally different meaning compared with what has
been common in science influenced by positivism. In the latter, law has meant
statements about universal empirical regularities. We argued, however, that a law
(e.g. the law of gravity) is a description of a mechanism existing as a property in

reality, but whose observable effects strongly vary depending on concrete circumstances. Hence laws should be analysed as tendencies. What are usually called a qualitative case study in the literature is a method very well suited for acquiring knowledge about such mechanisms or laws.

The division between the general and the unique has marked the discussion of qualitative and quantitative method. It is not uncommon in contemporary social science to take the position that qualitative methods provide knowledge about the specific and unique but that it takes quantitative methods to enable generalization. If we look at social science practice, however, we find that many of the generalizations appearing in the literature are grounded precisely in qualitatively orientated case studies. Let us give a few examples: Erving Goffman (1990) argues from qualitative studies that people's actions practically always have the character of performances where, with the aim of influencing other people's views of us, we hide certain things about ourselves and accentuate others. Through case studies, media researchers have been able to show that there are certain generally existing discursive structures and ideologies behind what on the surface appear as dissimilar texts and narratives shown on television (e.g. Fairclough 1995; Van Dijk 1997). By means of qualitative studies of power relations, researchers have been able to demonstrate that there are certain general power mechanisms recurring under totally different conditions (e.g. Ekström and Danermark 1991). Within the tradition of ethnographic research there have been many qualitative and descriptive case studies, including observations of situated everyday actions and interactions. However, as Silverman emphasizes, ethnography is not limited to descriptions of actions in different settings: 'On the contrary, ethnography shares the social science programme of producing general, possibly even law-like, statements about human social organisation' (Silverman 1993: 49). These are just four examples of research which, mainly with the help of case studies, has led to generalizable knowledge about structures and mechanisms.

In the second section of this chapter (cf. argument 2 above) we pose the question: how can we attain knowledge about the general from knowledge about particulars; or vice-versa, how do we get from particulars to generalities? As a suggestion for solutions to these problems we shall present four different modes of inference – deduction, induction, abduction and retroduction. We see these four as being complementary. They constitute central parts of the structure and logical preconditions of scientific reasoning, and are thus the core of the scientific method.

What we call 'inference' is descriptions of various procedures, ways of reasoning and arguing applied when we in science relate the particular to the general. Characteristic of inference is that from one thing conclusions are drawn about something else. It is important to emphasize one thing from the start: inference, as we use the concept, involves on the one hand formalized and strictly logical rules for deduction. Deductive logic is employed, e.g. to test whether conclusions we draw in an argument follow in a logically valid manner from the premises given to support the conclusion. We also use the concept of inference to denote various thought operations (e.g. retroduction) which are neither formalized nor strictly logical conclusions, but suggest a form of argument advancing from one thing to something else, e.g. arguing from individual observations to gain knowledge about general basic structures.

In everyday contexts we continually draw general conclusions from observations of individual cases. Some generalizations are well grounded in solid experiences. In other cases they may be manifestations of prejudices we hold, without being quite aware of it. Both in everyday discussion as well as in scientific argument it is important to take a critical attitude to unfounded generalizations. In science we are expected to apply well-reasoned and well-founded methods when we test the validity of a generalization. We will find the basis for these methods in the inferences and thought operations we shall examine in this chapter.

In the third and last section of the chapter we shall present two alternative models for an explanatory social science. The focus will lie in a demonstration of how the different forms of generalization and inference treated in the two previous sections are integrated in different explanatory models.

Generalization – two different meanings

So far we have been talking about generality (or generalization) without exactly defining what this concept means. If we look it up in a dictionary we may find the synonyms 'universal applicability' and 'universality'. Here we use these three concepts as synonyms. What do we mean, then, by generality?

Within science there are two fundamentally different ways of defining and using the concept of generality. We may call these the empiricist concept of generality and the realist concept of generality. According to the first, generality is a question of how large a group of events or other phenomena an empirical observation can be generalized to. In this case generalization is an extrapolation. Knowledge of a limited amount of events is extrapolated to, and is assumed to be valid for, a larger population. Generalizations can be made to larger populations over time, and to events in various sociocultural contexts. Empirical statements (and hypotheses) may in this sense be general to different degrees; they may claim to involve a few specific cases, but they may also refer to larger populations and circumstances of a more common nature. Let us exemplify this with two empirical statements differing in just this respect.

Statement 1:   During the last two weeks of the election campaign, mistrust of politics was expressed on several occasions in Swedish television news programmes.

Statement 2:   Distrust of politics is often expressed in mass media.

Naturally it takes different types of investigation to test the two exemplified statements. The first one is possible to test through a well-defined empirical study. The second statement is hardly possible to test comprehensively. Statements of this type are based on extrapolation to a larger population from the knowledge about particular cases. Generalizations in science deal partly with this type of empirical extrapolation, but not exclusively.

The empirical extrapolation is confined to what was described in Chapter 2 as the empirical domain, and excludes the domain of the deep structures of reality (what we have also referred to as the transfactual conditions of the objects). According to the realist concept of generality, scientific generalizations largely refer to transfactual conditions, to the more or less universal preconditions for an object to be what it is. Bhaskar (1978: 227) expresses it in the following way: 'Scientifically significant generality does not lie on the face of the world, but in the hidden essence of things'. The difference between these two types of generality and generalizing is illustrated in Figure 3.

What Figure 3 tries to show is, in the first place, that something can be general in two different senses – either in the sense of a *generally* occurring empirical phenomenon/event, or in the sense of *fundamental/constituent* properties and structures. In the second place the figure is designed to show that there are different actions, methods and patterns of inference behind these generalizations. The empirical extrapolation is based on induction. Induction is a process where, from observations of a limited number of events or phenomena (E1, E2, E3, E4, etc.), universally applicable conclusions are drawn from a larger population. It involves drawing conclusions about all from knowledge about a few, without leaving the empirical level. The scientific methods in this context are techniques, e.g. for taking representative samples and assessing the statistical certainty of a generalization. Knowledge about constituent properties or transfactual conditions, on the other hand, is attained by means of transfactual arguments and what we shall later on describe as retroductive inference. Taking

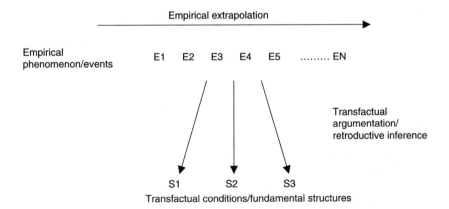

Figure 3 Two types of generalization

our starting point in the concrete we endeavour to abstract and isolate what is the basic constituent. We move from surface to depth, from the domain of the empirical to the domain of structures and mechanisms. These and also other modes of inference will be discussed in more detail in the next section.

Transfactual conditions are the conditions for something – a social relationship, an action, an institution or a social structure – to be what it is and not something completely different. Such transfactual conditions can be more or less general. Let us assume that an action is to be explained. A philosopher, who emphasizes intentionality as something universal for human activity, expresses herself very generally by focusing on the most transcendental – and in that sense universal – preconditions for human action. A social scientist, e.g. Giddens or Archer, who describes principally the relationship between structure and agency, is almost at the same level of generality. A sociologist, who analyses the prerequisites for a certain action in terms of the structures characteristic of a specific organization (e.g. family or school), or a person's internalized dispositions for action (habitus), is still looking for knowledge about general structures, however, not structures of the same universal character as those the philosopher analyses. It is important to see that all these analyses imply the ontology we described in Chapter 2 in terms of 'the three domains of reality'. The analyses do not restrict the search for knowledge to either the domain of the empirical or the domain of the actual.

This way of considering the two aspects of scientific generalization is in line with much of human and social science practice. Within science there are often formulations describing and conceptualizing transfactual conditions, without any claims of demonstrating an empirical generalization (extrapolation).

In scientific contexts, as well as in everyday life, we constantly use concepts implying generalizations – what are usually called universal concepts ('universalia'). Universal concepts express general properties, which distinguish them from concepts expressing something particular/individual. In the methodology of social science it is important to distinguish between two types of universal concepts: empirical categories and abstract concepts. An empirical category comprises a larger population of individual phenomena sharing a formal property. The universal concept of 'women' as an empirical category includes all people of a specific gender; 'elderly' refers to all people who have reached a certain age. Abstract concepts are universal concepts in another sense. They identify something which is universal in the sense of 'constituent'. Concepts like alienation, domination, social integration, ideology and reflexive identity describe more or less universal structures or mechanisms. These two types of universal concepts refer to the different forms of generalization we defined above. Empirical generalizations are expressed by means of empirical categories. Transfactual conditions are expressed by another type of universal concept, that is the abstract concept. We shall now proceed to the question of how the individual and the general are related to each other within the framework of different modes of inference or thought operations.

Scientific inference and thought operations

That reality does not speak for itself, that science can never limit itself merely to observing, registering and reporting, is a well-known fact. Reasoning, our ability to analyse, abstract, relate, interpret and draw conclusions, is a fundamental precondition for all knowledge and knowledge development. Philosophers of science have also emphasized feeling and intuition, as well as imagination and creativity as essential features of the cognitive process.

Thinking is a prerequisite if we are to make sense of what we observe, if it is to mean anything to us, to enable us to interpret the particular in a context, to enable us to draw conclusions about the general from observations of the individual. In this section we shall try to show that scientific method mainly revolves around different modes of inference. The concept of inference or thought operation refers to different ways of arguing and drawing conclusions – moving from something and arriving at something else – having in common that we thereby link observations of individual phenomena to general concepts. Inference is a way of reasoning towards an answer to questions such as: What does this mean? What follows from this? What must exist for this to be possible?

In order to test the validity of different modes of inference, to understand their possibilities and limitations, we must know their fundamental structure. Scientific inference is partly about following formalized, strict rules for logical argument and argumentation. The principal resource demanded of the researcher is the ability for logical reasoning. But scientific inference, in the sense of thought operations, also involves different ways of reasoning, interpreting and drawing conclusions without following strictly formalized rules. Here the researcher's powers of abstraction, as well as imagination and creativity, can be crucial.

We distinguish between four different modes of inference: deduction, induction, abduction and retroduction. Each of these represents a different thought operation, a different way of moving from one thing to something else. Deduction and induction (and, according to some, also abduction) are also concepts in formal logic. 'Formal' implies following the logical form of inference, not the substantive contents. As we shall see, this is manifested in the formalization of inference through different models, and also the use of symbolic language. In the real sense of the word, only deduction is valid as a strictly logical mode of inference. We shall shortly demonstrate what this means. However, we would like to say from the start that we consider the different modes of inference as complementary in research practice. Deduction, for instance, gives us universal guidelines for what is necessary for a logically valid argument, guidelines that can be used to test the validity of the conclusions drawn by means of, for example, retroduction. The account in this section can be summed up in Table 1. We recommend that the reader begin by surveying the table and then return to it as the different modes of inference are discussed in the text.

Table 1 Four modes of inference

	Deduction	Induction[a]	Abduction	Retroduction
Fundamental structure/thought operations	To derive logically valid conclusions from given premises. To derive knowledge of individual phenomena from universal laws.	From a number of observations to draw universally valid conclusions about a whole population. To see similarities in a number of observations and draw the conclusion that these similarities also apply to non-studied cases. From observed co-variants to draw conclusions about law-like relations.	To interpret and recontextualize individual phenomena within a conceptual framework or a set of ideas. To be able to understand something in a new way by observing and interpreting this something in a new conceptual framework.	From a description and analysis of concrete phenomena to reconstruct the basic conditions for these phenomena to be what they are. By way of thought operations and counterfactual thinking to argue towards transfactual conditions.
Formal logic	Yes	Yes	Yes and no	No
Strict logical inference	Yes	No	No	No
The central issue	What are the logical conclusions of the premises?	What is the element common for a number of observed entities and is it true also of a larger population?	What meaning is given to something interpreted within a particular conceptual framework?	What qualities must exist for something to be possible?
Strength	Provides rules and guidance for logical derivations and investigations of the logical validity in all argument.	Provides guidance in connection with empirical generalizations, and possibilities to calculate, in part, the precision of such generalizations.	Provides guidance for the interpretive processes by which we ascribe meaning to events in relation to a larger context.	Provides knowledge of transfactual conditions, structures and mechanisms that cannot be directly observed in the domain of the empirical.

Table 1 Continued

Limitations	Deduction does not say anything new about reality beyond what is already in the premises. It is strictly analytical.	Inductive inference can never be either analytically or empirically certain = the internal limitations of induction. Induction is restricted to conclusions at the empirical level = the external limitations of induction.	There are no fixed criteria from which it is possible to assess in a definite way the validity of an abductive conclusion.	There are no fixed criteria from which it would be possible to assess in a definite way the validity of a retroductive conclusion.
Important quality on the part of the researcher	Logical reasoning ability	Ability to master statistical analysis	Creativity and imagination	Ability to abstract
Examples	If A then B A Thus: B	From an investigation of the attitude of a representative sample of Swedes, draw the conclusion that 30% of the Swedish population is in favour of the EU.	Karl Marx reinterpretation/redescription of the history of humankind from the historical materialist view.	For a ritual to be just a ritual there must exist, *inter alia*, emotionally loaded symbols and common notions of inviolable/sacred values.

Note.

ᵃ The concept of induction has been used in partly different ways by different philosophers/theorists, and within different disciplines. Here we are talking about induction in the sense of inductive logic. In social science the concept of inductive is also used to describe a certain form of research procedure. We shall return to this research procedure in the next chapter. It is important not to confuse inductive logic with inductive research, since these concepts in part imply totally different things.

In what follows we will first present deduction and then induction as two forms of formalized logic for inference. In social science one talks, however, also about the inductive and the deductive method as terms for research approaches. In this case the issue concerns different ways of viewing the research process and its design, and how empirical observations are related to theories. Characteristic of an inductive approach is that research starts in relatively unprejudiced observations of reality without being bound to a specific theory. Then, step by step, the researcher develops different categories and concepts from collected data. The best-known inductive research approach is probably the 'grounded theory' approach. In contrast, the deductive research process takes its starting point in established theories. Through deduction, hypotheses are derived from these theories, and in the next step they are tested on an empirical material. These two different ways of relating empirical data to theory are something we shall discuss in more detail in Chapter 6. It is important not to confuse deductive and inductive logic respectively, with a deductive and inductive research approach, since they concern in part different things.

Deduction

The concept of deductive inference can be used as equivalent to inference where the conclusions follow in a strictly logical way from given premises. Deductive logic holds a unique position in science, since it is applied (or at least should be applied) when we examine the logical validity in all scientific argument, regardless of which research methods are being used or which research tradition we are following. It is fundamental for scientific argument that we substantiate our conclusions with various assertions, observations, etc. Deductive logic is used not to decide the reliability of these statements; rather it is used to test the logical validity of the conclusions we draw, given that the statements are correct. In that case the statements are called premises. A logically (deductively) valid conclusion is a form of inference where the conclusion must be true if all the premises are true. Deducing is synonymous with derivation. We may use a good definition of derivation taken from Føllesdal *et al.* (1990: 290, our translation): 'By derivation we mean the transition from premises to conclusion, i.e. an action or a type of action that you perform when arguing' (what the authors term 'action' is what we have chosen to call thought operations).

Within the framework of deductive logic a great number of formalized examples of deductions have been developed, which can be used when we test the validity of our own argument and that of others. Deductive logic is generally divided into different parts, of which propositional logic and predicate logic form two main parts. Propositional logic is the part of logic that examines the validity of an argument, where the propositions are related to each other by the words 'not', 'and', 'or', 'if … then'. The most common forms are modus ponens and modus tollens:

Modus ponens:	*Modus tollens*:
If A then B	If A then B
A	not B
Thus: B	Thus: not A

Propositional logic is used not only when we examine the validity of a scientific argument. It also constitutes the foundation in a scientific method called hypothetical deductive method (see Chapter 5). To test hypotheses (H) one deduces consequences (C) from these hypotheses – consequences that can be tested against various kinds of knowledge and empirical observation. If we conclude that the consequences are false we can infer that the hypothesis, too, is false. The logic behind this is modus tollens and can be expressed as follows:

Premise 1	If H, then C
Premise 2	not C

Conclusion	not H

Predicate logic examines inference also containing terms like 'all' and 'no'. The propositions in predicate logical language further consist of, first, what are called individual terms, and second, a predicate stating the properties of what the individual term states (Prawitz 1991). Inference building on predicate logic can have the following form:

All A are B
C is A
Thus: C is B

Deduction is usually presented as the opposite of induction in that it takes its starting point in what is the conclusion of induction, namely a universal/general law. Deduction can thus be used to deduce the particular from the general/a universal law. Here we give an example showing how predicate logic can be applied in such deduction (within brackets we note the symbols we have used so that it will be easier to compare with the formalization above):

Premise 1 (universal law/general statement):	All statements about something (A) *are* relative (B)
Premise 2 (individual observation):	Relativism (C) *is* a statement about something (A)

Conclusion (logically necessary conclusion):	Relativism (C) *is* relative (B)

Given that the premises are true it would be a logical contradiction to state that the conclusion is false. If we in an argument argue that all statements about reality are relative in relation to a social, conceptual or discursive context (i.e. not universally valid), we can by deductive logic conclude that this relative validity involves the statement itself. This has actually been one of the fundamental arguments against relativism, what has been called the 'inward collapse' of relativism (cf. Chapter 2).

A common criticism of Freud's psychoanalysis has been that Freud regards all people as governed by irrational instincts while at the same time presupposing that the theory, put forth by himself, is rational. Without taking a stance on the issue of whether this critique is based on a correct interpretation of Freud, we can reconstruct the critique by means of the fundamental structure of deductive logic. For the argument to be logically valid, the requirements are, as said before: if premises 1 and 2 are true, the conclusion must also be true.

Premise 1 (universal law/general statement):	All people's ideas (A) *are* manifestations of irrational instincts (B)
Premise 2 (particular observation):	Freud's psychoanalysis (C) *is* the idea of a person (A)
Conclusion (logically necessary conclusion):	Freud's psychoanalysis (C) *is* a manifestation of irrational instincts (B)

Deductive logic can be used in different ways in concrete research practice. In the first place we can start with propositions (universal basic assumptions) that we suppose (or know) are true, and from these deduce a great deal of specific knowledge which logically follows from these basic assumptions. In mathematics (but more seldom in social science) scientists devote their time to showing how a great deal of information can be deduced from a few basic assumptions (the so-called axiomatic method). Second, we can use deductive logic to deduce, from hypotheses, empirically testable consequences and through these indirectly test these hypotheses. Deduction is the core of what is called the hypothetico-deductive method. But deduction is not only associated with specific scientific methods. Deduction can also, in the third place, be utilized when we examine the logical validity of all scientific arguments, regardless of what research methods are being used.

The strength of deductive logic is that it provides rules for what is a logically valid conclusion based on given premises. The limitation of deduction is that it does not tell us anything new about reality beyond what is already in the premises. Deductive conclusions are analytical conclusions. By this we mean that the validity of the conclusions is dependent on our following the logical rules for deduction, independently of what reality is like. In analytical inference the conclusion is implicit in the premises. This means that it does not give us any guidance on how we, from observing particular phenomena, can gain knowledge of the abstract structures and mechanisms that make these phenomena possible. The three modes of inference we shall discuss may be called synthetic forms of inference (cf. Habermas 1972). Synthetic means that the conclusions add new knowledge about reality, which is not implicit in the premises/propositions. The validity of synthetic inference is thus dependent on what reality is like.

Induction

Inductive inference has been central in science ever since Aristotle, who is usually mentioned as the first philosopher who attached great importance to developing the logical structure of empiricist-orientated science. Inductive logic – as well as deductive logic – comes under formal logic. There is, however, one big difference between them. In inductive inference the conclusion does not necessarily follow from the premise. On the contrary, this conclusion entails addition of new knowledge beyond what is in the premise. We start from something known and given and draw conclusions which reach beyond this.

Inductive inference implies that from a number of observations of individual phenomena we draw general conclusions assumed to be true of a larger number of phenomena than those we have observed. Inductive inference can be a generalization over time and also of a larger population. Let us assume, for example, that we have a kettle filled with water on the stove and a thermometer in the water, and make the following observations:

On occasion one, when we heat this water to 100 degrees centigrade it starts to boil.
On occasion two, when we heat this water to 100 degrees centigrade it starts to boil.
On occasion three, when we heat this water to 100 degrees centigrade it starts to boil.

From this we conclude:
Always, when we heat this water to 100 degrees centigrade it starts to boil.

Here we have made a generalization over time. It states that the connection between heating the water to a certain temperature and the water's boiling, which has been observed on several occasions, exists on all occasions. This implies that the general conclusion – if it is valid – also makes it possible to predict something which has not yet taken place. If we plan on another occasion to boil this water, we can predict that it will boil at exactly this temperature.

Let us assume instead that we have three kettles filled with water and a thermometer in each kettle.

When we heat the water in kettle one to 100 degrees it starts to boil.
When we heat the water in kettle two to 100 degrees it starts to boil.
When we heat the water in kettle three to 100 degrees it starts to boil.
Conclusion: *all* water that is heated to 100 degrees starts to boil.

Here we have made an inductive generalization, meaning that from the observation that three separate entities of water have a certain quality, we conclude that all water has just this quality.

This mode of inference is often used in social science. The most common form of induction is perhaps when conclusions are drawn about an entire population from studies of a sample of investigated units (people, organizations, tests, etc.). The crucial question is whether the studied cases are representative in relation to the entire population. The samples that are examined must be of a certain size, and one must use sampling methods ensuring that the samples are representative. In statistics and research methodology, sampling and calculating methods have been developed with the object of dealing with just this induction problem. Another form of inductive inference, common in social science, is involved when we, from studies at a particular point of time, draw conclusions about other points of time.

The inductive mode of inference has limitations of two different kinds. One concerns the uncertainty of such inference, the risk of drawing the wrong conclusions although the premises are true. We call these the internal limitations of induction. Further, there is knowledge we will never reach, regardless of how well grounded the inductive premises are – conclusions we will never be able to draw – by means of induction. These can be called the external limitations of induction

The internal limitations have been the subject of lively discussions in philosophy. The core of the induction problem is rather simple. We cannot on logical grounds be certain that a description of observed occurrences (no matter how many they are) is true also of unobserved occurrences. This means, as the Scottish philosopher David Hume pointed out in the eighteenth century, that empirical generalizations are always linked to uncertainty. Nobody has come up with a real solution to this problem. However, statistics provide methods for calculating the degree of uncertainty in generalizations, given different assumptions.

But the internal limitations should not only be discussed in relation to logic and statistics. The possibility of making well-founded empirical generalizations depends on what the reality under investigation is like. To put it simply: when we draw conclusions about a fairly stable reality, the risk is comparatively small of generalizations turning out to be false. In spite of the induction problem (as Hume formulated it) we can in practice conclude that water under normal circumstances will boil at about 100 degrees the next day also, and even in a hundred years' time. If the air pressure is changed the boiling point will naturally change, but then it concerns conditions that are rather simple to control and account for (since air pressure can easily be measured and since there is a definite mathematical relationship between air pressure and boiling point).

In studies of an open and changeable reality, the induction problem has more serious consequences, however. The social reality at the level of events is often very unstable; the effects of social mechanisms depend on numerous concrete circumstances. Concerning for example people's actions, attitudes and values, scientists have indeed been able to show some relatively stable patterns. But people's actions and views, and even things like economic structures, the political structures of different countries, etc., still very much depend on a range of particular circumstances giving us little opportunity to draw empirically general conclusions from individual observations (cf. Chapter 3 and the discussion of open and closed systems).

An example of this can be taken from so-called reception research. Here, media researchers have sought knowledge about how people interpret and regard, for example, different television programmes. The investigations have often been conducted as group interviews, where the group has first watched a selected programme. One problem in this kind of research has been obvious, namely that the way an audience describes and discusses a television programme they have watched is very dependent on a number of circumstances: who the other co-watchers are, how they watch and what they are doing while watching; what questions the interviewer asks; what the people happen to know about the particular topic of the programme. All inductive inference under such circumstances is subject to great uncertainty. The concrete reality is simply too complex and changeable (cf. Ang 1991).

That inductive inference is associated with uncertainty is of course basically due to the fact that the conclusions do not logically follow from the premises, and that by inductive generalizations we speak about something beyond what we can observe here and now. This is the limitation of inductive inference compared with deduction, but at the same time it is its strength. A science that is only engaged in strictly logical derivations, or that only says something about known observations, would be a very narrow science indeed.

So far we have concentrated on the internal limitations of induction. However, it is no less important to consider the external limitations. Induction is closely associated with empirical science. It has been developed by philosophers attached to some form of empiricism (e.g. Francis Bacon, David Hume, John Stuart Mill). Induction gives no guidance as to how, from something observable, we can reach knowledge of underlying structures and mechanisms; it is limited to conclusions of empirical generalizations and regularities.

We do not suggest, however, that inductive inference as such should be ruled out in research. On the contrary, this mode of inference is part of scientific practice. But we attach less importance to induction than has often been the case, if we look at most of the literature on social science methodology. Our notion is that the objects of science are not primarily empirical regularities, but structures and mechanisms. It is also in these structures that we find the foundation for the fairly stable and lasting (but not unchangeable) character of nature as well as of social reality. 'On the realist view', says Sayer (1992: 158), 'nature's uniformity – to which many scientists have appealed – derives not from the "accidental" regularities of sequences of contingently related things but from the internal relations, structures and ways-of-acting of things themselves.'

We shall now proceed to the presentation of two modes of inference – abduction and retroduction – which in our view constitute a necessary complement to induction and deduction in a social science seeking knowledge of structures and mechanisms. Neither abduction nor retroduction is a logically valid mode of inference in the sense that deduction is. Both these types of inference represent a more comprehensive way of reasoning, arguing and relating the individual to the universal/general, that is, what we have called thought operations. With reference to the central role played by abduction and retroduction in scientific practice, plus the fact that they have seldom been mentioned in the literature on social science method and methodology, we will discuss them in more detail than we have done with induction and deduction.

Abduction

What is common to the objects of social science is that we can describe them as both individual phenomena, and as manifestations of – or parts of – general structures. This is true about social activities as well as the products of these activities, such as texts, pictures, buildings, situations where people meet, etc. Many of the concepts we use allegedly identify those general structures. Table 2 gives examples of what we mean by this distinction between individual concrete phenomena and general structures.

The difference between what is described in the left and the right columns, respectively, is a difference between on the one hand observable events, and on the other, structures not directly observable. Knowledge of the latter requires concepts and theories. But there is also a difference in generality. In the left column it is a matter of individual phenomena, which can look rather different from time to time. In the right column there is a description of the more general, universal, but not unchangeable dimensions of social reality.

How do we actually make the assumption that individual events may be part of a general, more universal context or structure? What makes us see universal structures in individual events? What is it in, for example, a particular funeral

Table 2 Individual events and general structures

Individual events/phenomena	General structures
Men and women who communicate at a place of work, in the home or at a political meeting	Gender structures, internal relationships described in terms of gender theories
Pupils and teachers meeting in a classroom	Norms and rules making school a specific institution
The manifest content of a text	Implicit ideological meanings of the text
A building as a physical object	The power structures that certain buildings can be regarded as embodying
A funeral, people greeting each other, or a morning meeting in a newsroom	Rituals creating social cohesion by means of internal relations and mechanisms

service that makes us see something general, which we call ritual? How does a social scientist discover that certain behaviour is a manifestation of a normative structure? How can a media researcher, who first sees a news item as a concrete description of an event, in the next instant see that what is manifested in the news text is part of an ideological structure? In the following we shall try to provide some answers to this kind of question.

Neither deductive nor inductive logic can inform such discoveries. Deductive inference is analytical and, as we have pointed out, says nothing new about reality. According to induction, general inference is a generalization of properties already given in particular, observed data. But the examples given above involve discovering, or drawing conclusions from, circumstances and structures that are not given in individual empirical data. There must be other processes, another mode of inference behind such conclusions.

To describe the process behind these modes of inference that are neither deductive nor inductive, the American philosopher Charles S. Peirce worked out the concept of abduction. Peirce, who was active in the latter part of the nineteenth and at the beginning of the twentieth century, was a logician and a pioneer of American pragmatics and semiotics.[2] Here we will concentrate on Peirce's contribution to the concept of abduction.

Abduction is a concept which is in part difficult to capture. One reason is that Peirce describes abduction on the one hand as a mode of inference with a defined logical form comparable to induction and deduction, and on the other hand as a more fundamental aspect of all perception, of all observation of reality. The humanists and social scientists who have applied the concept of abduction in recent years, inspired by Peirce, have further emphasized that abduction involves what has been called redescription or recontextualization. These three different ways of defining the concept of abduction are not contradictory, but stress different aspects of scientific inference. When Peirce writes about inference he does not exclusively allude to inference in the sense of strictly logical derivations. He rather alludes to ways of reasoning, thinking and arguing in a wider sense (Habermas 1972: 113). So far his use of the concept of inference corresponds to our use of the concept.

We will start by presenting abduction as formalized inference. Then we will proceed to abduction as redescription/recontextualization, and conclude by showing that abduction can also be understood as a central element in all perception.

Peirce (1932, see also Bertilsson and Christiansen 1990) presents the difference between the logical structures of deduction, induction and abduction by means of the example shown in Table 3 (over the page), and we include it mainly to show that abduction, too, can be formalized.

The last proposition in all logical inference is the conclusion of the two premises. In deduction the result is a logically necessary consequence thereof. A general rule is our starting point, we observe the individual case, that the beans are from this sack. Given that the rule is true, the result, that the beans are white, follows strictly logically. In induction the rule is a conclusion valid with some

Table 3 Deduction, induction and abduction – the formal structures of inference

Deduction	Induction	Abduction
Rule: All beans from this sack are white	Case: These beans are from this sack	Rule: All beans from this sack are white
Case: These beans are from this sack	Result: These beans are white	Result: These beans are white
Result: These beans are white	Rule: All beans from this sack are white	Case: These beans are from this sack

Source: Peirce 1932 (see also Bertilsson and Christiansen 1990)

probability. We note that the beans are from this sack (what Peirce calls the case) and that the beans are white (what Peirce calls the result), and from this we draw the inductive conclusion that all beans from this sack are white. The conclusion may be wrong, because we have not examined all the beans in the sack. If we know, on the other hand, how many beans there are in the sack and how many we have examined, we can estimate the statistical probability of the conclusion being correct. In abduction the case presents a plausible but not logically necessary conclusion – provided that the rule is correct.

Abduction differs from induction in that we start from the rule describing a general pattern, and it differs from deduction in that the conclusion is not logically given in the premise. Abduction is neither a purely empirical generalization like induction, nor is it logically rigorous like deduction (Collins 1985).

Peirce's example with beans and sacks is in fact not quite relevant when it comes to the application of abduction within social science. The formalization above indeed demonstrates something central to all abduction – that we (1) have an empirical event/phenomenon (the result), which we (2) relate to a rule, which (3) leads us to a new supposition about the event/phenomenon. But in social science research the rule is most often a frame of interpretation or a theory, and the conclusion (the case) is a new interpretation of a concrete phenomenon – an interpretation that is plausible, given that we presuppose that the frame of interpretation is plausible. In Peirce's example there is one true fact: either the beans are from the sack or they are not. We may proceed from the assumption that they are white, and look for other clues and eventually be able to conclude that the beans really come from the sack. We may also examine the rule and see if it is true, and that all the beans from the sack really are white. When we apply abductive inference in social science and interpret a phenomenon in the light of a frame of interpretation (rule), the frame of interpretation constitutes one of several possible frames and the interpretation of the phenomenon one of several possible interpretations. What is common for all abductive inference, however, is that the conclusion provides new insight as an outcome of our interpreting or explaining something with the help of what Peirce calls the rule. But this is always a fallible insight, a form of hypothesis.

The conclusion is one of many possible conclusions following from the fact that we relate different ideas and knowledge to each other (Denzin 1989: 100). A decisive difference between deduction and abduction is that deduction proves that something must be in a certain way, while abduction shows how something might be (Habermas 1972: 113).

We can further clarify the essence of abduction by proceeding from a quotation from Randall Collins (1985: 188): 'in Peirce's view abduction, too, is a mode of inference – of logic in the largest sense – by which one moves from one set of ideas to their conclusions in another set of ideas'. The last part of the quotation captures something quite central. Abduction is to move from a conception of something to a different, possibly more developed or deeper conception of it. This happens through our placing and interpreting the original ideas about the phenomenon in the frame of a new set of ideas. What was called rule in the formalization above, is precisely this set of ideas, which we apply to be able to understand and interpret something in a different way. In scientific work this set of ideas may have the form of a conceptual framework or a theory.[3]

Another way of expressing just this is to talk about abduction as redescription or recontextualization (Jensen 1995: 148). To recontextualize, i.e. to observe, describe, interpret and explain something within the frame of a new context, is a central element in scientific practice. The history of social science contains many well-known recontextualizations. Marx recontextualized the history of man and society from a materialist conception of history, according to which man's way of producing the necessities of life, and the way of organizing this work, constituted the very momentum of history. Durkheim recontextualized suicide as a phenomenon by regarding it as a social fact. In his book *Modernity and Self-identity*, Giddens recontextualizes anorexia as a manifestation of what he denotes reflexive identity, which has become characteristic of postmodern society. He writes: 'Anorexia represents a striving for security in a world of plural, but ambiguous, options. The tightly controlled body is an emblem of a safe existence in an open social environment' (Giddens 1991: 107).

The revolution of recontextualizations is that they give a new meaning to already known phenomena. Social science discoveries are to a large extent associated with recontextualization. Social scientists do not discover new events that nobody knew about before. What is discovered is connections and relations, not directly observable, by which we can understand and explain already known occurrences in a novel way.

Peirce also used a method used by detectives in solving crimes, to exemplify the logic of abduction. The activities of various people, observations at the place of the crime and statements in interviews, are interpreted and gain a significance within the frame of an overall hypothesis about how the crime may have been committed. An experienced, insightful and creative detective is able to recontextualize what she knows about the crime (the clues) within the frame of different possible scenarios of how the crime could have been committed. In a similar way, doctors use abductive logic when interpreting symptoms described by the patient. By relating to a rule/pattern that the doctor finds conceivable, he or she can also make a reasonable analysis of the causes of the symptoms. A mechanic listening to a jarring noise from the engine likewise recontextualizes the noise within the frame of several possible patterns he or she is familiar with. In social science we interpret actions by regarding them in relation to different theories of social action. An action is described in two completely different ways, depending on whether it is recontextualized within the frame of a theory of rational choices or a theory of ritual action. The detective, the doctor, the mechanic and the scientist have this in common, that they test different frames of interpretation. In some cases several frames of interpretation can be used to complement each other; in other cases they can be integrated. In still other cases, after working through material, we may suddenly be struck by an insight, get a hint of how different circumstances might be connected in a way we never thought of before.

Even if social science research may be similar to the work of a detective, there are some important differences. The detective may find the final solution to the crime. Abductive conclusions in social science are seldom of the nature that we can ultimately decide whether they are true or false. This becomes obvious if we go back to the examples in Table 2 above. When we interpret or recontextualize a text as a manifestation of ideological structures, an action as a manifestation of normative structures, or a building as a manifestation of power structures, the abductive inference is at the same time an abstraction isolating certain aspects of the object. One and the same phenomenon can always be recontextualized in different ways without it being possible to say that one of these is more true than the other. On the other hand we can of course examine a particular recontextualization with regard to how valid it is.

Peirce has argued that it should be possible to verify hypotheses generated through abduction, by the use of experiments and inductive logic (Peirce 1990: 244). The question is, to what extent is this possible? In accordance with the metatheory we presented in Part I, abduction becomes a manner of acquiring knowledge of how various phenomena can be part of and explained in relation to structures, internal relations and contexts which are not directly observable. Such structures cannot be derived either inductively or deductively. Abduction has been given an independent status in the research process, as it provides a type of knowledge that cannot be acquired either through deduction or inductive generalizations. Social science analysis is essentially a matter of using theories and frames of interpretation to gain a deeper knowledge of social meanings, structures and mechanisms. In this way we build up knowledge that cannot be reduced to empirical facts and thus cannot be tested in line with the same logic as the testing of empirical predictions.

However, Peirce too emphasizes that abduction cannot at all be reduced to induction or deduction. The fundamental difference between induction and abduction he describes in the following manner: 'But the essence of an induction is that it infers from one set of facts another similar set of facts, whereas [abduction] infers from facts of one kind to facts of another' (Peirce 1986, in Jensen 1995: 150).

Umberto Eco (1984) distinguishes between three different types of abduction: overcoded, undercoded and creative abduction. They all represent different ways of relating studied phenomena to some form of classification system, frame of interpretation or code giving meaning to the phenomena (Jensen 1995: 158).

Overcoded abduction, according to Eco's typology, is a mode of inference characterized by automatism and naturalness. It is a matter of spontaneous interpretations, which we make from a culturally and socially grounded prejudging. Both in ordinary life and within science we constantly make such interpretations. What is regarded as a natural interpretation in one cultural/social context may be something utterly controversial in another context with other prevalent codes. All observations involve such an abductive process, which is a precondition for the observed phenomenon to have any meaning at all.

Undercoded abduction implies that we choose between a number of possible frames of interpretations or theories. In social science we can ask: What difference does it make if we interpret a particular behaviour from the viewpoint of a theory of ritual action on the one hand, or from a theory of rational choice on the other? Which of several existing theories about the development of history should we take as our starting point when we interpret a particular historical occurrence?

Eco's typology also contains a third type of abduction, which he calls creative abduction. It is characterized by being unique and innovative. In the context of social science it is a form of creative abduction when a researcher observes something from a frame of interpretation that nobody has used before, or which at least opposes conventional interpretations. Charles Darwin's redescription of the evolution of species, Goffman's interpretation of social interaction as a manifestation of dramaturgic action, and Freud's interpretation of people's dreams within the frame of a theory about the unconscious, are all examples of such creative abduction.

In a more fundamental sense, all abduction builds on creativity and imagination. This is the essential difference between abduction and the two other modes of inference we have discussed so far. In their application in social science research, different abilities are required on the part of the researcher. Induction primarily calls for mastery of a specific statistical analysis. Deduction demands the power of strictly logical reasoning. The foundation of abduction is chiefly creativity and the ability to form associations. Besides comprehensive knowledge of established alternative theories, models and frames of interpretation, abduction requires a creative reasoning process enabling the researcher to discern relations and connections not evident or obvious – to formulate new ideas about the interconnection of phenomena, to think about something in a different context, an ability to 'see something as something else'.

The concept of abduction captures a central aspect of the research process, something that has been underlined even by philosophers and theorists of science who do not explicitly take only Peirce's theories as their point of departure. What these theorists have in common is that they emphasize that science not only involves description but also 'redescription' and detection of meanings and connections that are not given in our habitual way of perceiving the world. Theories and models expressing (assumptions about) more general contexts are indispensable resources in redescription and recontextualization. As an example, Uggla sums up Max Black's and Mary Hesse's views on scientific models in this way:

> For the use of models in science is not motivated by the ability of these models to empirically describe a pure reality. The strength of scientific models lies instead in their ability to break away from a descriptive discourse and provide a possibility to *see 'something' as 'something else'*. Since the purpose of using models in science is to explore reality by establishing new relations in it, the scientific model has a heuristic function in producing new hypotheses and so *discovers new dimensions of reality*.
>
> (Uggla 1994: 400, our emphases and translation)

Abduction is, as Habermas (1972) says, a mode of inference broadening our knowledge and stimulating the research process. It is through thought operations that new ideas are introduced, and thus they are more important for scientific progress than, for example, deduction.

A question that immediately suggests itself is, of course, how do we know if these redescriptions provide better knowledge about our object of study? We shall in part come back to this question in Chapter 5. But we would for the moment like to once again stress that abductive logic, applied in social science, very seldom (if ever) leads to definite truths – not even in combination with induction and deduction. Abduction is more associated with a way of viewing the relation between science and reality, implying that there are no ultimately true theories, and therefore no rules either, for deciding what is the ultimate truth. On the other hand there is the possibility for increasingly better knowledge, and this is meant in two senses. First, redescriptions can provide a deeper knowledge about the particular case under study; second, one can also gradually test, modify and ground theories about general contexts and structures by relating these theories to ever new cases.

In Table 2 above we illustrated the relation between particular phenomena and general structures with some examples. One of them was this:

Individual events / phenomena	*General structures*
A funeral, people greeting each other, or a morning meeting in a newsroom	Rituals by means of internal relations and mechanisms, creating social cohesion

We can now see that abduction in these cases is a matter of redescribing/recontextualizing concrete events from a set of ideas, or a theory of, for example, rituals. Theory provides deeper knowledge of the particular event. From the theory we can in this example understand events and social situations as rituals, and thus detect relations and mechanisms in these situations that we would not otherwise have discovered. It is not enough, however, to ask: What does the theory say about different events? The purpose of studying different events (of performing new case studies) should not merely be to demonstrate how more and more events can be interpreted and redescribed with the help of a readymade theory. Equally important is the question: What do the events say about the theory? Studies of new, particular cases are essential if we are to test and develop theories about social relationships, structures and mechanisms. When we take our starting point in studies of various concrete situations (funerals, spectators at sports arenas, meals in homes and at restaurants, common ways of greeting known and unknown people, etc.), then a theory of rituals can be modified and refined. In a research practice guided by abduction, the interplay (dialectic) between theoretical redescriptions of cases and case-study-based theory development is absolutely central.

We have now examined two ways of describing abduction – as formalized logic and as redescription/recontextualizing. Peirce also discusses abduction as an interpretative element which is an absolute condition for all perception. In a broader sense, abductive inference can be seen as an overall term for all forms of interpretation made from a pattern or system of classification. According to Peirce it is in the nature of all perception to be interpretative. Perception, or empirical observation, if you like, demands that we give meaning to what we observe, by interpreting or classifying it in a certain way. Classification in its turn means that the object is arranged into general classes or concepts. Even the simplest observation of something is thus linked to a generalization (Peirce 1990: 231ff). Perhaps we do not usually think about it, but we always see something general in the individual. This way of regarding empirical observations is manifested in what Eco calls overcoded abduction. It is also in accordance with a critical realist view of empirical observation. Such observation is part of the transitive object of science; the observation contains an interpretative element. Empirical observation can never be the same thing as an actual reality, which is independent of the cognitive subject. The meaning of two observations of one and the same phenomenon can therefore differ (sometimes in a very radical manner), depending on preunderstanding and conceptual starting points (see Chapter 2).

In a critical scientific analysis it is important to employ the abductive inference for redescription, so that we can interpret particular phenomena as part of general structures. But it is also important to problematize the inference made in a more automatic way (overcoded abduction). Scientific observations and analyses are based on classifications. There may be good reasons for questioning some classifications and conceptualizations as manifestations of ideologies and hegemonic values. The difference between the interpretative/classifying element included in our spontaneous, everyday observations of reality, and the abductive inference we apply in theoretically guided redescriptions, is that the former is very often 'beyond the sphere of criticism', to use Peirce's formulation (Peirce 1990: 232).

Retroduction

Abduction is thus an inference where redescription or recontextualization is the central element. By means of abduction we recontextualize and reinterpret something as something else, understanding it within the frame of a totally different context. In this way we introduce new ideas of how individual phenomena are part of the structure and internal relations. We shall now focus on retroduction, which in this context can be described as a mode of inference, by which we try to arrive at what is basically characteristic and constitutive of these structures. That is to say, what are the basic characteristics of the general structures from which we start, in abduction, when we interpret and recontextualize particular actions and events? In concrete research practice such inferences can sometimes be difficult to distinguish. Nevertheless they represent two different modes of inference that it is essential to discriminate between when the core of the methodology of social science is to be described.

Before describing the specific character of retroduction we will – in order to avoid misunderstandings – clarify in what respect retroduction is an inference and in what respect it is not. Unlike deduction, retroduction is not an inference in the sense this concept has in logic, that is, logically valid inference, from premise to conclusion. Retroduction is not, as are deduction, induction and abduction, a formalized mode of inference (cf. Table 1). But it resembles deduction, induction and abduction insofar as it is a thought operation through which we can move from knowledge of one thing to knowledge of something else.

For the development of knowledge in social science, retroduction as a mode of inference is indispensable, provided that we take our starting point in the metatheory presented in Chapters 2 and 3. This realist metatheory emphasizes the difference between observable events and the domains of structure and mechanisms. Social reality consists of structures and internally related objects containing causally operating properties. Knowledge of this social reality can only be attained if we go beyond what is empirically observable by asking questions about and developing concepts of the more fundamental, transfactual conditions for the events and phenomena under study. Retroduction is about advancing from one thing (empirical observation of events) and arriving at something different (a conceptualization of transfactual conditions).

The core of retroduction is transcendental argumentation, as it is called in philosophy. By this argumentation one seeks to clarify the basic prerequisites or conditions for social relationships, people's actions, reasoning and knowledge. The term 'conditions' here means the circumstances without which something can't exist. In such argumentation we try at the same time to separate the necessary conditions from contingent circumstances (cf. Chapter 3).[4] As this argumentation means that we go beyond the empirical, it is also called transfactual argumentation. Transcendental philosophy has been severely criticized by those who maintain that the only thing we can have knowledge about is what is given, that is, reality as we spontaneously experience or observe it. Critical realism, however, repudiates a science that reduces knowledge to knowledge about the directly given or observable.

One of the best-known proponents of transcendental philosophy is the German philosopher Immanuel Kant. He argued that there are some foundational conditions on which all knowledge is built. One is that all our experiences and all knowledge are structured in time and space. According to Kant the human mind is endowed with such conditions. Therefore Kant's philosophy is called transcendental idealism. Bhaskar's transcendental realism differs from Kant's philosophy in at least two important aspects (cf. Collier 1994: 21):

1   Bhaskar discards idealism and argues that our knowledge of reality is possible just because reality is constructed in a certain way. He means that we ought to look for the transcendental conditions, not in our minds (as idealism does) but in reality, as it exists independently of our search for knowledge.
2   Unlike Kant, Bhaskar does not claim to describe universal and unchangeable conditions for our knowledge of reality. Transcendental knowledge, like all knowledge, is fallible. In addition, the foundational structures we are trying to comprehend by means of transcendental arguments are changeable in themselves.

We do not mean that social science should be oriented towards a philosophical argumentation. What we do mean is that retroduction, as a mode of inference, is central, regardless of whether we as theorists devote ourselves to the most fundamental conditions for social activity and formation of society, or if we as social scientists analyse and try to explain concrete social events. The fundamental question in both cases is: How is any phenomenon, like an action or a social organization, possible? If we call this phenomenon X, we may formulate our question thus: *What properties must exist for X to exist and to be what X is?* Or, to put it more briefly: What makes X possible? In the first part of the book we showed that critical realism regards the objects of social science as (mainly) relational. Social phenomena are what they are by virtue of the internal relations they have to other phenomena. Taking this as one's starting point, retroduction becomes a matter of trying to attain knowledge about what internal relations make X what it is.

There is no reason to leave this way of asking questions to philosophers; quite the reverse. On second thoughts we may affirm that retroduction is continually being used in analyses at different levels of abstraction – from philosophy to concrete social science analysis. What do we mean by different levels of abstraction in this context? Well, the question 'What makes X possible?' can be answered by referring to conditions/structures differing in degree of abstraction and in how fundamental they are. The question of how a certain action is possible can be answered by referring to (philosophical) theories of intentionality as a universal condition for all human activity. But the question can also be answered by attempting to reconstruct the system of social positions, the norms and rules, or the social and culturally acquired dispositions (habitus) structuring a particular action. There is no sharp dividing line between philosophy and social science if we consider the way transfactual argumentation or retroduction is used. Nor is there any reason why strict boundaries should be called for. It is a matter of differences in degree.

Retroduction is used in social science both by researchers who side with critical realism, and researchers who in their practice share the same view in many important aspects, but who would probably not side with critical realism in every respect. Let us give three examples that illustrate how widely this mode of inference or thought operation is accepted in the social sciences today – both as analyses at a very high level of abstraction and as analyses of more specific conditions for social processes. We shall start with an example of an analysis at a high level of abstraction, in the borderland between philosophy and social science.

Example 1

Jürgen Habermas has developed a theory of universal pragmatics, which has also been called formal pragmatics. The concept of pragmatics here alludes – to somewhat simplify – to the pragmatic aspects of language, that is, our way of using language in an act of speech, in communication where someone talks with somebody about something. The theory is universal or transcendental, as it claims to reconstruct universal conditions for communication (Habermas 1984; McCarthy 1988).

When language is used in practice we always relate our speech acts, according to Habermas, first to an external reality (a reality which we can describe either truly or falsely), second to an inner reality (the individual's intention of her actions, which can be expressed truthfully or dishonestly), and finally to collective norms and values (which can be conceived as normatively right or wrong). Every speech act expresses claims to validity; claims to comprehensibility; truth, truthful and normative/moral rightness. The universal preconditions for a rational use of language are thus:

1   that we can use language representatively and distinguish what is from what seems to be;
2   that we can use language expressively and distinguish between what the individual is and what she pretends to be;
3   that we can use language to develop common values and distinguish what is from what ought to be (McCarthy 1988).

Habermas holds that communication would be impossible without universal claims to validity and without what he calls the ideal speech situation as a regulative notion, inherent in our way of using language. In this speech situation we are making claims of validity but are also expected to meet such claims when they are questioned. Habermas' theory is abstract and has been developed through transfactual argumentation. Abstract, here, does not imply that it describes anything divorced from reality. On the contrary, the theory describes something inherent in language and concrete communication.

Habermas uses the term 'reconstructive science' as a designation for a methodology oriented precisely towards reconstructing the fundamental preconditions of a rational communication (McCarthy 1988: 276). We interpret 'reconstructive science' as almost synonymous with what we, after Bhaskar, call retroduction. Habermas is not a pronounced adherent of critical realism, even if there are close points of similarity (Outhwaite 1987). He has a realist approach in the sense that he claims to lay bare real deep structures and rules, which are the underlying preconditions for communication.

Example 2

In his book *Modernity and the Holocaust*, Zygmunt Bauman (1989) gives some explanations of the Holocaust by asking the question: What made the Holocaust possible? In his sociological analyses Bauman has adopted a post-modern position, which is essentially different from that of critical realism. However, his aim is the same as that of realism, namely to identify foundational conditions behind concrete historical events, and the essence of his argument is what we have described as retroduction. Bauman begins his analysis by discarding those explanations of the Holocaust which amount to it being a specifically German (a result of the economic and political situation), or a specifically Jewish, problem (a result of increasing anti-Semitism). Bauman discards them because they do not draw attention to what he sees as the fundamental condition of the Holocaust, that is the structure of rational modern society. Characteristic of this society, according to Bauman, is that it is a 'gardening culture' – a culture marked by strategies to control and create perfect order, on certain principles, removing that which does not fit in. Racism is one of several manifestations of this. What is also characteristic of modern society is the elaborate, bureaucratic hierarchy, with routines for division of labour and fixed roles, distancing the actions from the consequences of these actions, thus reducing the responsibility of the individual to a matter of playing one's role. The social control associated with these bureaucratic systems of authority is another typical feature. These were the fundamental conditions making the Holocaust possible, the structures making the Holocaust what it was.

Example 3

Randall Collins (1990) has developed a theory – partly from analyses of concrete situated determined interaction – answering the question: What must there be for a ritual to be a ritual? The question could also be posed like this: What is it that makes this particular interaction a ritual? For an interaction to be a ritual, according to Collins, there must be a group physically meeting at a certain place; they must focus on a common object or an activity, sharing certain emotional moods and sacred objects. The ritual interaction is constituted by mechanisms, producing (if the ritual works) social cohesion, group selectivity, emotional energy, and membership symbols charged with strong emotions. Symbols convey holiness (what must not be questioned) and mark boundaries between those who belong and those who do not belong.

We find that Collins in his analyses of social interaction also poses a more fundamental question: What is the ultimate precondition for social solidarity – indeed for society to exist as a society? What holds society together? Collins, strongly influenced by Durkheim, answers: Rituals with mechanisms producing moral solidarity and a strong emotional power. By saying this we have shown that the retroductive inferences that Collins makes (as we interpret him) focus on both the preconditions for concrete forms of social interaction in specific situations, and on the issue of transcendental preconditions for enabling a society to be a society.

Common to the three studies in our examples above is the fact that they have been seeking the basic conditions for the phenomena under study, looking in social structures and relations. Retroduction serves as guidance in the argumentation behind the conclusions drawn by Habermas, Bauman and Collins. Retroduction is in some way the core of their scientific method. The concrete methods they use, however, are very different.

So far we have described and illustrated the specific way of asking questions and of arguing within the frame of transcendental arguments and retroductive inference. But what is the working process itself like when we are working with such an inference? How do we arrive at the conclusion that certain structures and mechanisms but not others make up the conditions for X to be possible? How can we distinguish between the necessary conditions for X (the constituent properties) and the more contingent circumstances affecting the particular case under study (cf. Chapter 3)? There is no universal method for this. On the other hand there are several strategies which can guide us when we are drawing retroductive inferences, as we will now demonstrate.

What is common to these strategies is that they can help us discern structures and mechanisms in an open reality, where these seldom or never appear in a pure form; in principle they are always part of a complex interaction with other mechanisms under more or less specific circumstances. The traditional experiment requires that causal mechanisms can be studied in a closed system.[5] In Chapter 3 we showed why this possibility hardly ever exists in social science. The strategies we shall now present, together constitute powerful alternatives to the traditional experiment. We will examine five (complementary) strategies, which have often been used in research, regardless of whether the research has been in line with critical realism or not. They are: counterfactual thinking, social experiments, studies of pathological cases, studies of extreme cases and comparative case studies. We would like to emphasize that these six strategies are powerful alternatives to the traditional experiment. They are not to be seen as inferior or less satisfactory versions of an ideal which social science has not been able to reach. To the contrary, social science has been able, among other things, by means of these strategies, to produce broad and well-founded knowledge of social structures and mechanisms.

Counterfactual thinking

Counterfactual thinking is fundamental for all retroduction. We ask questions like: How would this be if not … ? Could one imagine X without … ? Could one imagine X including this, without X then becoming something different? In counterfactual thinking we use our stored experience and knowledge of social reality, as well as our ability to abstract and to think about what is not, but what might be.

Counterfactual thinking is fundamental in scientific practice, as we understand what something is in relation to what it is not. In our understanding of the world, presence and absence are constitutive of one another. Correspondingly, we can only discern the necessary, constitutive properties of something by relating these properties to what is not constitutive (but rather an accidental circumstance). To understand the specific and constitutive for X – a social identity, a social ritual, a way of life, an institution, a linguistic genre, etc. – we must also have some idea of what X is not. If we consider presence and absence, the necessary and the contingent, the constitutive and the non-constitutive as opposites, we can say that counterfactual thinking is at the same time dialectic, since in this reasoning we examine something in relation to its opposite.

Here is an example. Counterfactual thinking can serve as a guideline when we examine what properties are constitutive for news journalism as a linguistic genre and institution. Television news would not be what it is if it was not presented in an impartial and unambiguous language by a newscaster in a defined environment. Television news would not be what it is without the set of discursive strategies, by which facts are construed as facts, and the claims of objectivity and neutrality on the part of the news institution are upheld (Heritage and Greatbach 1991; Potter 1996). At the same time, through counterfactual thinking we can arrive at the conclusion that it is not in line with this genre and institution to have a cheering audience in the studio, to enact the contents as a drama, to allow the reporter in the studio to use ironic language or introduce the items by saying, 'Well, we can't be quite sure about this. It could be interpreted in many different ways. Anyhow, my opinion is that … '

Social experiments and thought experiments

In ethnomethodology, a scientific tradition initiated by the American sociologist Harold Garfinkel, a form of experiment has been carried out which could be a fruitful strategy for retroductive inference (Garfinkel 1967). Ethnomethodology in many ways deviates from critical realism. It repudiates analytical dualism, and can scarcely accept the realist notion that structures exist somewhat independently of individual activities. Ethnomethodology focuses on locally situated activities, and claims that structures do not exist outside people's everyday activities but only as intrinsic qualities in these (Zimmerman and Boden 1991). But there are also similarities. One is that ethnomethodology, too, aims at tracing the *conditions* for social interaction to be what it is. What are the constituent properties of everyday conversation? What in people's social interaction and conversation causes social order and stability to be maintained? Why does social interaction hold together?

Ethnomethodologists have explained this by pointing to the mechanisms by means of which people in a day-to-day routine maintain a social order. To be able to interact adequately in different social situations it is necessary for the participants to have access to methodological competence and common, taken-for-granted assumptions of the situation. Conversation constitutes a central part of the social interaction. An example of the mechanism, which has been identified as important in everyday conversations, is repair. Conversational remarks which might disturb the order – misunderstandings or expressed disagreements – are often treated as a joke or met with methods of remedy and repair.

How can we attain knowledge of the taken-for-granted assumptions forming the foundation of ordinary social interaction? How can we attain knowledge of the fundamental rules and mechanisms of conversation? Well, by social experiments, among other things, where we examine what happens when in various ways we break with what is expected of us. The following is an oft-used example: let us say that next time I meet a friend, I will answer his way of starting the conversation in the following manner (quoted from Garfinkel 1967: 44):

> How are you doing?
> How am I regard to what? My health, my finances, my school work, my peace of mind, my … ?

My friend would probably be either very confused, perhaps offended or angry, or he would quickly collect his wits and repair my violation against the order by regarding my answer as a joke. What can we learn by such experiments? Well, that a basic quality of ordinary conversation is that we expect others to understand what we mean when we say something in a certain situation without further explanation, even if we express ourselves vaguely. Ordinary conversations take a common understanding of the situation for granted. From such experiments, where we *provoke* an action by threatening the order of things, we can also examine the methods that are put into practice in everyday conversation to repair that same order.

Garfinkel also shows that in many cases it is enough to imagine what would happen if one acted in a certain way, without trying this in practice. To show that ordinary interaction is based on fundamental and tacit expectations and common understanding, he asked his students, among other things, to spend between fifteen minutes and an hour in their own homes watching what happened, but the whole time on the supposition that they themselves were lodgers. The students saw how difficult this was to do, and this experience confirmed that shared understanding and people's ability to immediately recognize a situation as a particular type of situation is a precondition of meaningful social interaction.

In Chapter 3 we expressed doubt about the possibility of using experiments in social science to study the effects of causal mechanisms. How does this square with the fact that we now consider social experiments to be a successful methodological strategy? Well, first, these examples refer to studies of social mechanisms that are so strong, so fundamental for ordinary conversation, that an experimentally produced violation of order tends to have the same effect in different situations, regardless of the fact that we cannot study the mechanisms in a closed system. Second, it is only in combination with a transfactual argument that these social experiments can provide knowledge of causal mechanisms and their effects. Knowledge of the constitutive conditions for ordinary conversation and social cohesion cannot be obtained solely by observed regularities. Third, traditional experiments are usually performed in a constructed situation (some form of laboratory or the like). In that setting, other social mechanisms specific to the experimental situation will influence the outcome. What we here call social experiments, however, are carried out in natural situations. The experimental element lies in the circumstance that the researcher consciously provokes a situation in order to study how people handle it.

There are, of course, ethical aspects to be considered before putting social experiments into practice. The thought experiment as a type of counterfactual thinking is often preferable. Usually it suffices to consider the consequences of a certain action to understand the conditions for a social order. We can imagine what it would imply if we broke certain rules and rituals in ordinary life. We can imagine the consequences of not showing the expected regard for symbols in a particular situation. It is not least our ordinary social experiences that cause us to know what we cannot do without threatening the social order and to understand how such a break of order would probably be received. Often it is unnecessary to actually carry out an experiment. Ordinary social experience is a necessary resource in much retroductive inference within social science.

The starting point, or the very material, for retroductive inference is usually conditions that are wellknown from social practice. The task of science is not primarily to detect new social events or activities, but to reconstruct (and detect) the preconditions for these well-known social situations to be possible. It is these discoveries we can make through retroduction. This means that in scientific work we can and should use experiences we have acquired both in research practice and in ordinary life. Now and then students ask themselves: Can I use other data besides those which I have collected in this particular investigation? The answer is: Of course! Nobody manages in a single empirical investigation to collect the experience needed for a well-grounded retroduction. Naturally, it is important to collect, by well-reasoned choices, new material for one's procedure and to apply scientific methods in the data collecting. However, scientific method is at least equally concerned with what the researcher makes of her data and her experiences, or more precisely, how she applies different modes of inference and scientific argument.

If we reflect a little we realize that the work of such theorists as Marx, Mead, Goffman, Habermas, Bourdieu and Giddens is pioneering not because it describes empirical situations we did not know about before; on the contrary, it is because we recognize the empirical circumstances that the theories are rendered valid in our eyes. The pioneering part is that they reconstruct the prerequisites, the structural conditions, of what we recognize from social practice. To a large extent the same thing is true of the great discoveries in connection with the natural science revolution in the seventeenth century, a revolution usually declared to be the starting point for the development of modern scientific methods. Galileo's theories were principally about a physical reality familiar to people. The questions he tried to answer by his experiments were of the kind: What mechanisms constitute the fundamental preconditions for bodies to fall in the way they do?

Studying pathological circumstances and extreme cases

To get an answer to the question 'How is X possible?' we can study various cases where the preconditions for X appear much more clearly than in others. There are at least two types of case where social conditions and mechanisms are very obvious: first, those where the conditions are challenged and the mechanisms are disturbed; and second, extreme cases where mechanisms appear in an almost pure form.

Carrying out what we have described above as social experiments mainly involves challenging the conditions of normality, to remove certain mechanisms and provoke others to appear. But there are also cases where the conditions are challenged without the researcher having to provoke anything. Collier describes this in terms of 'the methodological primacy of the pathological' (see Collier 1994: 165). Collier also quotes the following pertinent description by Bhaskar:

> It might be conjectured that in periods of transition or crisis generative struc-
> tures, previously opaque, become more visible to agents. And that this,
> though it never yields quite the epistemic possibilities of a closure ... does
> provide a partial analogue to the role played by experimentation in natural
> science.
>
> (Bhaskar 1989a: 48)

The point of this kind of case study is that we can learn much about structures and mechanisms by studying pathological or critical situations. Mechanisms, which are usually hidden as they are counteracted by other mechanisms, become very clearly apparent in certain situations. The force of gravity would, as Collier writes, be much more obvious than in normal circumstances if it were brought to act in full force and the ceiling above our heads fell down.

This is also the methodological strategy that Freud employed when he developed a theory of how the human mind is structured, partly in the light of what he had learnt from the study of neurotic patients. In social scientific research practice we can think of many situations where this strategy could be applied. On television, for instance, the assignment of roles, directed by staff, and the structure of a debating programme become obvious when a participant suddenly challenges them by not conforming to the otherwise hidden structure. Norms never become so apparent as when someone breaks them, perhaps because they do not know them. The emotional charge of symbols becomes evident from the fierce reactions aroused when someone violates them. The conditions for social cohesion become obvious in times of disintegration, and the conditions for the legitimacy of national authorities may well be studied to advantage in situations when that legitimacy is seriously threatened. The difference between what we call pathological cases and social experiments is that the latter are based on the researcher's provoking the pathological situation, while this situation in the former case happens anyway.

Another common methodological device is to go to extremes in order to support a retroductive inference. The strength of experiment in natural science is that you can study, in a constructed laboratory, certain mechanisms as they appear in a purer form. An alternative, employed in social science, is to study real cases where mechanisms manifest themselves in a purer form than usual. For instance, we can study mechanisms connected with a ritual interaction by focusing on some social interaction which is extremely ritualized – a funeral or a baptism – and then examine if the same mechanisms also characterize other forms of social interaction. We can examine an extremely bureaucratic organization to obtain knowledge of mechanisms characterizing other organizations too, but in less obvious ways.

Common to both these types of case – pathological and extreme – is that through them we can learn about the conditions for the normal by studying the abnormal.

Comparisons of different cases

Studies with the aim of describing, by means of retroduction, the fundamental conditions for anything to be what it is may well be organized as comparative studies. The researcher chooses to study a number of cases which are all assumed to manifest the structure she wishes to describe, but which are very different in other aspects. If the researcher wants to develop a theory of the ritual element in social interaction (to hold to the example we used earlier), she will preferably endeavour to compare several completely different interaction situations in order to be able to discern the structure all these cases have in common. In this way it can be possible to distinguish the necessary, constitutive conditions from more accidental circumstances. What makes it so productive to compare different cases is precisely this, that comparison provides an empirical foundation for retroduction, a foundation to sort out contingent differences in order to arrive at the common and more universal.

In other situations where researchers ask the question 'What qualities must there be for X to be what it is?', they can, by comparing different cases, infer that totally different qualities or structures are involved. From case studies of various talk shows on television, for example, researchers have concluded that such programmes can be structured following the pattern of three different genres: a debate, a narrative or a therapy session. In concrete cases it may be difficult to discern these three forms, and it can also happen that they are mixed. Through systematic comparisons and transfactual argument, however, these qualitatively different forms can be distinguished. Each one of them has different constitutive qualities and presents different conditions for the concrete production. They structure the production in different ways and affect the way events are related, how the talk is conducted and staged, how the host behaves, what guests are invited, and so on (Livingstone and Lunt 1994).

Critical realism has been restricted in a way, as it has to a large extent been occupied with criticizing the experimental science which assumes that social mechanisms can be studied in closed systems, while at the same time saying very little about alternative methodological strategies. We have therefore here demonstrated five powerful alternatives to the traditional experiment. They may well be combined in different ways in concrete research practice. As we have shown, strategically selected case studies are a very important feature of a social science founded on critical realism.

Two models for an explanatory social science

In the introduction to this chapter it was stressed that social science in essence aims at explaining social conditions. In this section we will describe two completely different methods for an explanatory social science. The first one is a model usually presented in the literature of social science method and epistemology. It is called the Popper–Hempel explanatory model after its originators, Karl Popper and Carl Hempel (Popper 1959; Hempel 1965; Keat and Urry 1978). Other designations of the same model are the covering-law model or the deductive nomological explanatory model (Ekström 1992).

The second model has been developed within critical realism, especially by Bhaskar. An essential difference between these models, as we shall see, is that the first mainly builds on deduction and induction, whereas abduction and retroduction constitute the central modes of inference in the second model. There are of course other models, too, for explanatory social science. Our aim in this chapter, however, confines itself to presenting a model developed within critical realism, a model which is an alternative to the very influential, but seriously criticized, Popper–Hempel explanatory model.

Basically the Popper–Hempel model goes back to the empirical definition of causality such as it has been described by David Hume (Hume 1966). Causality has to do with empirical regularities. Hume assumes that causal conclusions are based on observations of how something is repeatedly followed by something else in time, that is to say universal/law-like regularities between events.

According to the Popper–Hempel model, all explanations are based on knowledge of universal conformity to law or at least law-like regularities. The structure of this explanatory model can be described thus (Gilje and Grimen 1992: 135):

Explanans: Universal law(s)
               Framework condition(s)
               Triggering cause(s)
Explanandum: Description of what is to be explained

Explanans are the conditions we refer to in order to explain the event (Explanandum). The law expresses a postulation of how two events (Y and X) are connected. The framework condition describes the preconditions for this law to be valid, that is, what is necessary for event Y to be followed by event X. The triggering cause is what makes the event take place, given that the law is true and the framework condition is met. We will illustrate this by a concrete example.

Explanans: All objects that are dropped will fall to the ground (universal law).
                    Sarah is holding a bottle and there is no object which can stop Sarah's bottle from falling to the ground, if she drops it (framework condition).
                    Sara drops the bottle (triggering cause).
Explanandum: The bottle falls to the ground.

An objection that immediately suggests itself in relation to this explanatory model is the fact that there is hardly any conformity to law within social science other than the fact that most regularities between events occur with a certain probability. However, according to Hempel the same model can be applied even when we explain something in relation to statistical probability instead of deterministic laws. The difference is that the conclusion (explanandum) in such cases cannot be inferred by strictly logical deduction from the premise; the conclusion in this case is valid with a certain probability. This can be illustrated by an example from Føllesdal *et al.* (1990):

Explanans: There is a high probability that patients infected by streptococci will be cured if they are treated with penicillin (statistical law).
                    Per had a streptococci infection and was treated with penicillin (triggering cause).
Explanandum: Per was cured.

In this example we cannot deduce from the premise that Per was cured, only that it is highly probable that he was.

Regardless of whether it is an issue of statistical or deterministic laws, the deductive inference is central in this explanatory model. To explain something is to deduce consequences from premises assumed to be true. But how do we arrive at the law from which the explanation originates? Either it says that event Y is always followed by event X, or that event Y with a certain probability will be followed by event X. It thus expresses an empirical inductive generalization. Inductive inferences are central in the empiricist philosophy of science on which this explanatory model rests. One can imagine that it is through a number of observations of how objects that are dropped will fall to the ground, that the law 'all objects that are dropped fall to the ground' can be formulated; it may also be from a series of observations of patients, who have been treated with the medication penicillin, that the law of the relation between penicillin and cured streptococci infections can be formulated. But we do not gain knowledge of law-like relations through occasional empirical observation. Both Popper and Hempel argued for a hypothesis-testing method. Since we will discuss this method in Chapter 5, we will here just briefly say something about its basic structure. The method is based on the formulation of hypotheses. From the hypothesis, empirical consequences are inferred. An empirical consequence is something which follows from the hypothesis and which can be ascertained to be true or false by means of observation. If the observation is in correspondence with the empirical consequence, the hypothesis has to some extent been supported (it is not falsified, at least); if the observation is not in correspondence, the hypothesis is falsified. A leading idea in Popper's philosophy of science is that science should be oriented towards falsifications. Hypotheses expressing general-izations or laws should never be regarded as finally proved, according to Popper. On the other hand, their validity increases as they are exposed to still more attempts of falsification without being falsified.

Critical realist questioning of the Popper–Hempel explanatory model is radical and comprises its application in both natural and social science. The most important part of this critique is:

1   That this model is limited since it takes its starting point in an empiricist ontology, which reduces reality to the domains of events and empirical observations; causality is understood as regular connections between observ-able events.
2   What is said to be an explanation does not actually explain anything; it just describes a law-like/statistical relation and the explanations do not identify any causal mechanisms.

This is very obvious in the examples presented above. In the first example we are told nothing of what makes an object fall to the ground, and in the second example we are not told what it is in penicillin that has the power to cure certain diseases. The critique of the empiricist perspective has been treated at some length in Chapters 2 and 3, and thus there is no need to go into detail here.

Instead it is time for us to present a model of an explanatory social science taking its starting point in critical realism. Such a model should be guiding the research that is trying to attain knowledge of constitutive qualities and causal mechanisms generating events, but also knowledge of how different mechanisms cooperate and, under specific circumstances, contribute to the production of concrete events and processes. Bhaskar (1978, 1989a; see also Collier 1994) has presented two different models (called RRRE and DREI) which can be said to correspond to these types of cognitive interest. Separately they are complicated, and an explanation in this context would lead us too far. Furthermore, we are not fully convinced that the division Bhaskar makes is fruitful. We will therefore instead present a model that claims to integrate the essential parts of Bhaskar's reasoning.

It is important to elucidate a few things before we start examining this model. Compared to the Popper–Hempel explanatory model it represents a more comprehensive approach, pointing at key elements for an explanatory social science. In this approach abduction and retroduction play central roles, instead of induction and deduction. (However, we will once more emphasize that deductive logic can and should be used in analyses of all scientific argument, regardless of what methodology is behind the results presented.) The approach further rests on the presumption that the fundamental structures of explanatory social science can be described as a movement from the concrete to the abstract and back to the concrete. The Popper–Hempel model shows how empirical laws can be related to particular events. The explanatory model of critical realism provides guidelines for how to relate in research practice the concrete to the abstract and the abstract to the concrete.

We especially wish to emphasize that this model (containing six different stages) should be seen as a guideline and not as a template to be followed to the letter. Research processes can and should be structured in different ways. The separate stages can also be intertwined and need not follow each other in a strictly chronological order. In research practice it can often be necessary to switch between the different stages. In a concrete study there may also be reasons for concentrating on certain stages and touching upon the others more lightly. The model we present (Table 4) represents a radically different way of regarding the research process, compared to the models most frequently mentioned in books on social science methods. On the other hand, much of social science research to some extent goes along in practice with precisely the model we present here.

The model describes the research process as a way from the concrete (stage 1) to the abstract (stages 2–5) and then back to the concrete (stage 6). Every stage (except the first) in itself involves such a swing between different levels of abstraction. Abstraction and concretization provide two different types of knowledge about reality, both important but not to be confused or reduced to one another (cf. Chapter 3).

Table 4 The stages in an explanatory research based on critical realism

Stage 1: description

An explanatory social science analysis usually starts in the concrete. We describe the often complex and composite event or situation we intend to study. In this we make use of everyday concepts. An important part of this description is the interpretations of the persons involved and their way of describing the current situation. Most events should be described by qualitative as well as by quantitative methods.

Stage 2: analytical resolution

In this phase we separate or dissolve the composite and the complex by distinguishing the various components, aspects or dimensions. The concept of scientific analysis usually alludes to just this (analysis = a separating or dissolving examination). It is never possible to study anything in all its different components. Therefore we must in practice confine ourselves to studying certain components but not others.

Stage 3: abduction/theoretical redescription

Here we interpret and redescribe the different components/aspects from hypothetical conceptual frameworks and theories about structures and relations. This stage thus corresponds to what has been described above as abduction and redescription. The original ideas of the objects of study are developed when we place them in new contexts of ideas. Here several different theoretical interpretations and explanations can and should be presented, compared and possibly integrated with one another.

Stage 4: retroduction

Here the different methodological strategies described above are employed. The purpose is for each one of the different components/aspects we have decided to focus on, to try to find the answers to questions like: What is fundamentally constitutive for the structures and relations (X), highlighted in stage 3? How is X possible? What properties must exist for X to be what X is? What causal mechanisms are related to X? In the concrete research process we have of course in many cases access to already established concepts supplying satisfactory answers to questions of this type. In research practice, stages 3 and 4 are closely related.

Stage 5: comparison between different theories and abstractions

In this stage one elaborates and estimates the relative explanatory power of the mechanisms and structures which have been described by means of abduction and retroduction within the frame of stages 3 and 4. (This stage can also be described as part of stage 4.) In some cases one might conclude that one theory – unlike competitive theories – describes the necessary conditions for what is to be explained, and therefore has greater explanatory power (see also Chapter 5). In other cases the theories are rather complementary, as they focus on partly different but nevertheless necessary conditions.

Stage 6: concretization and contextualization

Concretization involves examining how different structures and mechanisms manifest themselves in concrete situations. Here one stresses the importance of studying the manner in which mechanisms interact with other mechanisms at different levels, under specific conditions. The aim of these studies is twofold: first, to interpret the meanings of these mechanisms as they come into view in a certain context; second, to contribute to explanations of concrete events and processes. In these explanations it is essential to distinguish between the more structural conditions and the accidental circumstances. This stage of the research process is of particular importance in an applied science.

We shall conclude this chapter by presenting an example of how these different stages can permeate a concrete study. It is a sociological study of gender segregation in the labour market (Roman 1994). Roman aims at examining whether, within knowledge companies, there is another relation between the male and female parts of the workforce, besides that found in traditional business. One of the aims of the thesis was to examine whether there are gender-segregating mechanisms in these knowledge companies. With the help of Figure 4 we can illustrate the basic idea of the process.

The first stage of the research process consists in describing the phenomenon. In the example, gendered division of labour in the Swedish labour market is described with the help of extensive studies (though not performed by the author herself). In the second stage the phenomenon (gender segregation in the labour market) is divided analytically into a number of imaginable causal components. A social phenomenon is very seldom unambiguous. As a rule one can analyse a number of dimensions or different aspects. In the example gender-typical lines of action, and negative special treatment, are some such components. These phenomena are the empirical manifestation of a great number of cooperative and counteractive mechanisms – for example, gendered

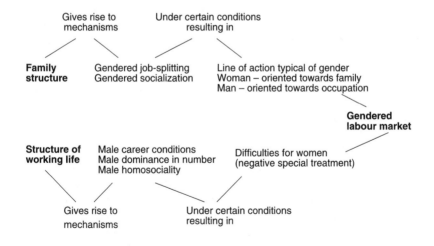

Figure 4 Illustration of conceptualizations in the research process

Source: Roman 1994: 84

division of labour, gendered socialization and male career conditions – which in a specific context together constitute one or more unobservable structures. In this way the studied phenomenon can be described as a result of several causal mechanisms. These mechanisms are located partly in the family structure, partly in the working life structure. It is at the social level that mechanisms arise (emergent powers) and under certain circumstances their effect results in a gender-segregated labour market. What one does in the research process is try to identify these possible causes.

Each such part can then be related to different ideas and causal theories. A redescription of each part is carried out using the respective theories (the third stage). These descriptions make it possible to find a number of possible underlying causes. Plausible explanatory models are discussed. The author points out several possible theories. She rejects, however, theories at non-social levels (particularly biological theories). In critical realist terms we can say that she is looking for the emergent powers at the stratum where her study object is.

As the reader can see, we are moving backwards in the figure. We go from the empirical concrete phenomenon towards the generative mechanisms. (We shall soon turn back from the abstract concepts to the concrete level.) Since we are dealing with open systems, there is a great number of possible mechanisms cooperating. All of them are not, however, equally plausible. Roman writes (1994:37): 'My starting point is that the phenomenon is best explained by reference to the processes producing it. A question which should be asked is thus, *what* in different social structures is it that *can* produce gendered segregation.' We have now come to the fourth stage in the above model. Roman identifies and describes several fundamental generative mechanisms that can explain the phenomenon. At the fifth stage these are weighed against each other regarding, among other things, their relative explanatory power. She argues that some of them are more important than the others (see the figure). Within the frame of the sixth stage she then examines how these mechanisms manifest themselves in the concrete reality.

A central question of the thesis is: Are the previously identified gender-segregating mechanisms operating here, too (for example, we would add, in knowledge companies)? The answer is that these mechanisms manifest themselves in contexts where one would expect to find counteractive mechanisms, such as lack of manpower in the business. As we have pointed out before, it is important to distinguish between structural conditions and contingent circumstances. The author here employs both intensive and extensive designs in her data collection. The emphasis, however, is on the intensive part. The 'test' of the hypotheses of the generative mechanisms is carried out by means of a theoretical and an empirical confrontation. At the same time as Roman establishes that the gender-segregating mechanisms do seem to operate, there are also counteractive mechanisms. These are discussed at length, and their importance is evaluated. She does this by switching between theoretical and empirical arguments.

Conclusion

In this chapter we have considered three central themes in the methodology of social science – generalization, inference and explanation – and within the framework of each one of them we have described important methodological implications of the epistemology and ontology presented in Part I of this book. In discussions about social scientific method, generalization is very often placed on an equal footing with empirical inductive generalization. This will supply a very limited understanding of society, since generality is not just about – and not even in the first place – empirical regularities. The general must also be sought in the structures making up the constituent properties of social relations. Knowledge of these structures requires transfactual argument, or what we have also called retroduction. Retroduction can be seen as a mode of inference or thought operation, beside other forms of inference: deduction, induction and abduction. They should be seen as complementary, and together they constitute the foundation of different scientific working procedures. The four forms of thought operation represent fundamental courses of action we must follow in order to reach the overall goal of social science: to be able to explain conditions in society with true knowledge of reality. At least that is our argument in this chapter. Each one of these modes of inference at the same time represents different ways of relating the specific to the universal and general. By deduction, knowledge of individual phenomena is derived from universal laws. By induction, inference is drawn about larger populations from individual observations. By abduction, individual phenomena are recontextualized with the help of general concepts and categories. By retroduction, accidental circumstances are abstracted in order to arrive at the general and universal. Deduction – unlike the others – is a formalized inference, in which conclusions are drawn in a strictly logical way from premises. On the one hand, deduction has become the hub of some scientific methods in particular, such as the hypothetico-deductive method. On the other hand, deductive logic defines formalized rules that are universal and applicable to the examination of all scientific argument. Scientific inference, where we from something draw conclusions about something else, cannot be reduced either to strictly logical inference (deduction) or to empirical generalization (induction). Scientific inference is not only about applying formal logic; it also involves reasoning, creativity, the ability to abstract, and theoretical language in order to see meanings and structures in the seemingly unambiguous and flat empirical reality. This is obvious, not least if we consider what social science practice in fact looks like. To be able to detect meanings, relations and coherence, to be able to gain knowledge of social structures and transfactual conditions, those modes of inference are required, which we have described in terms of abduction and retroduction. In our view, scientific development and rethinking would hardly be possible without these thought operations. It is through them we alter ordinary ways of reasoning. By abduction and retroduction we can see connections and structures not directly obvious in the empirical reality. In the last part of this chapter we have also shown how abduction and retroduction can be integrated in a model of explanatory social science. The discourse in this chapter has several times touched upon another central theme – the role of theories in research practice and the relation between theory and empirical data. We shall discuss this in Chapter 5.

5 Theory in the methodology of social science

In Chapters 2 and 3 we highlighted conceptualization as being absolutely crucial in social science research. In Chapter 4 we suggested that generalizations, inferences and explanations build on different ways of employing theories in research practice. Abduction, just to mention one example, could imply recontextualizing empirical phenomena within the framework of alternative theories. It is now time to more explicitly examine the role of conceptualization and theory in social science methodology.

Undergraduates writing research papers are often told that they must take their starting point in theories. However, as supervisors we often fail to explain what this means. Why are theories necessary? How should one use them in practice? It is not uncommon to find papers (and doctoral dissertations) containing extensive theoretical passages without any clear link to empirical analysis. From the paper-writing student's point of view, theories at the worst become something they have to add to satisfy what they regard as academic snobbery, which makes the paper boring reading, especially for people outside the academic sphere.

If, however, one learns to integrate theorizing into the research in a fruitful way, it will contribute to new knowledge and insight, thus making the research paper exciting and thought-provoking to writer and reader alike. This is one of the most important and decidedly most difficult challenges in practical research. The difference between a good and a not-so-good research paper often depends, perhaps even in most cases, on the writer's ability to apply theoretical concepts. The aim of this chapter is to demonstrate how theories can be used in social scientific research.

In social science it is common to deal with theory and method separately. Universities may of course be justified in having separate courses in theory and methodology. Yet it is restricting if method is primarily associated with methods of data collection and empirical analysis, since an essential element of the craft, the method, is about employing and developing theories. One should regard theorizing as an integrated part of research methodology, or, as Sayer so pertinently puts it, 'Any serious consideration of method in social science quickly runs into basic issues such as the relation between theory and empirical observation and how we conceptualize phenomena' (Sayer 1992: 45).

Social scientific skill in essence is a matter of analysing and developing the theoretical language and of employing it in empirical analysis.

There is also another reason why method and theory should not be treated as two separate elements of social science. The value of different methods depends on how we theoretically define our research object. We must ask ourselves what we are going to study before we can answer how to set about it.

The outline of this chapter is as follows: first there are two sections aimed at clarifying what a theory is, from the perspective of critical realism. Then we proceed to the components of theories – concepts. The following sections will describe different ways of relating theory to empirical research in practice.

Three comprehensive perspectives on theory and observation

Regarding the relation between theory and empirical observation, two different views have often been polarized. On one view, the role of theory is to order, explain and predict facts (Sayer 1992: 45). Theories present hypotheses of relations between observable events/phenomena. The validity of a theory is assessed when it is tested against empirical data. This view has been developed within the positivist research tradition.

On the second view, all theories are regarded as constructions creating imagined relations between phenomena. Theories can never be submitted to decisive empirical tests, since there are no facts independent of the theories to test them against. Under the influence of Kuhn's studies in particular, of the history of science, it has been a common argument that we always understand reality – and define our data – within the framework of theories that are more or less taken for granted. Therefore theories cannot be true or false; yet they can be more or less useful. In postmodernism the conception of theories as constructions has been taken to such extremes that it seems totally pointless to evaluate different theories in relation to empirical data. Here there is a tendency to reduce theories to nothing but rhetorical constructions, without any valid reference to a reality independent of the theory.

Critical realism represents a third position in relation to these two standpoints. We have already described this position in Chapter 2. Still, let us briefly review some of the central starting points of critical realism concerning the relation between theory and observation/data.

1   We can never understand, analyse or categorize reality without using a theoretical language of concepts.
2   These concepts are constantly being developed.
3   The development of concepts presupposes an (intransitive) reality independent of these concepts.
4   The relation between theories/theoretical concepts and the properties or objects the concepts are referring to is not unambiguous and simple; nor is it arbitrary. All theoretical descriptions are fallible, but not equally fallible.

5   Theories and theoretical concepts are developed in relation to the experiences we obtain when we use them to understand reality.

Theorizing and development of concepts have a key role in ordinary research practice. The reason for our maintaining this is actually quite simple. To a large extent the objects of social science are such social situations, relations, processes and structures that never appear as given facts or as something directly observable. Social relations and structures can only be understood by means of concepts. It is a fairly common notion that our knowledge increases primarily through data collection and surveys. With Bhaskar's terminology we can say that such a notion is based on a double reduction. Our knowledge of social reality is reduced to knowledge of events, which in turn is reduced to empirical observations of these events.

Development of knowledge presupposes development of the language we use in order to understand and explain the social reality, that is to say, our concepts. Development of theories and concepts is not only a means to improving empirical studies but is also a goal in its own right for a social science aiming at insights into basic social structures and mechanisms. Theories should be apprehended in an undogmatic way; they are fallible and changeable and there will always be a number of competing theories.

Scientific method is essentially a matter of switching between different levels of abstraction, but it is also about relating these levels to one another. Theories are abstractions that can never be put to a direct test against objective facts. If our observations are to mean anything at all to us, we need a language. Scientific work implies a conscious attitude to the theoretical language of science. Further, theories must not become arbitrary constructions; they must be founded on experiences of concrete reality. The ability to switch between abstract theorizing and observations of concrete reality, without yielding either to arbitrary theorizing or to short-sighted observation, is at the core of social science working procedure.

What is a theory?

> Like so many words that are bandied about, the word theory threatens to become meaningless. Because its referents are so diverse – including everything from minor working hypotheses, through comprehensive but vague and unordered speculations, to axiomatic systems of thought – use of the word often obscures rather than creates understanding.
>
> (Merton 1967: 39)

There is a good deal in Robert Merton's reflection on the concept of theory. The concept is still being used – many decades later – in many different ways. This has partly to do with the fact that the concept of theory has been given different meanings in different competing metatheories and research traditions.

The concept of theory is also a superordinate concept for a variety of different types of theory – from very general abstract ones, bordering on philosophy, to more concrete theoretical hypotheses of specific phenomena. In Merton's formulation there is an unmistakable critique of what he and many others have regarded as too general and speculative social theories. Building on this critique Merton argued for so-called middle-range theories, theories that are concrete enough to enable tests (to be verified or falsified) against empirical data, by certain procedures. Merton's critique was not unjustified and is hardly less relevant today. Too much of social scientific work is devoted to speculative theorizing and constructions of new concepts, barely contributing to any development of knowledge.

The fact that there exist completely different types of theory (and theoretical language) is not a problem, however, but rather a resource, which ought to be employed in social scientific practice. We can distinguish between four different types of theories, which can partly be demarcated with reference to their degree of abstraction. Raymond Morrow and David Brown (1994: 40) answer the question 'what is theory?' by distinguishing between three different theoretical languages existing in social science: metatheory, normative theory and descriptive theory.[1] By also distinguishing between two types of descriptive theory – on the one hand theories confined to specific areas of inquiry, and on the other hand general theories – we arrive at four instead of three types of theory.

Metatheory is theories about the foundational assumptions and preconditions of science. Critical realism, phenomenology, hermeneutics and positivism are metatheories building on different ontologies and epistemologies. The whole of this book views scientific working procedure from a specific metatheoretical standpoint.

Normative theory refers to the theoretical language and argument which examines as well as supports various ideas of how something ought to be. It can be a theory focusing on moral, political or ideological issues. In many social scientific concepts and theories there is an inherent normative critique, in that concepts provide tools by means of which we can understand reality in new ways, can reflect, problematize and relativize. Informed by concepts like socialization, cultural code, symbolic capital, hegemony, gender stratification, ideology, etc., we can see that the sociocultural conditions we tend to regard as natural in everyday life are in fact created by various social processes. The existence of competing theories in social science forms the base for a reflecting social science, that is, a science which offers alternative ways of understanding society. At the same time, theories are being developed to make it possible to identify mechanisms that tend to create and also justify dominance relationships and social inequality. In this respect social science has a critical emancipatory potential.

A critical science often takes its starting point in notions that improvement of society is possible. This does not mean that science can provide simple, clear-cut solutions. Social life – as many contemporary theorists have observed – is marked by ambivalence and fundamental dilemmas, making such simple solutions impossible (Sayer 1994; Bauman 1991).

One might say that the normative dimension of social theory has experienced a revival in social science in the past few decades. We have already mentioned that Habermas and Bhaskar emphasize the critical and emancipatory potential of social science. Habermas is also one of the many contemporary theorists who have contributed to a situation where issues like rationality, democracy, citizenship, equality, morals, ethics, etc., are at the centre of attention in social science (see also Bauman 1991, 1993; Benhabib 1992; Kellner 1995 – to name just a few examples). The distinction between fact and value, so central in positivism, has been questioned, not least within critical realism. It is, however, beyond the scope of this book to examine this issue more closely (see Archer *et al.* 1998: part III).

By *descriptive theories* one means theories claiming to be able to describe and characterize more fundamental properties, structures, internal relations and mechanisms. Such theories thereby suggest how we may interpret and explain different social phenomena. We can distinguish at least two different types of descriptive theory, first, theories demarcated for specific objects of research (unemployment, residential segregation, drug abuse, professionalization, etc.), and second, more general theories, marking fundamental aspects of social activity, social interaction and social development processes. Goffman's theory of dramaturgic action, Mead's theory of symbolic interaction, and Giddens' structuration theory, are all examples of general theories.

Concerning descriptive theories, Sayer (1992) makes another distinction, capturing something essential with regard to social scientific research practice. He distinguishes between theory as *ordering framework* and theory as *conceptualization*. In line with the first view, theories are 'a way of ordering the relationship between observations (or data) whose meaning is taken as unproblematic' (Sayer 1992: 50). This type of theory is often presented in the form of a formalized model pointing out, on the one hand, the variables included in the theory, and on the other hand the assumed relations between these variables. Quantitative (statistical) relations between different, empirically measurable conditions are studied by means of such models. Hellevik refers to this perspective when he discusses causal analysis:

> A causal analysis falls into two parts, a theoretical and an empirical one. In the theoretical part the scientist defines her ideas of causal relationships in a model showing what variables are assumed to be relevant and what influences are assumed to exist between these variables.
>
> (Hellevik 1984: 11, our translation)

There are probably few scientists who would say that a theory is the same thing as a causal model or an ordering framework. But in their practical work researchers very often assume that theories are tested by measuring correlations between variables from such models. In this case theories are comprehended as assumptions of general (causal) relations between observable events. We will come back to this viewpoint later when we consider different ways of relating theorizing to empirical research.

Within the framework of critical realism, theories are not first and foremost regarded as ordering frameworks but as conceptualizations (Sayer 1992: 50). Ordering events or phenomena in models is of minor importance. What is important is that we conceptualize events, mechanisms and internal relations in a certain way, with the help of theories. Conceptualizing is the same thing as abstracting and isolating fundamental qualities (see Chapter 3). The concepts provide an abstract language enabling us to speak about qualitative properties, structures and mechanisms.

The difference between a theory and an individual concept is that the former conceptualizes the relations between several central concepts in a rigorous and reasoned fashion. Theory is, as Jensen (1991: 7) writes, 'qualitative, insofar as it represents a configuration of interrelated concepts'. If we link this with what we have said in the previous chapter, we see that what was there called abduction and retroduction concerns simply conceptualization. Abduction can be redescribing and giving meaning to events, taking one's starting point in a theory, a coherent system of ideas or concepts. Through retroduction, concepts and theories are developed which can provide answers to such questions as: What characteristics make X what X is? Social theories are abstractions, crystallizing the necessary conditions for social structures to be what they are. Sayer (1989: 258) expresses it thus: 'Theory is no longer associated with generality in the sense of repeated series of events but with determining the nature of things or structures, discovering which characteristics are necessary consequences of their being those kinds of objects'.

Theories are utilized in science to explain events and actions (cf. Chapters 3 and 4). A particular understanding of causal explanation is actually often directly related to a particular understanding of scientific theory. This becomes very clear if we compare positivism and critical realism:

> For the positivist, science is an attempt to gain predictive and explanatory knowledge of the external world. To do this, one must construct theories, which consist of highly general statements, expressing the regular relationships that are found to exist in that world.

> Thus, for the realist, a scientific theory is a description of structures and mechanisms which causally generate the observable phenomena, a description which enables us to explain them.
>
> (Keat and Urry 1978: 4 and 5 respectively)

From a positivist perspective, explanation is to explain one event by relating it to an empirical regularity. Theories articulate assumptions of such general regularities, formulated as law-determined or law-like relationships between events. We described this in Chapter 4 when we discussed the Popper–Hempel explanatory model. A fundamental idea in critical realism is, as we have already shown, that causality involves properties, structures and mechanisms that can only be identified through retroduction and by means of abstract concepts and theories. Even here explanations relate to general conditions, but this time in the sense of fundamental structures. We can now summarize our answer to the question: What is a theory? We will do so in the form of five statements:

1   Theory is a language, indispensable to science (see Chapter 2).
2   The theoretical language always includes an interpretation of the social reality. We see and understand the world with the help of theories. Theories here serve as an interpretative framework.
3   Theories are indispensable when it comes to explanation, since they conceptualize causal mechanisms.
4   Theories are abstractions; they describe phenomena with reference to certain aspects, which have been separated from other aspects also characterizing concrete events or phenomena.
5   Theories can be metatheories, normative theories, and also general and more specific descriptive theories. These different types of theory are all of great importance in social scientific research practice.

Theoretical concepts

Social theories build upon concepts and relations between concepts. A concept refers to a particular body of thought, to a certain meaning. The concept must be distinguished from the term we use to express this meaning, and from the object or the properties in reality, to which the concept is supposed to refer.

The relation between terms and concepts, that is to say the meanings the terms signify, is in principle arbitrary, not natural. This relationship is determined by linguistic and cultural agreements that are changeable, for instance agreements within the scientific community. Several different terms can denote the same meaning. Different languages can be used to talk about the same thing. The English word 'alienation', the German 'Entfremdung' and the Swedish 'främlingskap' are three terms used for one and the same concept.

An insight usually ascribed to the Swiss linguist Ferdinand de Saussure, and which has later been developed in semiotics, is the circumstance that the meanings of concepts are created through relationships. The basic relationship is the relation of opposites. Concepts are, Saussure (1966: 117) writes, 'purely differential and defined not by their positive content but negatively by their relations with the other terms of the system'. When we develop concepts in science we do so precisely by differentiating, by separating and specifying the meaning of one concept in relation to another. By scientific concepts we strive to specify qualities in relation to other qualities, in a way that gives us a deeper knowledge of social reality.

The relational character of concepts is also manifested in the triadic conceptualization, so common in social science. It has been most clearly expressed in dialectics by Friedrich Hegel and then in Marxism, by the concepts of thesis, antithesis and synthesis. Thesis and antithesis represent concepts that are defined precisely as each other's opposites. Synthesis is a concept whose essence of content is an integration of, or a relation between, thesis and antithesis.

Much of social theory is built on triadic conceptualizations. Feminist theory builds on a differentiation between male and female and a third concept for the relationship itself between them, for example concepts like patriarchy or gender stratification. Giddens' structuration theory is one of many theories dividing structure and agency and then developing a third concept – structuration – to characterize the interrelation between the two concepts. In Bhaskar's theory the corresponding classification of the interrelation between structure and agency is transformation. This way of defining concepts as opposing each other and then creating concepts for the mediation itself or the relationship between them is a fundamental feature in social scientific conceptualization. In ordinary research practice, the application of this triadic logic as a guideline for conceptualization can be very productive.

Numerous concepts and conceptual distinctions are presented in scientific literature. There is sometimes a tendency among scientists, in their respective fields, to successively develop their own models with different conceptual distinctions. Not least sociologists have been quite good at creating four-column tables by combining two variables and then labelling the combinations of qualities that arise. But it is important that conceptualization is not reduced to superficial empirical categorizations.

As we are taking our starting point in critical realism, we have specific expectations of conceptualization, and this is very important: concepts define, distinguish and discern certain properties. Conceptual differentiation should strive to discern those properties that are decisive for social activities, relationships and institutions to be what they are and not something qualitatively different (Sayer 1992: 82). It is essential not to confuse abstract concepts with empirical categories. The former distinguish mechanisms and structures, while empirical categories instead divide reality into different types of events and empirical characteristics. Conceptualization is something other than labelling empirical categories. When we examine theoretical models and concepts, one question is central: What mechanisms do these concepts highlight, that no other concepts have highlighted? In many cases it is more fruitful to develop and work with already existing concepts than to come up with new ones.

In other words, how we divide and conceptualize reality is far from arbitrary. We might say that a good concept is one that has 'punch', that is, it should be sharp and forceful. A concept that has punch is one that functions in practice, that provides deeper insight and has strong explanatory power. What punch the concept in fact has will be revealed when we use it in practice to analyse reality.

Metaphors are often very important in scientific conceptualization (Sayer 1992: 63). Metaphors build on analogies, conveying meanings from one thing to another. We describe something unfamiliar by referring to, giving a depiction of, something familiar (Berger 1982: 32). With the help of metaphors one creates images of circumstances which are otherwise hard to understand. Metaphors elucidate properties in an illustrative and illuminating way. They function well in communication, as they create opportunities for common associations. Metaphors, like abstractions, are a way of defining certain aspects of a phenomenon.

Everyday language is full of metaphors – 'he's as strong as a bear', 'it's cold as ice', etc. But metaphors are also used in science. Let us give four examples:

1   In media research there are discussions about what impact the media message has on the audience. In recent years criticism of earlier impact research has become increasingly stronger, since it is assumed to build on what has been called the 'injection model'. The injection needle has been a metaphor for a certain way of looking upon mass communication. It is immediately associated with certain characteristics of media; they are supposed to penetrate people's minds in a way against which people cannot protect themselves.

2   Organization theorists have used metaphors to crystallize various ideas of the nature of organizations. According to Morgan (1986) we can under-stand different aspects of complex organizations by using metaphors. He lists the following metaphors: an organization is like a machine, organism, brain, culture, prison, constant flow, instrument of dominance, political system. Each of these metaphors draws attention to different aspects of organizations, according to Morgan.

3   Goffman's use of the theatre and the dramaturgical performance as a metaphor for social interaction has been very important for social scientific conceptualization.

4   In political economy the market is often used as a metaphor for describing the context of social action. Some economists, for example, have illustrated the relationship between construction companies, house owners and resi-dents with the picture of a marketplace where people come to buy supplies. At a market individuals choose where to buy. They look at several stalls where different goods at different prices and of different quality are for sale. At a market the sellers at the same time adapt to other sellers and to the actions of the customers.

However, the strength of metaphors also entails a risk. Through the associa-tions and 'aha experiences' they create, they may also tempt people to go too far in utilizing them. The problem is that it is hardly possible to modify a metaphor. One must be able to modify and develop scientific concepts. It is fundamental for a scientific attitude always to be open to revise one's ideas in the light of one's experiences of reality. Regarding a metaphor, however, we must either keep it or abandon it completely. The image of the marketplace is either a good one that helps us understand the relationships in the housing sector, or it is simply misleading. There is no way of revising the image without it losing its value as a metaphor. Metaphors can contribute to the maintenance of deceptive conceptions. Empirical analyses from metaphors risk being reduced to predictable, one-sided interpretations.

Typical of metaphorical images is that they are based on immediate experiences of concrete situations: a syringe, a machine, a play, a marketplace. In Chapter 2 we argued that conceptualization and abstraction often require our breaking with the immediate and everyday conception of reality. Here there is a fundamental contrast between metaphorical images and abstractions which calls for our consideration.

At the same time scientists have argued that the language available to us for understanding reality is metaphorical and image-bearing by nature (Sayer 1992: 63; see also Denzin 1989). Science, like other activities where language is used to describe reality, is dependent on the capacity of language to create pictures of reality. Some theorists of science have also emphasized that metaphoric models can inform in creative discoveries and redescriptions of familiar phenomena. Bengt Kristensson Uggla (1994: 400), for one, writes that scientific discoveries can be understood 'as the fruit of metaphoric imagination, just as scientific revolutions can be connected to changes in the predominant metaphor' (our translation). The demand of science that concepts should constantly be submitted to critical examination and correction requires, however, that simple everyday metaphors are employed with great care.

Theorizing and empirical research: two leading traditions

It is now high time to address the question of how theories can be more specifically integrated in the research process. The aim of papers and other scientific work can be formulated in different ways: our objective is to *test* this theory; the empirical material will *elucidate* the theory; the aim is to *interpret* the empirical material in the light of the theory; the aim is to *develop* theoretical concepts from the empirical material. So theories can be used in a number of ways in scientific practice.

Different traditions in the social sciences have created a distinctive image for themselves in relation to others, partly just with reference to theories. Positivist-oriented science has tried to establish principles for how theories should be tested (be verified or falsified) against empirical data in line with a hypothetico-deductive logic. In the schools usually brought together under the designation of the interpretative paradigm – symbolic interactionism, ethnomethodology, ethnography – theories have been applied as the interpretative framework, but it is also within these schools that the more inductive strategies to generate (develop) theories from empirical data have been of great importance. In critical theory, theories have represented general (descriptive and normative) starting points for reflection and interpretation of current social problems. Here researchers have reinterpreted already completed studies and texts from a new perspective.

In the same year, 1967, two works were published that deeply influenced the discussion of the relation between theorizing and empirical research in social science: Robert Merton's *On Theoretical Sociology* with the essay 'On sociological theories of the middle range', and Barney Glaser and Anselm Strauss' *The Discovery of Grounded Theory*. These texts represent two different traditions, which are even today considered by some as the two main alternative research approaches.[2] They differ thoroughly regarding the question of how theorizing in practice should be related to empirical research. Merton's approach, influenced by positivism, indicates that theories should be tested against data. Glaser and Strauss develop a methodology for inductive theory generation. In the following we shall present and discuss these two approaches. In several respects they can provide important guidance for a social science based on critical realism. But we will also draw attention to some important limitations. In the section after that we shall present some other ways of integrating theory in concrete studies.

Middle-range theory: verifying theories with the help of empirical data

One of the most crucial contributions to the discussion of the role of theory in social scientific research practice is Robert Merton's argument for middle-range theory. Merton's approach has strongly marked a great deal of the theories of method in social science. A large number of papers have been published within the framework of the same comprehensive perspective, even though far from all of these have used the concept of middle-range theory.

In his essay 'On sociological theories of the middle range', Merton criticized the social science that is directed at developing grand theories, that is, very general and all-inclusive theories. The Marxist theory of capitalist society, and Talcott Parsons' theory of social systems and social action, are examples of the theories Merton alludes to. But he also repudiates a purely empirical social science, a science that collects data and tests empirical hypotheses without connecting them to theories. Theories are necessary for the explanation of different social conditions. Middle-range theory (MRT) is the designation of a certain type of theory and a specific methodology aiming at bridging the gap between general theories and empirical observation. Merton does not repudiate in principle the development of more all-inclusive grand theories, but he believes that grand theories are too speculative and without anchorage in empirical data. Much more substantial empirical knowledge about details is required before anyone can gradually systematize tested theories from different fields and develop comprehensive general theories. According to Merton, however, the problem of grand theories in social science is that they are of such a nature that it is hardly possible to test them. He maintains that it must be possible to test theories by carefully applied empirical methods.[3]

Characteristic of the kind of theory that Merton advocates is that it is restricted to specific social phenomena. Merton himself uses the theory of relative deprivation as an example. This theory is based on the fact that people look upon themselves in relation to what in social psychology are called reference groups. The theory suggests that people's experiences of some kind of deprivation is not only, or even primarily, related to how substantial this deprivation is from an objective viewpoint. Instead the experience is dependent on what these people's situation is like in relation to that of others, with whom they compare themselves. From this theory one can then at the next stage formulate testable hypotheses concerning particular situations, such as, for instance, people's experiences of a deteriorated material standard in connection with unemployment. Even if Merton himself mostly relates to social phenomena at the micro level, he emphasizes that this methodology is just as applicable when testing theories of macro conditions. Weber's theory of the Protestant ethic and the spirit of capitalism, as well as Durkheim's theory of suicide, can be seen as examples of MRT, according to Merton.

All theories comprise abstractions. According to the MRT approach, theories should be abstract enough to enable them to be applied to different social phenomena, but also concrete and specific enough to permit testing against empirical data:

> Middle-range theory involves abstractions, of course, but they are close enough to observed data to be incorporated in propositions that permit empirical testing.
>
> (Merton 1967: 39)

> Middle-range theories consist of limited sets of assumptions from which specific hypotheses are logically derived and confirmed by empirical investigation.
>
> (Merton 1967: 68)

Theories should be close to observable data. This proximity has essential implications for social scientific method. A theory has two basic components – concepts and the assumed relations between them. This means, first, that it should be possible to reformulate the theoretically defined concepts into operationally defined concepts (variables) without the theoretical concept essentially losing its meaning. It must be possible to find a valid indicator of concepts like class, status or social role. Second, it must be possible to carry out empirical testing of the assumptions of relations between the concepts. Within the scientific tradition to which Merton adheres, this testing is done by studying the existence of empirical quantitative relationships. MRT thus builds on the foundational assumption that the relations between concepts, formulated in the theory, should be studied in the form of quantitative relationships between variables. The existence of such empirical relationships is crucial when theories are tested.

What does this approach imply, as regards the orientation of the concrete research process? Merton himself is not very clear as to what he means by the testing of a theory, let alone how it should be done. In social science, however, methods have been developed for a theory and hypothesis testing research, which correspond well with Merton's approach. From the 1950s up to the present, an exhaustive amount of literature has been published, with the common ambition to develop and present methods of testing theories empirically. Some of this literature builds on fairly advanced logic and statistics (accounts of which go beyond the scope of this book). There are also other, more elementary books on method, describing ideal images of research design. In Chapter 6 we shall give a concrete example of the latter. To show what the MRT approach can mean in practice we will, however, now draw attention to the central stages in a research process directed at testing theories. Through these stages theory, hypothesis and observation of general relations (empirical regularities) are made to relate to one another.

1   In this research approach a theory is usually regarded as a system of propositions, which can be reduced to a number of testable hypotheses, by means of deductive logic. A theory is not testable in itself, only indirectly so by the more specific hypotheses that are derived from the theory.

   We illustrate this by reconstructing part of Emile Durkheim's study of suicide (used by Merton himself as an example of MRT). Durkheim's far-reaching theory can be summed up thus: changes and differences in the suicide rate can be explained by social facts, or more precisely, the degree of social integration and collective control. This theory Durkheim tries to confirm by empirical testing of some more concrete hypotheses.

   From an assumption that the family provides social integration for the individual, the following hypothesis can be deduced from the theory: after the age of twenty, married men and women are better protected against suicide than unmarried persons. If one further assumes that there is a higher degree of social integration among Catholics than among Protestants, the following hypothesis can be derived from the theory: suicide is more frequent among Protestants than among Catholics. Our example is a crude simplification. Durkheim's theory involves many more hypotheses. What is important in this context, however, is the principle. By deriving hypotheses from a more comprehensive general theory, the theory can be tested indirectly.

   Social science theories are more abstract than empirically testable hypotheses. Hypotheses can be derived from the theories, but their contents never correspond completely to one another. The same theory can always be tested by indirect means through several different but nevertheless valid hypotheses. It is not uncommon that some hypotheses are verified while others are falsified, despite the fact that they have been formulated to test the same theory. A falsified hypothesis is not necessarily a falsified theory. In the example of Durkheim's theory of suicide, for example, it might be true that the theory of social integration having an effect on suicide is correct, even if the hypothesis of differences between married and unmarried persons turns out to be wrong. The theory points at an abstract mechanism and the hypothesis at a more concrete circumstance. The more abstract a theory is, the greater the distance between the theory and the empirically testable hypothesis. The MRT approach is an attempt to find a middle course: on the one hand it repudiates an empirical social science that does not concern itself with abstract theory at all but devotes itself solely to directly testable empirical hypotheses; on the other hand it repudiates theories that are so abstract that they can hardly be tested by a hypothetico-deductive method.

2   An important stage in any research process oriented towards testing theories is operationalization. Operationalization means making hypotheses testable by constructing indicators that can be used to measure what the theoretical concepts express. When we have selected and defined an indicator, we have proceeded from a theoretical definition to an operational definition of the concept. There have been lively discussions within the philosophy of science concerning whether it is possible to translate theoretical language into such indicators (or what has been called a language of observation) (see e.g. Coniavitis 1984). The notion that theoretical concepts and empirical indicators should correspond with each other as far as possible is at least an ideal in research that is oriented towards testing theories.

Even this kind of problem can be illustrated by means of Durkheim's studies on suicide. The concept of social integration is central to his theory. In the hypothesis highlighted above, there is a first step of operationalization, as social integration here is expressed in terms of married or unmarried. This variable becomes measureable when Durkheim in the next step employs data from population statistics as an indicator of who is to be regarded as married or unmarried, respectively. The question is how well these data capture the concept of social integration. Another central concept is of course that of suicide. Durkheim's theoretical definition of suicide is: 'As suicide we regard all deaths that are the direct or indirect result of a positive or negative act (that is, failure to act), performed by the deceased, and which he knows will have this result' (Durkheim 1979). As the operational indicator Durkheim mainly uses information about suicide in official statistics. The problem here is of course that one cannot count upon this information being built on definitions of suicide consistent with Durkheim's own theoretical definition.

3   Characteristic of the theory-verifying method is that theories are tested against empirical relationships between variables. The relationship studied is a quantitative one, which permits measurement and statistical analysis. In some cases this quantitative aspect is already inherent in the theoretical formulation. Hubert Blalock (1984: 12), who has made influential contributions to the development of methods for theory-testing, gives the following example of a theoretical proposition: ' "The higher a white person's social status, the lower his or her prejudice toward blacks" '. The central concepts of the theory are simply considered as variables here, that is, properties capable of adopting a number of different values, which can be ranked and quantified. If we go back to Durkheim's theory by way of example, we notice that on the one hand it describes qualitative (substantive) relations

between different social conditions – it describes certain qualitative characteristics in the social integration, which are assumed to either counteract or support people's inclination to commit suicide. But on the other hand it is a theory assumed to explain quantitative variations in the variable 'suicide' (changes and differences in the suicide rate), by showing how this co-varies with quantitative variations in other variables (that is, indicators of high/low social integration). When the theory is tested, it is tested against statistical connections.[4]

In this methodology there is a strong connection between theory verification and preference for quantitative/statistical methods. The basis for this is the connection between causality and empirical regularities, which we have problematized before. Durkheim's theory includes an assumption of a crucial causal mechanism behind suicide, namely the degree of social integration. In his argument he presupposes that this mechanism, if it has causal significance, will manifest itself in empirical regularities. If no such regularities can be observed, one should, in accordance with this research approach, be forced to reject the theory of any causal significance of social integration. In a research based on the assumption that theories express qualitative properties and mechanisms, operating in an open system, it is, however, not self-evident that theories should be tested against quantitative connections between variables (cf. Chapter 3).

4   In practical research involving theory verification, it is never sufficient to study the correlation between just two variables. Theories usually contain assumptions of causality. The testable statements derived from the theory contain assumptions of how one variable affects another. To be able to say anything of whether a correlation between two variables is also a causal relation, one must take into consideration other relevant variables. To be able to discard the possibility that a certain correlation is actually a spurious correlation, some variables are kept constant. By means of a more or less advanced statistical method, one also tries to study several cooperating causes of a particular phenomenon. Within the framework of this research procedure, models are developed indicating which variables are to be included in the empirical investigation, and how these variables are supposed to be related to one another. In some cases the concept of theory is equated with just these models. The theories become what Sayer (1992) calls ordering frameworks.

By way of summarizing, we can say that the decisive elements in this research design are the methods and logical arguments we apply to relate the theory to testable hypotheses, and the testable hypotheses to the empirical quantitative data that has been collected. The relation between theorizing and empirical research becomes a question of deduction following logical rules on the one hand, and of operationalization on the other. These two elements will be absolutely decisive, since the validity of theories in this perspective is considered as totally dependent on the results achieved when the theory is tested against observations of quantitative correlations and regularities.

Grounded theory: generating theories from empirical facts

It is hardly an overstatement to regard grounded theory as the most elaborate and best-known alternative to the theory and hypothesis testing approach summed up in the previous section. Grounded theory (GT) stems essentially from the work of Glaser and Strauss (and their co-writers), but it has also been applied and developed by a range of scientists in various disciplines such as sociology, psychology, ethnology, business economics, media and communications research. The core of GT, what makes it a relatively uniform approach, is first that it takes its starting point in inductive theory generation, and second that it suggests various different methodological guidelines and procedures, which have been developed with the object of making theory generation more systematic and well reasoned. Without any pretensions of giving an exhaustive description of GT, we will in this section examine what, in our view, are the central and distinguishable aspects of this research approach. Then we will discuss the limitations of MRT and GT in relation to critical realism.

Inductive theory generation

As Glaser (1978: 15) points out, a standard question in sociological research is: What is the relation between theory and empirical research? We might also ask: How should theorizing and empirical research be linked to one another? Compared to Merton, Glaser and Strauss answer these questions very differently. Instead of deductive theory verification, they advocate inductive theory generation. GT is primarily a qualitative research approach, with strategies that serve as guidelines for an inductive generation of theories, with their roots in empirical data.

What does inductive mean, then, in this context? First and foremost it means that the researcher must start by thorough studies of empirical phenomena, and from them successively elaborate theories that are well grounded in data. Grounded theories should be useful not only for the researcher but also for the people involved in the social practice under investigation. The theory becomes grounded and useful, according to GT, if it fits the data and is a relevant way of conceptualizing specific fields/situations. Theories should fit data and not vice-versa. The conceptual categories that are developed should closely correlate to, and express the meanings of, data, which requires that one does not adapt one's interpretations to predefined categories. According to GT we should approach data in an open and relatively unbiased way. This has been interpreted and criticized as a sign of naive inductivism. On the one hand Glaser and Strauss argue for a research which permits data to speak for themselves and avoids analysis derived from already defined concepts. On the other hand they maintain that the reading of social scientific literature provides knowledge about possible concepts, thereby contributing to the theoretical sensitivity, which is a vital resource for analysis of data.

Grounded theory is also described as dense. A theory is dense and substantive if it is able to integrate multiple data from different situations and if it is based on a sample making it applicable in many concrete contexts. To Glaser and Strauss the opposite of a dense theory is an abstract theory, in the sense of being fairly void of empirical content. At the same time they often emphasize – and this is important – that even a grounded theory must be abstract and not superficially descriptive if it is to integrate multiple data. Conceptualizing, writes Glaser (1978: 6), is to surpass empirical data and to create concepts which on a more abstract level point to relations between seemingly separate events. It is by integrating multiple data at a higher level of abstraction that a theory can operate and become instrumental for explaining and understanding what happens in different social contexts.

It is an essential starting point for GT that conceptualization should be grounded in an individual's own everyday understanding of reality, such as it appears in specific social and cultural contexts and discourses. It is somewhat uncertain to what degree Glaser and Strauss hold that theory development should surpass this everyday understanding. On the one hand they stress that grounded theory should be accessible, instrumental and relevant for the individuals who are studied or who operate within the field of study. One might also interpret their outlook to indicate that a theory should correspond to everyday understanding. On the other hand, as we have seen, it is emphasized that conceptualization implies some form of surpassing. What distinguishes GT, anyhow, is the notion that theories must be inductively derived from the study of the phenomena they represent (Strauss and Corbin 1990).

Some central methodological procedures

It is far from uncommon that the systematic scientific method is believed to be mainly about the probing/testing of theories, while the discovery or generation of these theories is believed more or less to originate from creative guesses. By contrast, GT argues that theory generation is a result of a research process, which provides the best results if one follows certain procedures in a rigorous and systematic way. We shall briefly sum up a few central procedures that have been formulated with the aim of informing the development of grounded, integrated and dense theories. They can be compared to the central procedures in the theory-verifying approach (deduction of testable hypotheses from theories, operationalization, measurement, and the search for statistical correlation between variables).

Coding, or rather different forms of coding, is the core of GT. Theories are developed from data via coding, which means developing categories that discern and label common properties in data. This categorization or conceptualization should be grounded in exhaustive examination and careful data analysis. Coding is the way towards grounded abstraction. Codes are simply the concepts that give data a certain meaning and constitute the building bricks of the theory.[5]

This conceptualization of data Glaser (1978) also calls substantive coding, to distinguish it from theoretical coding. In the latter the substantial codes (the concepts) are related to one another. In this way theoretical codes indicate how concepts can be related and thus form an important part of theory development. As guidelines for this theory generation, Glaser (1978) also presents several so-called coding families, which point at possible ways of conceptualizing the relations between substantial concepts. We shall now discuss some of these that appear to be more comprehensive and particularly important in social science theory development.

1 Causality, consequences and conditions   According to Glaser this is the first comprehensive code one should bear in mind in theoretical coding. Here the relations between different situations are conceptualized as relations of causes and consequences. Other categories can be coded as preconditions for the indicated consequences to appear. Expressions like 'causes', 'leads to', 'depends on', 'follows from' and 'is an effect of' are different ways of denoting these theoretical codes.

2 Process   Here the relation between different concepts is conceptualized in the form of stages, steps, phases, courses of events, transitions, etc. All of them focus on processes and change over time. These theoretical codes are closely related to the problem of causality and are very common in social scientific theory.

3 Dimensions   Characteristic of this type of theoretical code is that it relates different concepts to one another as parts of a greater whole. A comprehensive category is reduced to different dimensions, sectors, parts, aspects, levels, and so on.

4 Strategies and motives for action   When people's actions are conceptualized, a special kind of theoretical code is used, relating motives to actions, means to ends, etc. Here concepts of the type 'aiming at' and 'strategies for' are used. These theoretical codes are central for rational choice theory and Goffman's theory of dramaturgic action, to mention just two.

To differentiate phases in the coding process, GT distinguishes between open and selective coding. As suggested by its name, *open coding* is a coding where the researcher approaches data without any defined conceptions or concepts. The aim is to create concepts, which give meaning to data, and categories, which bring together different concepts at a higher level of abstraction. This is a huge effort, taking a great deal of time. The material one works with must be examined several times, thoroughly and in detail. The first step, according to Strauss and Corbin (1990), is to break down the material into sentences or paragraphs and label different incidents, ideas, etc.: give them names that communicate what these elements of the material manifest or represent. The next step is to develop categories which integrate different concepts which seemingly describe the same type of phenomenon. Each category turns into a new concept, but this time at a higher level of abstraction. The qualitative content of the category is then developed, as the researcher identifies from the material the different properties that seem to be characteristic of that category.

Data do not speak for themselves. Strategies are needed to enable the discovery of concepts and categories. Two fundamental strategies presented in the literature are, first, constant posing of questions to the material; and second, different forms of comparison. Strauss and Corbin (1990) give examples of questions that could be posed to the material in order to, as they put it, open up data to enable rethinking potential categories and their properties. The fundamental questions that should be asked are: Who? When? Where? What? How? How much? Why? These questions can guide the formulation of more specific questions, which are continually asked as the coding is elaborated.

Comparison is fundamental in the GT approach, both in open and selective coding. By systematically comparing different cases and clarifying their similarities and dissimilarities, concepts and categories are developed, providing new insight into a phenomenon and at the same time being well grounded in data. Contrasted with something else, specific meanings may emerge in a clear way. The cases may be people, situations or moments. Let us for instance assume that we are interested in conceptualizing and categorizing the watching of television as a social activity. Our question is: What is the meaning of this activity? Guided by the comparative method we endeavour to collect data (by means of interviews and participant observation), which enables us to compare different people/groups of people and their television watching, different occasions and situations when they watch television, different programmes they watch, etc. In the coding phase a set of questions can be asked regarding the various situations, thus guiding the comparison.

Selective coding differs from open coding in that it is more focused on integrating the categories into a refined theory (Strauss and Corbin 1990). The coding is concentrated on what seem to be central categories for understanding and explaining a certain type of problem. Central categories are those to which other categories can be related and which can integrate other categories at a higher level of abstraction. The work with analysis – and possibly supplementary addition of new cases and data – is now delimited with the aim of developing a theory that will point out certain relations as being more fundamental than others. This also requires that the main problem, which the theory should explain, has been more clearly identified than in open coding.

As we have already hinted, GT advocates a flexible interaction between coding/analysis, sampling and data collection. In continuously new encounters with reality, concepts and theories are successively elaborated. New samples are continually made as a result of questions arising in the analysis. This is called *theoretical sampling*, since the samples are directed by the comprehensive question: What other people, cases or situations do we need to examine to be able to develop and ground the concepts and the emerging theory? In principle the coding – sampling – process should continue until one has developed a saturated theory. A theory is saturated when new cases and analyses no longer provide new knowledge relevant to the categories on which the theory builds, at the same time as the relations between the categories are well grounded in data.

Substantive and formal theory

Not least in view of the discussion about the limitations of GT, which we will presently look into, it is important to pay attention to another aspect of the research approach developed by Glaser and Strauss, namely the relation between substantive and formal theory. This is an essential element of GT, but it is often neglected when others apply this approach. By substantive theory one refers to theories developed for a specific area of inquiry. It could be theories of unemployment, the social situation of the hearing-impaired, or the impact of journalism on politics. Formal theory is theories built on abstract concepts, which are applicable to a range of subjects – theories of, for example, stigma, socialization, legitimacy and power.

Glaser and Strauss look upon substantive theory as a springboard in the development of formal theory. In social science this is not infrequently done by what is called rewriting. Theoretical conclusions grounded in a specific area are rewritten using more abstract theoretical wording. By way of example Glaser and Strauss mention how it is possible, by changing concepts, to rewrite a theory grounded in studies of the relationship between a doctor and his or her patients, so that it applies to relationships between professionals and clients. Thereby the generality of the theory is increased and it claims to be applicable to a number of concrete situations. However, one question must be asked: is the theory satisfactorily grounded? Rewriting can be a productive instrument in theory development; however, it should principally be viewed as a hypothetical assumption, until a more complete material is at hand. Formal theory can be developed and successively grounded by a combination of rewriting and attempts to integrate substantive theories. One can look upon the difference between formal and substantive theory as a difference in degree. It is, ideally, a question of an ongoing process of abstraction, resulting in formal theories whose generality successively increases, as the theory is grounded in more and more substantive areas (Glaser 1978).

Middle-range theory and grounded theory: limitations of these approaches

Both the theory-verifying approach (MRT) and the theory-generating approach (GT) offer important guidelines for social scientific research. The merit of the first approach is above all that it draws attention to the demands on logical clarity, valid operationalization and precision in empirical measurements, things we should always strive to attain in hypothesis testing. In social scientific research the testing of theoretically grounded hypotheses is not an inessential element.

Important developments in method are constantly being made, but it is beyond the scope of this book to discuss this issue here.

The GT approach has many great merits. It suggests a range of appropriate strategies for a large part of social scientific method, namely conceptualization and theory development. Theory development becomes an important goal in its own right. With the guidance these strategies offer, it becomes possible to develop concepts and theories which are abstract but at the same time integrated and grounded in data. The work with empirical data is focused on identification of properties and substantive relations instead of statistical connections between variables. It is also an essential point that theory development is presented as a natural part of ordinary research practice. Unlike the MRT approach, which presupposes that theories can be submitted to decisive tests, theory development in GT is an ongoing process. The core of this process is a flexible interaction between conceptualization and analysis of constantly new empirical data.

But neither of these approaches can claim to be sufficient in itself, or superior to other ways of directing scientific work. They are both limited. Let us imagine that social science up till now had followed these two approaches exclusively. In all probability we would then lack a great deal of the knowledge we have about social structures and mechanisms. The theories developed by classical scholars like Marx, Weber and Durkheim, or modern theorists like Habermas, Bourdieu, Giddens and Collins, would not exist as theories valuable to social science, nor would all the empirical analyses that have been made based on these or other general social science theories. The remaining part of this section will be devoted to a constructive critique of the two aforementioned research approaches. We shall dwell most on GT, since we consider it to have the most to offer a social science based on critical realism. Two types of limitation will be highlighted: first that the approaches have an empiricist bias; and second that the significance of general theory has been disregarded (cf. Layder 1993; 1998). In the section thereafter we will present examples of how one can work with general theories within the framework of a research going beyond both deductive theory verification and inductive theory generation. Here we argue that abduction and retroduction are fundamental and indispensable features in theorizing, and in the processes by which theorizing and empirical research are related to one another.

Empiricist bias

In a research practice informed by MRT, empirical observations are given priority. Empirical facts are assumed to be decisive when the validity of theories is assessed. Theories that cannot be tested empirically are discarded in this science. The approach implies a mainly empiricist epistemology, as it is assumed to be possible to test abstractions against empirical data through logical deduction and operationalization. Abstract theories describing transfactual social structures and qualitative properties cannot, however, be reduced to concrete, observable events or general quantifiable regularities. Two types of knowledge are involved. When abstract concepts like social integration, alienation, class or ideology are rewritten into empirical indicators and hypotheses of statistical connections, they lose essential aspects of their original meaning (Ekström 1993). Abstract social theory is a language with a value of its own, and cannot be reduced to hypotheses of empirical connections by means of logical derivations and operationalization. On the other hand, such hypotheses can be formulated within the framework of a comprehensive theory.

GT is often mentioned as an alternative to a positivist-oriented social science. Hence it may seem somewhat paradoxical that GT can justifiably be said to imply an empiricist epistemology, which is otherwise regarded as characteristic of precisely positivism. The following methodological ideals, however, make GT empirically biased: the inductive approach, the priority given to the work of coding and labelling of data, the argument that concepts should emerge from data and from the investigated individuals' notions of reality, and the idea that theories should represent reality and fit data (cf. Layder 1993). Here there is room, however, for different interpretations and, above all, for different ways of applying GT.

The methods and strategies developed in GT – and what enables us to talk about this as a specific methodology – no doubt represent an inductive ideal. There is a tendency to regard established theories as an impediment rather than a resource, when arguing that concepts should emerge from data through relatively unbiased coding. At the same time another feature is stressed as being very important, what has been called theoretical sensitivity, that is, the ability to analyse and give meaning to data. This sensitivity may be derived from a number of sources, from personal experience to knowledge of established theories (Glaser and Strauss 1967; Strauss and Corbin 1990). The research process is probably most productive when we manage to combine a fairly open attitude towards data with the use of established concepts as a resource. The theoretical language of science works like other structures: it is limiting in some ways, but it is also the medium that makes possible deep and creative interpretations of social reality.

Coding without the guidance of theoretical concepts runs the risk of being short-sighted, shallow and naive. Empirical data is always categorized data, and theoretical concepts are the scientific instruments necessary to find alternatives to common-sense categories. The critical potential of science is partly to be found here. Strauss and Corbin (1990) present a special strategy to employ in coding, which they call 'waving the red flag'. By this they mean that in the work with analysis and conceptualization of data, we should always react to (wave a red flag at) formulations like 'it is common knowledge … ' or 'it is obvious that … '. Any formulation implying that something is natural or normal should be meticulously examined by the researcher. The principle should be not to take anything for granted. Ideas of reality as representing the normal, the taken-for-granted within a certain sociocultural context, are particularly difficult to identify and conceptualize, but it is nevertheless important to do so. Glaser (1978) also stresses that theory development involves going beyond the empirical, the immediately given, developing theories at an increasingly higher level of abstraction. The question is, however, whether this is consistent with the demand that theories should fit data and be accessible and usable for people working in the social practice under investigation. Anyhow, it is obvious that GT does not consider the significance and consequences of the double hermeneutic of social science (see Chapter 2), and the problematic relation between an everyday understanding and scientific abstractions. Concepts describing fundamental social structures and mechanisms will always go beyond, relativize and problematize individuals' everyday experience.

There is room for different ways of interpreting and applying GT. It is particularly important not to reduce research work to a short-sighted, common-sense-influenced labelling and sorting of data. One should instead employ the strategies developed by Glaser and Strauss, with the aim of integrating data in the development of abstract concepts and theories. It is very doubtful whether it is at all fruitful to meticulously follow the various modes of coding as if they constituted a manual for scientific research. Such detailed inductive coding would be highly time-consuming and often needlessly inefficient. The risk is that there will be much work and comparatively little new knowledge. Still, there is a tendency in some research work to draw conclusions too fast without working with the empirical material. GT points to something important, namely that there are discoveries to be made if one takes the time to work on the material.

Existing concepts and theories should not just be used as a form of inspiration in the coding of data. In concepts and theories there is accumulated knowledge, which ought to be utilized. There is no reason to start from the beginning again, at every stage of the research process. Theories in particular contain knowledge of underlying structures and mechanisms, which can hardly be attained by the inductive method. There is in GT a strong tendency to tie theory development to our immediate impressions of the empirical reality as it appears in a relatively obvious way (Layder 1993). That is hardly the way to attain knowledge of fundamental social structures. Glaser and Strauss (1967: 34) react against what they call theoretical bias, a research that compels data into ready-made categories. Even if GT has developed since, one is justified to wave a red flag at the empiricist bias implied by this approach.

The significance of general theory

Within contemporary social science there is a fairly widespread and unfortunate division of labour between, on the one hand theorists who are engaged in developing and analysing general/formal theories, and on the other hand an empiricist-oriented research, which does very little to integrate the more abstract theories in its analyses (Layder 1998). We believe that it would be very profitable for researchers to make an effort in ordinary research practice to overcome this division.

In his book *New Strategies in Social Research*, Layder (1993) puts forward a constructive critique of the two strategies we have discussed here. One of

Layder's principal arguments against MRT is that this approach – through its demand for testability – excludes more general theories from social scientific research practice. According to Layder such theories are not speculative to the extent that Merton intimates, even if Layder, too, stresses that general theories should be empirically underpinned more often than is now the case. General theories must, however, and this is important, relate to the empirical reality in a totally different fashion, compared to MRT. They cannot be reduced to testable hypotheses, their validity cannot be totally dependent on empirical verification or falsification. They are instead evaluated with reference to how fruitful they are as interpretative framework, and to what degree they generate new and deeper knowledge of social structures. We shall discuss this more thoroughly under the heading 'The validity of theories'.

In our view, the GT approach, too, underestimates the value of general abstract theories. It is hardly possible to arrive at particularly general and abstract theories, if we take our starting point in a detailed unbiased coding of data; especially not within the framework of a normal research project. Glaser and Strauss do emphasize that formal theories can be generated from grounded substantive theories. However, it is questionable whether the general theories developed by Marx, Weber and Habermas, among others, and which constitute such an important part of social science knowledge, meet Glaser and Strauss' demands that theories be inductively grounded in data.

But what do we mean, then, by general theory or grand theory? This is not at all a clear-cut term, and Layder and Merton use it somewhat differently. We shall conclude this section by suggesting a specification.

The term 'general theory' can allude to at least three different characteristics of social theory. Layder uses the term by referring partly to theories conceptualizing more comprehensive processes and mechanisms in the evolution of society. Marx's theory of the capitalist society, Weber's theory of the increasing rationalization of society, and Habermas' theory of how the system colonizes the lifeworld, are well-known examples of such theories. Common for these theories is that they formulate assumptions of comprehensive historical social processes of change, at a macro level.

When Merton discusses general theories, or grand theories, which is the term he mainly uses, he is primarily alluding to something else (Merton 1967: 45). Grand theories to Merton are theories claiming to describe an all-encompassing total system, within which all types of social relationship and process can be placed. Such theories strive to totalize social science knowledge in a single system, from which it should be possible to explain empirical conditions in a range of different areas. It is thus the scope of the theory that makes it a general theory.

These two definitions of general theory may indeed be related to each other, insofar as a theory of comprehensive processes at a macro level may be relevant to many different, more specific areas and social scientific problems. But it is not self-evident that a theory of such processes simultaneously claims to present an all-embracing system. Common to the social theories usually brought together under the heading of postmodernism is, for instance, that they on the one hand emphatically question all totalizing knowledge, all unitary systems or grand theories, but on the other hand formulate assumptions of just such comprehensive processes of social change. One such process of change is characteristically enough what is considered as an ever-increasing fragmentation, which in itself almost makes grand theories impossible (see Denzin 1993). In the mid-1990s, as Ahrne *et al.* (1996: 17) write, 'nobody dreams of formulating an all-embracing theory of social development' (our translation). The theoretical discussion of comprehensive processes and tendencies in society, however, is just as lively today as it has ever been.

To these two definitions of the term 'general theory', we now add a third, emanating from critical realism such as we have described it in previous chapters. Many social scientific theories are general in the sense that they develop concepts that can make visible fundamental social properties, structures and mechanisms. This aspect should not be confused with the two others mentioned. There are many examples showing that such theories need not be either formulation of comprehensive development processes or all-embracing systems: Mead's theory of the development of self and identity in relation to social interaction and symbolic interaction; Goffman's theory of how people present themselves to one another and together define social situations; Bourdieu's theory of habitus and different forms of capital; Habermas' theory of the universal rules for our use of language – these are some examples of theories of general mechanisms. These theories focus on specific structures at specific levels of reality, contrary to theories claiming to incorporate a lot of different social mechanisms in an all-encompassing total system. Mechanisms and structures are general in the sense that they constitute the common foundational conditions for a variety of concrete, complex and diverse social processes, actions and relationships.

We can thus isolate three different meanings of the term 'general theory'. For the sake of clarity we sum them up:

1   theories of comprehensive social processes at a macro level;
2   theories claiming to represent all-embracing systems capable of integrating, in principle, all forms of social processes and relations; and
3   theories of foundational (transfactual) social structures and mechanisms.

Theories that are general, in the first and third sense, are an indispensable element of today's social science and should as far as possible be integrated in concrete research work. But there are at least two important objections to theories that attempt to integrate all knowledge in an all-embracing system. First, there is an imminent risk that such systems become all-embracing at the expense of depth and explanatory power. In other words they run the risk of being fairly void of substance that is valuable to our understanding of specific, social structures and mechanisms. Second, such systems can easily tend to be totalizing; the attempts to integrate empirical data from ever more specific areas into the same system come before everything else. In our view, however, theories should not totalize but open up. They should not be used to classify reality from pre-arranged systems but rather inform analyses, interpretations and explanations of the social reality. Social reality is a complex reality, consisting of different onto-logical levels and a variety of structures with their own specific properties. Different theories partly complement each other, since they focus on different levels, structures and qualities. Trying to integrate them in an all-embracing system seems futile.

General theories in social science research practice

There is a serious limitation inherent in MRT and GT, as both of them, in their own ways, motivate a social scientific research which in practice under-rates the value of general abstract theorizing. This is a result of, in the first case, the request that one should be able to break down theories into testable hypotheses (through deduction), and in the second case, the demand that theo-ries must be (inductively) grounded in data. In Chapter 4 we argued that abduction and retroduction are essential modes of inference/thought opera-tion alongside deduction and induction. In this section we shall demonstrate how general abstract theorizing can be integrated in the research practice through abduction and retroduction. The overall aim of this section is to emphasize those ways of theorizing in concrete research, which are more or less neglected within MRT and GT. We do this under two themes: Participating in the Theoretical Discussion, and Employing General Theory in Empirical Studies.

Before we start, however, we would like to draw attention to a distinction of importance in the discussion of general theories in social science. In his book *Sociological Theory: What Went Wrong?* Nicos Mouzelis (1995) emphasizes that we can see general theories, on the one hand as instruments/resources, and on the other as ready-made products. In the first instance, theory represents a certain way of viewing reality, a generally valid set of concepts that can be used when formulating interesting and relevant questions in concrete investigations, ques-tions which also take into account the more specific contextual circumstances not considered in the general theory. Theories thus become general in the sense that they have a general validity as instruments to be used in the interpretation and analysis of different concrete social situations. In the second instance, theories are perceived as more or less readymade explanations. They are made up of general statements about reality, assumed to have been empirically tested. These theories are general in the sense that they should enable prediction of various concrete courses of events and causal relationships. Mouzelis is critical of theo-ries claiming to be general in the latter sense, that is, as readymade explanations. That way of regarding theories may lead to explanations that are either shallow and trivial, or false, since they can never take into account the contextual and specific conditions influencing concrete cases. However, general theories – and Mouzelis among others mentions Parsons' theory of roles and institutions,

Giddens' structuration theory and Bourdieu's habitus theory – are very productive as instruments in concrete analyses. Mouzelis' argument is largely in agreement with the view we argue for in this book. However, we think it is important to clarify one thing. General theories developed in social science are productive instruments for a concrete analysis, only insofar as they are able to capture *real* social structures and mechanisms and the manners in which they are manifested in different social, cultural and historical contexts. This is the important realist addition to Mouzelis' argument.

Participating in the theoretical discussion

Every social practice and subculture to a certain extent develops its own language. Just like football players quite naturally talk about 4–4–2 to indicate a certain formation related to ideas about the game and the positions in the formation, and craftsmen develop their own terminology for different working operations, we in social science talk about macro structures, modernity, ideology, socialization, symbolic interaction, etc., in order to express complex ideas or concepts in a simple fashion.

Sometimes science is criticized for using an abstract language that no outsider can understand. Abstract is then in some cases equated with unnecessary intricacy. It is obvious that the theoretical language of science may function as a forcible means of strengthening the identity of the scientific community, while at the same time keeping out the uninitiated. But this is not unique to science; anyone who goes into a computer store to buy their first computer may have the same experience. And, what is even more important, the abstract concepts, which in part come from everyday knowledge but also go beyond it, are absolutely vital for the social sciences to be able to live up to the elemental expectations placed on science (see Chapter 2). The language of science may to an outsider seem very abstract and hard to understand. But conceptualization in particular is an indispensable element at the core of science, in a way that does not apply to other professions.

Social scientific theory comprises assumptions/hypotheses of the empirical reality. As we have seen, these hypotheses can to some extent be tested (verified and falsified) by means of defined research logic. But social scientific theory is also a language, which makes it possible to understand and communicate abstract relations. Theoretical language is not developed through decisive tests, verifying or falsifying. There is another logic behind this development. A language is continually developed as it is used in ongoing talk about society – in social theory literature, in seminars and in other situations. Of course, these theoretical discussions always take place in relation to one's experiences of the society one claims to describe, to some extent taken from concrete empirical studies, but also from other sources, open to anyone living in this society. A theorist who develops and uses concepts that do not give others a deeper understanding of the society they live in will hardly be successful. But the theoretical language is always taking place in relation to an already conceptualized reality. Established concepts are confronted with new ones, they are modified, reconstructed and surpassed. Concepts are developed, integrating the contents of many previous concepts.

There has been some contempt for abstract social theory discussions, probably for the most part rooted in an empirical and hypothetico-deductive research ideal. However, we have of late witnessed a renaissance of such social theory discussions, chiefly linked to different notions of how best to understand the radical changes in modern society. This discussion follows (as stressed above) a research logic essentially different from the logic of deductive hypothesis testing, as well as from that of inductive theory generation (cf. Carleheden 1996: 18ff).

How does this affect anyone who conducts social scientific studies or research? First, as scientists and students in an academic institution we are part of a scientific community and the theoretical discussions going on there, for example at different seminars. To be able to participate in these discussions, one must acquire knowledge of central social theoretical concepts. This is one of the purposes of reading and reflecting on both classic and modern social scientific theory.

Second, one can participate in the theoretical discussions by analysing established concepts and theories in papers and theses. If they are carefully defined, entirely theoretical studies may be appropriate even in more restricted paper assignments. In science there are especially strong demands on concepts being well defined. They should have an unambiguous meaning and be employed in a consistent manner. These demands are not always met. There are a number of concepts in particular which are employed with different meanings in different theoretical discussions, for example 'discourse', 'class', 'structure', 'ideology' and 'institution'. In social theoretical discussions new concepts are constantly being developed. Some of them may be justified, as they actually represent a new content of ideas and point to mechanisms not previously conceptualized in this fashion, but in other instances they may merely be new names for already known phenomena. To clarify different concepts – their content and relation to other concepts – is in itself an important research task. We could start, for instance, with a certain concept of particular interest to us and ask questions like:

- What is the real content of ideas represented in this concept?
- How is this concept integrated in a larger theoretical context?
- How does the meaning of this concept differ in the various influential theories where it is employed?
- What mechanisms are described by this concept that other concepts do not describe?
- Is it possible to integrate the different versions of this concept that exist in the literature?
- What actually is the difference between this concept and other similar concepts (for instance, how does the concept of discourse differ from conversation and ideology)?

If we take our starting point in a theory instead of an individual concept, the following questions may be relevant:

- In what context has this theory been elaborated and what does it claim to explain?
- How are the theoretical conclusions supported? Are there any obscurities in the argument, inconsistencies or contradictions in the theory?
- Is the theory undeveloped in any respect? Are there any vital gaps in the theory, relations that the theory has not yet conceptualized or defined?
- What conclusions, if any, can we draw from studies where the theory has been applied? What do they say of the validity of the theory?
- How does this theory differ from other theories claiming to explain approximately the same phenomena?
- Can these theories be complementary and perhaps integrated? What are the possibilities, for instance, of integrating different theories claiming to explain the same problem but doing it from the standpoints of different disciplines (for example, humanistic and social scientific standpoints respectively)?

These are examples of questions that can guide more wholly theoretical studies and discussions. To be able to participate in theoretical discussions it is of vital importance that we develop our ability to handle these kinds of question. Bearing in mind that theories have a crucial role in scientific knowledge development, the value of purely theoretical studies should not be underestimated. It is a matter of developing and refining the theoretical language, which can lead to deeper understandings and explanations of social reality. Theoretical studies can clear away obscurities and ambiguities impeding communication in social science, and can contribute to the development of concepts usable in concrete empirical analysis. We shall now address the question of how general theories can be applied in empirical studies.

Employing general theory in empirical studies

We shall now give a few examples of how general abstract theory can be integrated in concrete empirical studies. We start with what is commonly called problem formulation. Then we discuss how general theories can be used as interpretative frameworks and as tools in retroduction.

Formulating a scientific problem

The ability to formulate relevant and productive problems is fundamental in scientific work. A paper, as well as a thesis, is in part a test or examination of that ability. In this pursuit general theoretical perspectives and concepts are indispensable. Many forceful general theories have been elaborated in classical and modern social science, forceful because they present a way of looking at reality which opens up interesting questions. As David Silverman (1993) says, theories are the impetus for research. When a student is writing a paper, she has to exercise her ability to employ the theories she has met in previous courses.

In work on a paper or a research project, it is essential to distinguish between what is a scientific problem and what is a problem to politicians, proponents for an organization, the parents in a family, or what is described as a problem in, for instance, mass media. If information in a company does not work satisfactorily (from somebody's point of view), it may be a problem to the management, the workers and the organization in general. If there is disturbance in the stands, in connection with football matches, it may be a problem for those in the club who are in charge, for people directly hit by the disturbance, and for football in general. If in some groups of society fewer and fewer people read a daily newspaper, it may be a problem for the newspaper business and – as some people maintain – perhaps also for the progress of democracy. These are problems, but not scientific problems.

Still, such kinds of problem may be important starting points for the formulation of a scientific problem. Science should strive for relevance in society; that is to say, scientists should address issues that, for some reason, it is important to acquire knowledge of. The fact that we always choose (and must choose) a limited section of the social world – restricted by our notions of what is important to study – is something that Weber (1977) strongly emphasized. As we pointed out in Chapter 4 (Table 4), a scientific study may benefit by starting with an introduction, in which the reality we intend to examine is described, partly from the viewpoint of the people involved, that is, their own interpretations and descriptions. In other cases it may occur that the problem even at the outset crops up chiefly as an internal scientific discussion.

For a description of a problem, based on the everyday experiences of people involved, to become a scientific problem, the description of the problem must be analytically resolved and theoretically defined (cf. stage 2 in Table 4). In science theories are often called analytical tools. The concept of analytical tools is vague and can have several meanings. One meaning, however, is precisely that theories are used for analysis, in the sense of breaking down a complex and multifaceted reality and from here defining a scientific problem.

There are at least three comprehensive reasons for scientific problems to be grounded in theory:

1   Theories help us break down and limit our formulation of the problem in a conscious and well-thought-out way. Scientific problems should not only, or even primarily, be limited to defined empirical phenomena but to certain aspects, dimensions or mechanisms. Limitations are made in relation to different theoretical traditions and with the help of the abstract language of science. In the study of journalism, for instance, it is not enough to limit oneself to certain types of journalism, certain organizations, newspapers, etc. What is important is that we restrict ourselves to certain dimensions of journalism: the ideology production, legitimacy, narrative forms, discursive strategies, ownership structures, organization of production processes, or

some other dimension of journalism. If we choose to focus on, for example, the aspect of legitimacy, the problem formulation should be rooted in theories of legitimacy. We choose the theoretical points of departure, above all with regard to the relative explanatory power of different theories, and only second with regard to what the people involved may think are the most interesting issues. Theoretical concepts offer depth and precision to scientific problems.

2 Via its theoretical roots the specific study is at the same time related to more general knowledge. Science is not primarily a matter of solving individual problems, but of contributing to the development of general knowledge and theory, which in its turn may be usable for solving concrete problems (cf. Chapter 7).

3 Through theories, scientific problems are also related to more comprehensive social, cultural and/or historical conditions. Thereby a too-near-sighted perspective is avoided. Scientific problems should always be formulated in relation to a general knowledge interest, keeping individual actors' ideas and values at a distance. Journalism research, for instance, has formulated questions from different theoretical perspectives concerning the progress of journalism as an institution, its relations to other institutions, and the mechanisms by which journalism legitimates and reproduces its position (Ekecrantz and Olsson 1994; Ekström and Nohrstedt 1996). With theoretical perspectives, questions are asked about things that are taken for granted in the particular sphere of activity where one tries to find solutions to more concrete and immediate problems. Through their theoretical foundation, scientific problems become relativized in relation to normalized practices and taken-for-granted ideas.

In the process of formulating theoretically grounded problems, it is important to employ both more general abstract theories and theories focusing on the specific empirical object. A study of the power structures in the housing sector, for example, should try to find its theoretical point of departure both in theories of this particular sector and in more general theories of power. In tutorials we have often met students reasoning in this way: 'We are supposed to have theoretical points of departure, but we can hardly find any theories of the subject we are going to write about. What do we do then?' A relevant answer to that question would be, 'Avoid looking for a theory at too concrete a level. Try instead to find more abstract theories focusing on just those dimensions or mechanisms you intend to study.' As a rule there are always productive theories to start from.

In the actual work on a research paper it is very important to make a real effort to integrate the theoretical argument in the empirical investigation. This ought to be done in at least two ways. First, by clearly demonstrating how the theories have contributed to the formulation of the specific research questions. If you dedicate a separate section of a paper to theoretical entry points, it is appropriate to conclude it with a section dedicated to comparing the theories discussed, clearly illustrating how they are related to the research questions of the paper. Second, when the conclusions of the paper are considered, it is important that you connect back to the general theories and discuss what the outcome of the research study has to say with regard to these theories.

A final remark concerning a common dilemma in connection with research papers: one of the most important differences between research (a scholarly study) and investigative work is that research questions must be theoretically grounded. In an investigation it is the specific problem formulation of the interested party that takes precedence. To fulfil an investigative assignment within the framework of a scholarly study can therefore be a difficult enterprise, fraught with conflict. There are no simple solutions to this dilemma. In Chapter 7, however, we shall argue that interested parties in various fields of work often benefit more from theoretically grounded papers focusing on specific mechanisms, than from papers which set out to suggest how concrete problems should be handled in practice.

Applying theories as frameworks for interpretation and as tools in retroduction

> [T]heories are seen as tools that help us see, operate, and get around specific social fields, pointing to salient phenomena, making connections, interpreting and criticizing, and perhaps explaining and predicting specific states of affairs. … Social theories provide maps of societal fields that orient individuals to perceive how their societies are structured. … Social theories are thus heuristic devices to interpret and make sense of social life. … Social theories can also illuminate specific events and artifacts by analysing their constituents, relations, and effects.
>
> (Kellner 1995: 24f)

This citation from a book by Douglas Kellner nicely sums up how useful theories are to us, both as frameworks for interpretation and as tools, when we via retroduction attempt to identify constitutive properties of concrete phenomena, events and structures.

In Chapter 4 we used the concepts of abduction and recontextualization for the process in science by which we interpret and give meaning to specific occurrences and phenomena, taking our starting point in some form of interpretative framework. General theories can be used as such interpretative frameworks. Such interpretative frameworks contain fundamental social assumptions and cannot be subjected to decisive empirical tests. On the other hand we can formulate more concrete, falsifiable hypotheses within the framework of a particular theoretical context. We here present examples of two concrete research assignments where general theories are utilized as interpretative frameworks:

1 Interpreting/recontextualizing the same empirical data, starting from two different theories, could be one important undertaking. Irrespective of what we study, there is nearly always a number of theories that could be

relevant as frameworks for interpretation. Studies with this orientation can address the following comprehensive issues: In what respects can the theories chosen be said to correspond to one another (that is, lead to similar analyses of data), be openly competitive (entailing conflicting interpretations) or perhaps complementary? What meanings, connections and relationships are identified in one theory but not in another? What particular problems and questions for further research are brought to the fore by the different theories?

2   Applying established theories to partly new empirical fields would be a somewhat different research undertaking. One purpose of such an undertaking is to test the area of application of a certain theory. Is the theory productive when it comes to understanding even this area of inquiry? By thus bringing theoretical perspectives into fields where they have not been applied before, the theory could also contribute to new ways of understanding and thinking about something. For instance, when Gaye Tuchman in the early 1970s employed social constructivism in interpretations of news and news production, this resulted in creative insights into the social mechanisms affecting this production, insights which have had great impact on subsequent research (Tuchman 1980).

In retroduction, what is also called transfactual argument, general abstract theories are an indispensable resource. As pointed out before (in Chapter 4), the border between abduction and retroduction is not very distinct as regards concrete research. Retroduction, however, points to a specific field of use for abstract theories. The practical research undertaking could be as follows: We depart from a concrete phenomenon (an activity, a type of action, a text or a picture) and pose the question: What structures are fundamental for this phenomenon to exist and be what it is? When trying to answer this kind of question we can to some extent use the various strategies presented in the section on retroduction in Chapter 4. But we also have to use existing theories. Different theories can complement each other, since they focus on different structures. Theories describing the same mechanisms, although in different ways, should be compared so that we obtain some idea about their validity and explanatory power.

The validity of theories

We have given several examples of how general theories can be integrated in concrete studies. Such procedures are essential complements to the strategies associated with MRT and GT. Different ways of working with theories are grounded in different kinds of research logic, which also means that the validity of theories is evaluated by different criteria. Within the framework of GT, theories are generated whose validity is assessed due to their being grounded and saturated. Theoretical hypotheses tested in accordance with the scientific ideal of the MRT approach are evaluated with consideration given to whether they have been subjected to tests that meet the demands for logically valid derivations and precision in measurements. General social scientific theory discussions adhere to yet another research logic: they are evaluated with respect to such criteria as explanatory power, the ability of the theories to conceptualize fundamental social mechanisms and integrate central concepts from other theories, whether they are creative or not, and whether they are logically consistent. When general theories are applied as a framework for interpretation they are evaluated with respect to whether they are usable and generate new insight into the phenomena of interpretation.

Abstract general theories need not be either speculative or untried just because they have not been tested strictly deductively or been grounded strictly inductively. Abstract theories are tested and modified primarily by being used in research practice, in social theory discussions and empirical studies. Let us take Michel Foucault's theory of power, knowledge and discourse as an example. The theory has been criticized, but it has also inspired research in a range of concrete fields. Scientists from different disciplines (psychologists, geographers, media studies, sociologists, pedagogues, historians) have found it fruitful and have applied it, mostly in a partly modified form relevant to their particular object of study. It has inspired the development of more concrete theories connected to specific fields. The same could also be said of many other theories in social science.

It is of course important to avoid a dogmatic application of theories, making entirely predictable what we see and what we do not see. Theoretical frames for interpretation must constantly be subjected to critical analysis and internal scientific debate. It is essential to be open-minded to other general theories, both in the formulation of research problems and in the interpretation of empirical material. If talk about testing or evaluating a theory is to be meaningful at all, we must discuss the advantages of the theory, as well as its limitations and problems: To what extent can we, starting in the theory, understand and explain connections and processes of which we earlier had a more imprecise conception? Does the theory promote a deeper understanding of the phenomenon of interest? What can it explain or not explain, respectively? What experiences contradict the theory? Are there aspects/dimensions of the research object that cannot be conceptualized from the theory in question? What are its limits, compared to those of other theories? Theories should also be presented in a way that makes them open to critical examination. The foundational supposition of the theory, the base of experience referred to as supporting the theory, and the chain of argument behind the theory, must all be as clear as possible.

Conclusion

Scientific knowledge builds on systematic development and the application of theories at different levels of abstraction – this is how one might sum up, in a very simplified way, the recurring argument in this chapter. Theories make up a language, indispensable to science, informing interpretations and enabling explanations by conceptualizing structures and causal mechanisms. In this chapter we have presented a number of ways to integrate and employ theories in practical research. We have given much space to middle-range theory and grounded theory, as they represent two major traditions in social science and have been very influential in their way of regarding the relationship between empirical research and theorizing. These two approaches both contain important research strategies. At the same time they have essential limitations, having to do with what we have called an empirical bias, and having underestimated the significance of general theories in social science. For that reason we have in the latter part of the chapter given examples of how general theories are used in research practice, all within the framework of a research logic that is different from both middle-range theory and grounded theory.

We hold that there are strong arguments for taking a flexible and undogmatic position on the issue of how theories can and should be employed in research practice, which might sound like too simple a solution to a difficult and disputed problem. However, this position is not a manifestation of eclecticism but is based on certain principles. One of the essential problems of the methodology that has been influenced by positivism is in fact the view that research practice should follow a template for how theories should be tested, a template which is furthermore assumed to be common to social science and natural science. The result is a science which concerns itself with the testing of hypotheses, while at the same time disregarding the value of abstract general theory. Some researchers have applied the grounded theory approach, as if it presented the complete outline for a methodology which should be followed from beginning to end. The result runs the risk of becoming a rather trivial and shallow categorization of data.

Theorizing and conceptualizing, working with theories and concepts and in different ways relating them to empirical material, is fundamental to social scientific research. This work should not be reduced to a method. It involves reasoning with concepts, abstracting, interpreting, testing, modifying established concepts and developing new ones, grounding concepts and testing hypotheses – processes that can only to a limited extent be reduced to logical rules and standardized methods (cf. Layder 1998; Morrow and Brown 1994). In this chapter we have presented a range of strategies as guidelines for such work.

We have also tried to show that the different modes of inference/thought operation (deduction, induction, abduction and retroduction) described in Chapter 4 are foundational for the processes by which we in science develop, test and apply concepts and theories. Earlier, it was common procedure to differentiate between a deductive and an inductive approach when considering the relation between theorizing and empirical research. This is limiting. Retroduction is a key form of thought operation in theorizing and theory generation. When theories are used as guiding frameworks for interpretation, this is a mode of abductive inference which is an indispensable feature of much social science research.

6 Critical methodological pluralism
Intensive and extensive research design

In this chapter we will mainly discuss methodology issues in relation to some of the ontological and epistemological positions mentioned earlier, and also methodology issues in relation to the four different kinds of thought experiment presented in Chapter 4. In the previous chapters a number of fundamental concepts and trains of reasoning within critical realism have been presented and discussed: generative mechanisms, structures, powers, tendencies, closed as well as open systems, and abstraction. An understanding of these concepts is essential for the comprehension of the discussions in this chapter.

Every social science investigation involves metatheoretical, i.e. ontological and epistemological, assumptions. Sometimes they are clearly demonstrated, sometimes they are not. The researcher may not even be aware of them. Research is directed by explicit and implicit assumptions of society as a whole and by conceptions of what we can obtain knowledge about and how such knowledge can be obtained. It may seem trite but it is worth mentioning again how important it is that the choice of methodological approach and design is governed by the assumed specific qualities of the object or objects of study. There should be congruence between the object of study, the assumptions about society and the conceptions of how knowledge is possible, and one's choice of design and method, what we in Chapter 2 called 'practical logic'. If we assume – as critical realism does – that social science studies are conducted in open systems, that reality consists of different strata with emergent powers, that it has ontological depth, and that facts are theory-laden, then these are some factors that affect the choice of design and method.

Believing that critical realism can be applied unambiguously in practical research would, however, be a misconception. Critical realism is not a method. One might say that to a researcher whose reasoning is based on critical realism, some methods and approaches seem to be more productive than others. Or, to be more precise, that she knows how to use certain methods and knows what conclusions can be drawn from the results they produce. It seems natural, for example, to adopt a critical attitude towards

1   the claim that it is possible to understand and explain phenomena by using methods from the natural sciences, which presuppose more or less closed systems;

2   methods based on purely subjectivist assumptions, i.e. that social reality is
     nothing but a social construction and not an interpreted objective reality;
     and
3   approaches based on the objectivist assumption that subjective intentions
     should be excluded from a scientific study of society.

The outline of this chapter is as follows: we shall start by discussing the issue
of mixed methodologies. Then we shall summarize what are usually considered
as the two main streams in social science methodology: quantitative and qualitative method. We use these terms and this dichotomy by way of introduction,
since this is the traditional way of classifying methods. Qualitative methods have
many more nuances than the quantitative ones and are subsequently more difficult to describe in brief; they can involve historical analyses, ethnographic
methods, action research and discourse analysis, just to mention a few types. We
shall not be able to discuss them all but shall refer in brief to some of them in a
more general discussion about this type of method. For the rest we refer the
reader to the extensive literature on the two respective methods.

From our starting point in critical realism we shall try to lay a more systematic
foundation for the choice of method. Instead of discussing the quantitative and
the qualitative method as the basic division, we use the concepts of extensive and
intensive research design. We see practical research work as an ongoing interaction between them.[1] This will be described in a section dealing with these
approaches.

Combining methods

The dispute between advocates of the two methodological approaches is of long
standing. Sometimes it has been unrelenting and hardly constructive, sometimes
– and especially of late – it has been fruitful and productive. Scientists advo-
cating the quantitative view have criticized qualitative research. They consider it
imprecise, affected by the scientist's subjective attitude and unfit for making
predictions. The other side has retorted that quantitative research is based upon
a naive theory of objectivity and that it can neither describe the complexity of
social reality nor make it possible to understand agents' motives and efforts to
create meaning. We, and many others, are of the opinion that such a discussion
and polarization is not only fruitless, but that it is also misleading to oppose the
quantitative to the qualitative method. There are several reasons for this opinion.
The way in which the dichotomy has often been presented leads to its obscuring
fundamental metatheoretical problems, e.g. those concerned with the stratification of reality, the relation between structure and agency, and the intransitive as
well as the transitive dimensions of reality. Further, the dichotomy does not grasp
the practical research process, which often contains elements from both
approaches – even if this mostly happens without metatheoretical reflection.

We claim, first, that a particular method cannot be excluded beforehand, and
second, that it is profitable to combine methods in practical research work. This

must not, however, be confused with methodological relativism – on the contrary, we try to present concepts and assumptions that make a conscious choice of design and method possible. 'Anything goes', as Paul Feyerabend (1993) expresses it, but we would like to make the important addition: 'but all methods are not equally suitable'. We would like to designate this attitude *critical methodological pluralism*, in which the foundation for what is suitable or not is to be found in the relationship between metatheory and method. We are not the only ones to advocate a multimethodological approach and see its fruitfulness. Within the sociologist community the following views have been expressed and are widely supported:

1   that the distinction between quantitative and qualitative method is no longer relevant;
2   that there is no such thing as a 'universal method' – both approaches have their domains and relevance; and
3   that there is a great value in multimethodological approaches (see also Karl van Meter 1994). Layder (1993), for instance, discusses and advocates multistrategy research. Other terms for the same thing are 'method triangulation', 'combined operations' and 'mixed strategies'.

Nevertheless, we find that there is often a weak point in the discussion on mixed methodology. In his attempt to describe what mixed methodology is, Creswell (1995) writes that it 'represents the highest degree of mixing paradigms. … The researcher would mix aspects of the qualitative and quantitative paradigm at all or many … steps' (177–8). Creswell and others (see e.g. Tashakkori and Teddlie 1998) are critical of the paradigm-methodology link we advocate here. This is clearly shown in the way Howe (1988) formulates the problem: 'But why should paradigms determine the kind of work one may do with inquiry any more than the amount of illumination should determine where one may conduct a search?' (13). Howe holds that epistemology must not be placed above practical issues, nor the conceptual over the empirical. This is also a fundamental starting point in the pragmatic perspective. The practical and the empirical take precedence over the ontological and the epistemological, a view that the pragmatists themselves call 'the dictatorship of the research question' (Tashakkori and Teddlie 1998).

Although we sympathize with this pragmatic attitude to the issue, we would like to emphasize the importance of paying attention to the ontological-methodological link. We too want to see more methods in use – when necessary. However, there is a great risk that some conclusions will be drawn that cannot be drawn from the application of a particular method unless you have made the ontological base clear. At the beginning of this chapter we mentioned, for example, that if you presuppose that social science studies are conducted in an open system but nevertheless study the phenomenon using quantitative methods, which require a closed system, you must then be very observant about what conclusions can be drawn from such an analysis. We believe that if you separate the concepts about the nature of reality from the methods with which you can study it according to the pragmatic view, such a separation is an illusion and it entails great risks. It is an illusion because in the 'dictatorship of the research question' mentioned above, there is always an implicit or explicit conception of the nature of reality which has generated this particular research question. However much you want to take a pragmatic attitude to research practice, you cannot escape the ontological dimension. Even a pragmatist has a conception of what the reality is like that she wants to study. One cannot escape the ontological-methodological link. We also see the risks of a mix that is not guided by ontology, because the fundamental principles for the use of different methods are lacking. However, we do not want to exaggerate the differences between our viewpoint and the pragmatic one when it comes to the actual research process. We can characterize the perspective we shall expound in this chapter as 'critical methodological pluralism', and maintain that like the pragmatic viewpoint ours is also open to mixing methods, but this mix must be governed not only by the research question but, and more fundamentally, also by the ontological perspective from which you proceed.

Let us briefly illustrate what has been said by pointing out some of the purposes of mixing methods. Possibly the most common purpose is to try to validate a result. Through qualitative analyses one has found indications of connections or conditions that one wants to 'test' by means of quantitative methods. Such concepts as 'detection' and 'theory generating' are often connected to qualitative methods and 'control', 'evidence' and 'theory testing' to quantitative methods. Often a sharp distinction is made between the context of discovery and the context of justification.[2]

Another purpose of mixing methods is that one may use qualitative methods as a first step in an investigation. In an explorative-directed qualitative study research instruments are tried out; the researcher learns more about different aspects of the phenomenon, etc. The qualitative study is only a preparation for the 'proper' quantitative study, so to speak. A third purpose is to use quantitative and qualitative methods side by side in order to empirically elucidate a phenomenon in as much detail and as thoroughly as possible. A fourth purpose is to explore how common a phenomenon is that has been qualitatively studied, i.e. how common it is empirically. A fifth purpose, finally, may be theory development. A multistrategic approach opens up for the use of ethnographic methods, which will give a deeper understanding of the studied object. Moreover, quantitative analyses might indicate connections and conditions not to be found in qualitative analyses, thus furthering theory development.

From a critical realist perspective the first purpose, to validate, entails the epistemic fallacy, i.e. you fail to see that reality has ontological depth; you do not realize that an empirical connection in itself cannot identify the active mechanism or mechanisms, nor does it contribute to any profounder information about the interaction of the forces behind an observed pattern. Such interaction can only be detected through an intense and focused study of consciously selected cases. In other words, empirical regularities are pieces in the jigsaw puzzle of searching for mechanisms, not arbiters. When a quantitative approach discloses an empirical regularity, this is neither a necessary nor a sufficient condition for explaining a phenomenon. Further, if an expected connection cannot be found, this does not infer that a causal force (mechanism) is lacking. Forces that counteract each other might prevent the empirical manifestation of the mechanism in question.

The second purpose too, 'the preparatory purpose', can be criticized from the same standpoint. Still, a qualitative preparatory study can be conducted for other reasons, e.g. to give the scientist the necessary insight into a phenomenon new to her.

When it comes to the third purpose – describing a phenomenon – the qualitative method is often applied to give a more profound description of some elements of what has been analysed with the help of quantitative method. However, for such a study to be productive it needs to be conducted from strategically and theoretically selected different angles of approach; i.e. in making the descriptions one must take into consideration both metatheoretical assumptions and specific social science theories. Let us point out two conditions, which ought to determine the methodological approach: the notion of social structure and agency analysis (the realist transformation model), and awareness of how essential the time/space dimension is. Both these perspectives are manifested in Archer's model, which will be discussed in Chapter 7. As for descriptions, it is worth emphasizing the fact that quantitative descriptions sometimes serve a useful purpose, especially when macro phenomena are concerned.

The fourth purpose – the use of quantitative method to examine how common a certain phenomenon is – is often justified, e.g. within social statistics, and cannot be criticized *a priori* in view of the ontological or epistemological assumptions maintained by critical realism. It is important, though, that conclusions drawn on the basis of quantification do not surpass the information about the phenomenon reached through this approach. More about this later on.

As for the fifth purpose, theory development, we find this purpose, which we expounded in Chapter 5, absolutely crucial. We consider the search for generative mechanisms as the main undertaking in research work, in which both methods need to be applied – which is something we also shall discuss later in this chapter.

Quantitative method

What is designated quantitative method often rests on a logical positivist metatheoretical foundation,[3] and that is also the starting point of this section. However, we must not forget that quantifications and the use of statistical calculations and mathematical models are often features in research work not based on the metatheoretical assumptions of the positivist approach. One example of this is Göran Therborn's (1995) analysis of development in Europe after World War II. Quantification and the utilization of certain statistical methods are therefore not always synonymous with a positivist methodology.

From an epistemological perspective concerned with the search for scientific laws, there is no sharp division between the natural and social sciences. It is maintained that they both have basically similar objects of study. Advocates of this point of view, proponents of a unity of science, argue that research is ultimately concerned with finding correlations from observable data. The empirical regularities shall then serve as foundation for scientific explanations. Some of the proponents of logical positivism, for example Moritz Schlick, claimed that (scientific) statements were meaningful only as long as they were empirically verifiable. You cannot make any scientific statements unless they deal with things that can be experienced empirically. Such reasoning was, however, not undisputed among positivists. It is in fact impossible to satisfy such strict demands for verification. One of the critics was Otto Neurath; he was an ardent proponent of positivism and the idea of a unity of science, but he considered that these notions had been taken too far. He repudiated the concept that all science can be derived from physics, as he also rejected – which is more relevant in this context – the notion of one single method. He severely criticized his positivist colleagues for their 'verification absolutism'. (Likewise he criticized Popper for his 'falsification absolutism', thereby anticipating Kuhn's and to some degree even Feyerabend's critique of science.) He advocated methodological pluralism and tolerance. However, it has to be said that he was very clear in his opinion that social science should not contain any interpretative features. Thus there were limits to methodological pluralism.

In spite of the heterogeneous tendencies of logical positivism there is a common core, namely the notion that the foundation for our knowledge is the empirical domain, to use critical realist terminology. As we related in Chapter 4, this theory was developed methodologically by Hempel and Popper, who in the so-called subsumption model argued that an event can be explained with reference to, first, one (or more) earlier events, and second, to one or more laws, where the quoted law must cover the event one wishes to explain. This is also what has given the model its name, the covering-law model, also called, as we have seen, the Popper–Hempel model.[4] Even if it is worth emphasizing that the positivist view of the issues of a unity of science and of method was divided, the Popper–Hempel method has become predominant in practice.

The research process in this tradition could be described as follows: First, one characteristic is a scientific rationality emphasizing the need of 'law and order'. Rationality contains a demand for uniform rules. These rules of methodology must be designed to provide reliable knowledge. There is an established working procedure that should be applied to all research methods. Second, it calls for empirical verifiability through various kinds of measurement. Since it takes as its point of departure the empirical domain, thereby confining science to that domain, this demand is quite logical. A third aspect is the stance that explanations in terms of cause/effect are based on an assumed, not observable, conformity to laws. Hence it is a question of interpretation and of 'assuming', for (empirically and theoretically) well-founded reasons, that there exists a causal relationship between covariant variables. The empirical verification of such an assumption requires a statistic covariation as well as a logical chronological order. To identify a variable as cause, another necessary condition must be fulfilled: the influence of other variables on the effect-variable must have been controlled. The higher number of such variables that can be excluded, i.e. can be proved not to be covariate with the effect-variable, the more likely it is that the identified variable is the cause of the event. Finally there is a fourth characteristic of this work process; when the quantitative method is applied, researchers often take their starting point in methodological individualism. They do see human beings as depending on social relationships and susceptible to social influence, but the empirical base is always the individual. Social institutions and social structures are therefore regarded as constructions. 'Army is the plural form of soldier', as Jarvie expressed himself in a debate (quoted after Bhaskar 1989a: 27). The actions of an army will consequently be studied by studying its members. In a more general way one could say that social events and conditions are studied and explained by means of qualities at the individual level and the actions of individuals. Thereby qualities of social strata will be reduced to qualities of psychological strata, hence, according to some critics, making it impossible to study relations, which is one of the central objects of social science (see further Mouzelis 1995).

The quantitative working procedure can be illustrated in many ways. Here we choose a figure from a traditional book on quantitative method (Rose and Sullivan 1996). The figure is not at all new. It goes back to Wallace (1971). It describes something we might call the 'positivist circle': from hypothesis, observation and empirical generalization to a theory, which in its turn generates hypotheses, etc. The practical elements are research design, conceptualization, operationalization, data collection, coding, input and analysis, and then causal conclusions. The 'hub' in the figure represents technical methods.

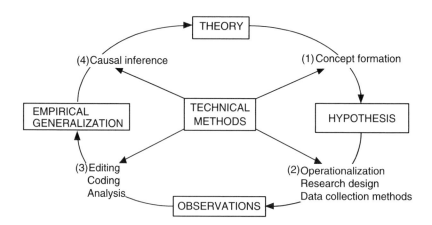

Figure 5 The positivistic circle

Source: Rose and Sullivan 1996, from Wallace 1971

One can see that the model covers induction and deduction; but there is no room for abduction or retroduction, which we discussed in Chapter 4. Nevertheless, the authors name it 'The logic of social science research'.

In analytical models inspired by positivism, mathematics (statistics and mathematical models) plays an important role. Mathematics is considered an effective tool in research since theory development, according to positivists, requires generality, precision and simplicity – qualities found in mathematics and statistics. We can discern two important fields of application for mathematics, one in questions connected to sampling problems, and the other in issues of theory development and modelling. The first concerns the tools needed to handle questions of selection, different kinds of measurement problems such as non-response, and the question of to what degree of certainty one can exclude the influence of chance (significance). It refers to estimates related to the so-called inferential problem, the difficulties that arise when, from the results of a small sample, you wish to say something about the conditions of a much larger population. This is generalization in the sense of empirical frequencies and regularities which we discussed in Chapter 4. In several descriptive branches of the social sciences, among them social statistics, the tools supplied by statistics are absolutely crucial. As it is often impossible to conduct overall investigations, statistical instruments are indispensable to enable any statements about, for example, the health of a population, political sympathies, etc., with a known degree of certainty.

Theory development and modelling refer both to mathematical representations of theories or models, and to statistical analysis models. As far as the mathematical models and analyses are concerned their proponents argue that mathematics is a powerful and flexible language for expressing models. It is often compared to a map – many details are missing, but enough remains to enable people to orient themselves (Doreian 1985). Mathematics leads to a high degree of precision by enforcing exactness in formulations. Simplicity is furthered by the formalism of mathematics, which facilitates the construction of simple theories, thus making theoretical work easier. Using Stephen Toulmin's (1992: 130) words, the essence of such a rationalist and mathematical position is that empirical data support, fail to support or partly support new hypotheses, as measured by numerical and probabilistic indices. To this end a number of tools have been developed, e.g. regression analysis and path analysis. Mathematical and statistical instruments have been developed for deciding when an association is considered to exist, by estimating the power and significance of the correlation. For instance, models have been developed which take into consideration the assumed causal consequence and interactive models.

The quantitative method also works with aggregates of units. When this method is used one studies not only single cases, for example an individual, but aggregates of individuals (compare an army and an aggregate of soldiers). The consequence is that the researcher brings together groups of individuals who have no other relation to each other than having in common one or more qualities of interest for the investigation. The individuals often do not compose a group in any theoretical sense, but are united by a formal relation in a taxonomical group – something we shall explain in more detail below.

To sum up what is characteristic of the quantitative method, it often uses statistical-causal analysis, variable-analysis, and aggregates of units where mathematics has a central role; and further gives priority to empirical observations.

Qualitative method

Qualitative methods can be seen as a generic term for a number of non-quantitative methods. Whereas the metatheoretical base for quantitative studies is often logical empiricism, the metatheoretical base for what is called qualitative studies varies. It is often maintained, though, that the metatheoretical base for qualitative research is phenomenology (see e.g. Merriam 1988). Sometimes also hermeneutics is mentioned. However, these metatheoretical 'derivations' can be misleading because of their simplistic notions. Both what we here call qualitative as well as quantitative methods can be used in research practice without necessarily linking them to the said metatheoretical base.

Significant for qualitative research is the focusing on particular cases – one or several. This means that you study, for instance, one or several persons' biographies, an institution or a whole community. The case can also be an event or a process. It is often emphasized that cases should be studied in their natural contexts, since the case gets its particular signification as part of this context. Case studies can be described in many different ways. Sharan Merriam (1988: 25) distinguishes among the various descriptions four common traits: they are particularistic, descriptive, heuristic, and inductive. Particularism focuses on a particular phenomenon, e.g. a person or an event. The descriptive factor implies that the description of the case is detailed. According to Merriam a case study should include as many variables as possible and describe the interaction between them over a long period, so called 'thick' description. The heuristic element results in the reader getting a more profound understanding of the case. The inductive element means that the experiences of the case can lead to certain conclusions, which are sometimes denoted as theory-generating. So far we can sum up qualitative method as having the following principal characteristics: a case study design, study of the cases in their natural environment, orientation towards understanding, 'thickness', and theory-generating.

Let us for a while consider one of the elements, the one directed towards understanding, since it is often pointed out as the main dividing line between the different types of method – 'verstehen' versus 'erklären', i.e. between on the one hand, methods aimed at understanding a phenomenon and interpreting it, and on the other hand at explaining a phenomenon. Proponents of a method grounded in hermeneutic philosophy emphasize interpretation and understanding. They often point out the objects of social science as essentially different from the objects of the natural sciences. Characteristic of the social world, 'culture' is its significance passed on by tradition. Therefore the meaning of the phenomena must be disclosed. This calls for specific methods, since you are looking for a meaning which is not immediately obvious. What is said in an interview or is observed in a classroom or a supermarket cannot be taken for granted – cannot be judged from appearance – what is important is to find the meaning behind utterances and actions. Generally speaking, hermeneutics is an absolutely central feature in social science as a whole, since the phenomena we study in some respect always convey a meaning. One might briefly describe the fundamental traits of this approach as focusing on the interpretation of mean-ings. The object of interest, the phenomenon, is sometimes called the 'text'. This may refer to a written text, a work of art, an action or some other phenomenon conveying a meaning.

We shall now briefly mention the two fundamental elements of the hermeneutic process. First, an interpretation is dependent on the researcher's earlier experiences, her theories, frames of reference, and the concepts she uses in the interpretation of the studied object. Together this constitutes what Hans-Georg Gadamer calls 'prejudice or pre-judgement'. This concept has affinities with 'hopeful conjectures' (Popper), 'scientific paradigm' (Kuhn), and 'general background theories' (Feyerabend). Prejudice among other things comprises one's own experiences, language and ideological conceptions. One must take such prejudice of the phenomenon into consideration and incorporate it in one's analysis. Second, one is constantly involved in interplay between the parts and the whole. A fact must always be put into a larger context so that its significance becomes clear. For instance, we cannot understand a person's actions unless they are related to his or her biography. In the writings about method there is a frequently used example: if you try to explain to a native of the Trobriand Islands in the Pacific what you do when you withdraw money from a bank, you end up having to describe the whole of modern society. Every action gets its meaning in relation to other actions and in this way the web grows from a single detail to a comprehensive social web. There is a constant interplay between the whole and the parts. All interpretation is contextual in time and space, i.e. the knowledge we acquire is grounded in specific contexts. Starting from the concepts of text, prejudice and context, the foundation of the hermeneutical work process is often illustrated as a circle (Figure 6).

Beside hermeneutics, phenomenology is perhaps the most important metathe-oretical starting point for qualitative methodology. Ethnomethodology, with Alfred Schutz and Harold Garfinkel as its most prominent researchers, emanates from this metatheoretical base. The starting point for a phenomenological perspective is perception, the intuitive ability to see things or facts. A phenome-nologist should try to get behind what has been experienced. This can be done with the help of abstraction. The mode of abstraction we are dealing with here differs, however, from the one we described in Chapters 2 and 5. Abstraction in that sense meant isolating in one's mind a particular aspect of an object or a phenomenon in order to gain knowledge about the causal powers. The phenome-nologist abstracts in order to find the essence of the phenomenon. Generalizations can be used in a similar way. By the term generalization a phenomenologist means something partly different from what has been previously

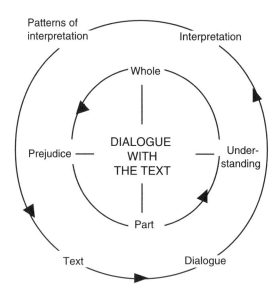

Figure 6 The hermeneutic circle

discussed. Generalization in our perspective has been described in Chapter 4 (see Figure 3), where we pointed out, among other things, that generalization has to do with transfactual conditions – the more or less universal conditions for an object to be what it is supposed to be. A phenomenologist instead emphasizes what various objects have in common.

Another important element in phenomenological method is the endeavour to obtain knowledge about the whole phenomenon. It seldom appears in its entirety but must be sought either by means of imagination or by change of perspective, which provides new experiences. Perhaps the most central aspect of the phenomenological method is a process called reduction. This must not be confused with reduction in the sense that an explanation of a phenomenon in a stratum can be derived from phenomena in another stratum, e.g. that emotions are reduced to biological mechanisms. Reduction is performed in three steps: in the first step the subjective apprehension is transformed into an objectively given phenomenon. The second step involves an endeavour to find, through abstraction, the properties constituting the essence of the phenomenon. In the third step, finally, attention is directed towards the subject of knowledge, i.e. the researcher. The idea is to observe oneself critically and discover whether the abstractions and generalizations one has made are valid. Through this critical consciousness we should be able to disregard the subjective and give a neutral description of the object.

In one sense phenomenology is positivistic and in another sense anti-positivistic. Among the positivistic features is the belief in an objective method (free from all prejudice) and the belief that sense experiences are the source of knowledge (proximity to empiricism). A pure science based on 'pure' facts and not on idle speculations is desired. What primarily distinguishes the phenomenologists from the positivists is their different perspectives: phenomenologists are seeking the whole and not, like many positivists, the parts. Another difference is the view held by the former that even though sense-data are the primary source of knowledge, it is by reasoning that we attain a deeper insight into reality – through introspection. In this process consciousness must be cleansed from the researcher's subjective thoughts. One can achieve this by letting doubt occupy the seat of honour. Phenomenology can therefore be characterized as close to empiricism and rationalistic; it takes its starting point in 'simple sense-data' and by means of pure reasoning it reaches true knowledge.

It should be emphasized that differences between hermeneutics and phenomenology exist, since they are sometimes linked in a way that conceals substantial differences. Even if a researcher like Schutz, a disciple of Edmund Husserl, has been influenced by Weber and his claim that social reality must be viewed as something meaningful, he sees this as a starting point and considers it possible to surpass the subjective dimension and arrive at an intersubjective description even of everyday social life. Another important difference between hermeneutics and phenomenology is the latter philosophy's strong emphasis on objectivity and rationality. As in natural science, phenomenology has strict demands on method and tries to avoid all forms of subjectivity.

In this context we also want to stress the fact that there are qualitative methods starting from other metatheoretical assumptions than those of hermeneutics and phenomenology. However, the greater part of research work employing qualitative methods has hermeneutics or phenomenology as its base – that is why we have mentioned these perspectives. Before turning to a description of another way of dichotomizing methodological work, we will sum up the characteristics of qualitative and quantitative research as they are traditionally presented (Table 5). The summary has been taken from Merriam (1988: 18). Similar summaries are to be found in a number of books on method. The reason we have chosen Merriam's description is not that we consider it the best one, but her key words provide a comprehensive picture of how the differences between the methods are traditionally understood.

Our aim is now to try to go beyond the dichotomy expressed in this picture. Instead of the dual concept of qualitative and quantitative method we shall introduce another dual concept: intensive and extensive design.

Intensive and extensive research design

Within social science, phenomena are contextually defined. In an open system we must take account of many influential powers. Besides, social science phenomena are inherently complex, i.e. they have many different socially important qualities and thus belong to a number of categories, e.g. woman, unemployed, young, cohabitant, immigrant, and uneducated. We are therefore often in a situation where we must choose. One choice is to study how a large

Table 5 Characteristics of qualitative and quantitative research

Point of comparison	Qualitative research	Quantitative research
Focus of research	Quality (nature, essence)	Quantity (how much, how many)
Philosophical roots	Phenomenology, symbol interaction	Positivism, logical empiricism
Associated phrases	Fieldwork, ethnographic, naturalistic, grounded, subjective	Experimental, empirical, statistical
Goal of investigation	Understanding, description, discovery, hypothesis generation	Prediction, control, description, confirmation, hypothesis testing
Design characteristics	Flexible, evolving, emergent	Predetermined, structured
Setting	Natural, familiar	Unfamiliar, artificial
Sample	Small, nonrandom, theoretical	Large, random, representative
Data collection	Researcher as primary instrument, interviews, observations	Inanimate instruments (scales, test, surveys, questionnaires, computers)
Mode of analysis	Inductive (by researcher)	Deductive (by statistical methods)
Findings	Comprehensive, holistic, expansive	Precise, narrow, reductionistic

Source: Merriam 1988: 18

number of qualities become noticeable in a certain situation, whereby we often find that only a few entities have all these qualities. The other choice is to study a large number of objects, which as a rule only results in obtaining a few qualities – both context and complexity suffer by this. We exclude many qualities, of which several could be of great importance for the subject matter of our study. However, it is not only a question of breadth on the one hand (little information of many entities), or depth on the other (much information about few entities), although methodology literature to a large degree has presented it as if this was the big issue. We shall discuss in more detail what is more relevant, i.e. different questions at issue, definitions, and the kind of knowledge that is gained.

So far in our presentation we, too, have taken our starting point in a traditional view of the relationship between metatheory and methodology, i.e. the view that quantitative methods are rooted in logical positivism and qualitative methods in subjectivist/phenomenological positions. We believe, like the pragmatists in the field, that this association has a restraining influence because it suggests that the only options are either a positivist or a hermeneutic/phenomenological science. Critical realism is a metatheory, which enables us to understand the importance of methodologies in a partly new way. That is also the significant difference between our view and the pragmatic one. The decisive question is how different methodologies can convey knowledge about generative mechanisms. As we have seen, mechanisms are regarded as tendencies which can be reinforced, modified or suppressed in a complex interaction with other mechanisms in an open system. The result may be that they cannot always manifest themselves empirically. In addition, the motive for action is regarded as a causal mechanism beside others, which makes the traditional division between a quantitative and explanatory methodology on the one hand, and a qualitative and understanding methodology on the other hand, limiting and misleading.

We suggest instead that one describe this part of the research process in terms of intensive and extensive empirical procedures, where both of these are meaningful – but in different ways – in the search for generative mechanisms, as well as in investigations of how mechanisms manifest themselves in various contexts. The way in which intensive and extensive procedures relate to qualitative and quantitative methods can be described thus: the intensive empirical procedure contains substantial elements of data collecting and analyses of a qualitative kind. The extensive procedure has to do with quantitative data collecting and statistical analysis. It is important to keep in mind that the different data collection and analytical methods are set in a particular metatheoretical context, that of critical realism. What we are discussing here is complementary empirical procedures and their being part of a greater whole, namely the research process guided by a critical realist ontology. We will now discuss in more detail how the procedures complement each other, but let us first sum up some of what we have been discussing in the previous chapters that is of vital importance for understanding the possibilities and limitations of the different methods; that is to say we shall repeat the foundations of the ontology-methodology link.

1   A central characteristic of reality is the difference between various domains – the real, the actual and the empirical – which we have described in Chapter 2. Mechanisms, events and experiences are the three basic concepts in this context. The methodology we advocate makes a leap, so to speak, from manifest phenomena to generative mechanisms. In the logical positivist approach, as well as in other empiricist approaches, e.g. grounded theory, it is experiences – i.e. the empirical domain – that form the base for the method in question. In critical realism it is mechanisms. Since they do not necessarily manifest themselves as experiences, the positivist nomological (law-seeking) method must be rejected (something we have advocated in Chapter 5). Nor is the answer any method inspired by phenomenology or hermeneutics, which we described earlier. None of these have rid themselves of the positivist idea that experiences are the primary object of knowledge (Bhaskar 1989a: 20).

2   In Chapter 2 we also discussed the issue of open and closed systems. As society cannot be regarded as a closed system, because of the interaction between mechanisms and because of individuals' conscious and reflective

actions, no methods based on the idea of creating a closed system can be used within social science. This also leads to the conclusion that the view presented by the covering-law model of explanation and prediction as symmetrical is not fruitful. Such a view may be valid for closed or nearly-closed systems, but never for open systems – i.e. never in social science. Consequently, experiment as a scientific method is not applicable in social science. As we have shown in Chapters 2 and 4, we must instead rely on conceptual abstraction, that is isolating certain aspects of reality in our minds – not trying to isolate them by manipulation of events. However, it needs to be emphasized that this does not lead to the conclusion that theories cannot be tested. Of course they can. That kind of relativism is not a feature of the critical realist perspective. The difference between, for example, positivists and critical realists lies in the question of how a theory should be tested, not of whether it can be tested or not. We discussed this in Chapter 5.

3   The fundamental aspects of social reality, which decisively affect the questions of method, are that society can neither be reduced to its individuals (Weber), nor to a social entity without individuals (Durkheim), but that the world is structured and stratified (we shall give an exhaustive account of this in Chapter 7). An important methodological conclusion is that we can discard two approaches: methodological individualism and methodological collectivism. The first sees existence as comprehensible only if it is reduced to dealing with individuals, and the latter claims that a phenomenon can be explained only if reduced to the whole of which it is a part. We have instead highlighted the relative autonomy of different strata. Strata cannot be reduced one to another: at the different levels there are emergent powers, which we cannot reduce to the level above or below the one in question. A practical methodological consequence of this is that the researcher, in order to understand a phenomenon, must allow the analysis to encompass a number of levels.

4   Another essential aspect is the view of man as agent. What characterizes most empirical social science studies is that they involve individuals who act consciously. Human beings act with intention and purpose, and they assign meaning to phenomena. The intentions must therefore be regarded as causes and be analysed as tendencies (see Chapter 7). All attempts to explain social phenomena must rightly take this into consideration. Thus it is important to understand the acting individual. The method must be able to incorporate this hermeneutic premise.

Strata and emergent powers, mechanisms, open systems and intentionality are consequently some of the central conditions determining the view of design and method in critical realism. As the nature of reality is stratified, the social science focus should be upon those elements of reality which can shed light on the generative mechanisms. In Table 6 we sum up a view of a methodology we find fitting.

Table 6 Intensive and extensive empirical procedures

Task	Identify generative mechanisms and describe how they are manifested in real events and processes	
	Empirical procedures	
	Intensive	*Extensive*
Research question	How does a process work in a particular case or small number of cases?	What are the regularities, common patterns, distinguishing features of a population?
	What produces a certain change? What did the agents actually do?	How widely are certain characteristics or processes distributed or represented?
Relations	Substantial relations of connections	Formal relations of similarity
Type of group studied	Causal groups	Taxonomic groups
Typical methods	Study of individual agents in their causal contexts, interactive interviews, ethnography, qualitative analysis	Large-scale survey of population or representative sample, formal questionnaires, standardized interviews. Statistical analysis
Limitations	Actual concrete patterns and contingent relations are unlikely to be 'representative', 'average' or generalizable. Necessary relations discovered will exist wherever their relata are present, for example, causal powers of objects are generalizable to other contexts as they are necessary features of these objects.	Although representative of a whole population, they are unlikely to be generalizable to other populations at different times and places. Problem of ecological fallacy in making inferences about individuals. Limited explanatory power.
Type of account produced	Causal explanation of the production of certain objects or events, though not necessarily representative ones .	Descriptive 'representative' generalizations, lacking in explanatory penetration.

Source: A slightly modified version of Table 1.1 in Sayer 1992: 243

In the following sections we will discuss some essential features of the empirical procedures. Our account also contains some critical comments on some features of the traditional ways in which different methods have been used; this will better illustrate in what way the process we advocate differs from those we have discussed earlier.

Research issues

As we have already said, in the practical research process very often both intensive and extensive approaches are needed in the search for answers to the
fundamental questions of generative mechanisms. These methodological tools
cannot, however, be used indiscriminately: they can only help to answer those
questions they are designed for. Intensive and extensive empirical procedures
apply to different kinds of problem. The intensive approach focuses on generative mechanisms. Most social science issues are complex, which often makes it
difficult to study a large number of cases, thus forcing the researchers to limit
themselves to fewer cases, which are then studied more intensively. Investigating
how a mechanism works in a concrete situation involves tracing the causal power
and describing the interaction between powers that produces a social
phenomenon. While seeking and analysing these mechanisms it may also be of
interest to discover how common a phenomenon is, what the characteristics of a
particular population are, etc. These are some of the things that are focused on
in the extensive approach. If we want to understand and explain the new
poverty in society at the end of the 1990s, it is highly relevant to ask ourselves
what poverty is like in this particular case, but also to ask how many people there
are among the new poor, and what is empirically characteristic of the new
poverty. Thereby we can get some idea of what empirical patterns are produced
by a particular mechanism or structure of mechanisms.

This combination of empirical procedures is of central importance in the
research process. One working model, suggested by Tony Lawson, is the
contrastive explanation. On a number of occasions we have pointed out that
mechanisms work in a dynamic and open social world. This means that mechanisms do not always appear empirically in their 'pure' form. Counteractive
mechanisms may be involved. Further, the mechanism in question might be
inactive. However, in real life mechanisms do not appear at random and unsys-
tematically. Lawson (1997) writes: 'Over restricted regions of time-space certain
mechanisms may come to dominate others and/or shine through', and these
mechanisms are 'giving rise to rough and ready generalities or partial generalities, holding to such a degree that *prima facie* an explanation is called for' (204).
Such partial regularities Lawson calls 'demi-regularities'. In the example of the
new poverty we can assume that it does not appear at random. The
phenomenon is related to other factors, for example class. These empirical
relations can also be assumed to be stable over time and space. Fundamental
demi-regularities are often very stable. Gender, class and ethnicity patterns
change very slowly in society. Gender-related segregation in the labour market,
the relation between class and health, and ethnic housing segregation are all
phenomena that are reproduced over a long timespan. Our task is to explain
these phenomena by identifying the mechanisms forming them. Together with
Lawson (*ibid.*) we claim that social scientific research is about identifying demi-
regularities and from them trying to find explanations. The contrastive part is
simply the fact that conditions for one group in society differ from that of

another group. For instance, there is a tendency that people from the working class have poorer health than those from the middle class. There is also a difference in the sickness profile. By contrasting systematic differences it is possible to identify differences providing clues to generative mechanisms. In this part of the research process the extensive empirical working method is of vital importance. Without such an approach it is difficult to detect interesting demi-regularities.

The next step in the research process is trying to explain these demi-regularities. We are looking for one or several mechanisms, which could account for the phenomenon we wish to explain. In Chapter 4 we explained how abduction and retroduction are the way to proceed. However, this phase of research also contains an important empirical feature. And this is where the intensive approach becomes useful, providing an in-depth study of one or a few cases focusing on specific circumstances. In social science we do not have access to experiment, i.e. the ability to close the system, and hence our alternative is abduction and retroduction in combination with empirical data from intensive procedures. When, in our endeavour to explain a demi-regularity, we have reached an explanation we believe is valid, it must also be empirically grounded in demi-regularities. This is not the same thing as saying that the latter part of the process is decisive for whether the explanation is valid or not. But it is a very plausible assumption that those mechanisms we assume generate the phenomenon under investigation have a certain duration in space and time. However, one must be aware of the fact that empirical manifestations are just that, demi-regularities.

This short description has made it clear that the research process involves both an intensive and an extensive element. For detection of the causal mechanisms the most important element, however, is the intensive procedure where retroduction plays a vital role.

Relationships and types of groups: what constitutes a social phenomenon?

In Chapter 2 we discussed at greater length the distinction between a substantive coherent relation (internal and external) and a formal relation of similarities. Substantive relations refer to factual relations interconnecting, e.g. landlord–tenant, husband–wife, whereas a formal relation is a relation of (dis)similarities, e.g. age or income. In a social network, for instance, individuals interact and are in a substantive relation to each other. The relations between the members of the network constitute the social network. If they cease to interact the network ceases to exist. If we look at the formal relations there is a totally different situation. For instance, a group of patients with the same diagnosis have the same characteristic (the diagnosis) and are formally related to each other. However, the patient group is not constituted by any social interaction between patients, merely by sharing the same characteristic.

Thus it is the type of relation which defines what type of group is studied, causal or taxonomic. In the intensive approach the focus is on causal groups.

This leads to the methodological inference that extensive approaches, where taxonomic groups are used as empirical material, can hardly expect to find the substantive relations. Let us illustrate this by anticipating the example we shall bring forward in the next chapter. Suppose we are interested in learning which mechanisms generate ill health among many elderly people in connection with forced relocation due to housing reconstruction. The contrastive demi-regulation here is the differences in mortality and morbidity among relocated and not relocated. Further, suppose that in an extensive analysis we do not find any empirical relation between biological gender and changes of health in these cases. Both men and women suffer from ill health in this 'forced relocation situation'. So there is no contrastive demi-regulation here. A natural conclusion would then be that gender is of no interest in this context and that it does not 'explain' anything. Such a conclusion would have been quite natural with a traditional quantitative working procedure. Other qualities would have been focused on instead, e.g. class and age. This type of conclusion is common in research dealing with this kind of problem. The conclusion is correct in the sense that both men and women suffer, but wrong as to the role of gender. The fact that it does not 'explain' anything in a statistical analysis does not by itself infer that it is of no importance when it comes to explaining ill health. On the contrary, gender may be of vital importance for understanding the mechanisms that generate ill health. We might, for instance, suspect that women through the traditional gender roles in society have tended to identify themselves more with their home than men have. Losing their home will then affect women more severely. But we might just as well assume that men find it harder to handle a removal, with all the practical and domestic work it involves as well as more stress – this, too, is a consequence of gender role. Both groups would suffer and the mechanisms can partly be found in the current (and historically determined) relation between the genders. If gender is treated as a biological property and women and men are treated as taxonomic groups, there is a risk that we might exclude essential elements from the analysis, thereby receiving imperfect explanations. If gender were on the other hand treated as a social and relational phenomenon, this would contribute to a better understanding of the phenomenon. The example also illustrates how restricted the extensive approach is. It can only capture contrastive demi-regularities between taxonomic groups.

Working procedures and sampling: why is contextualization important?

A concrete model for a methodology which tries to place a studied phenomenon in a context has been evolved by Layder (1993). In his so-called 'research map' he points out four different constituents, which are all studied in a historical perspective: context, setting, situated activity and self. To be able to explain we must study how mechanisms manifest themselves in concrete contexts. These aspects are comprehended by the 'research map', which is presented in Figure 7.

Research element	Research focus
CONTEXT	*Macro social organization* Values, traditions, forms of social and economic organization and power relations. For example, legally sanctioned forms of ownership, control and distribution; interlocking directorships; state intervention. As they are implicated in the sector below.
SETTING	*Intermediate social organization* Work: Industrial, military and state bureaucracies; labour markets; hospitals; social work agencies; domestic labour; penal and mental institutions. Non-work: Social organization of leisure activities, sports and social clubs; religious and spiritual organizations.
SITUATED ACTIVITY	*Social activity* Face-to-face activity involving symbolic communication by skilled, intentional participants implicated in the above contexts and settings. Focus on emergent meanings, understandings and definitions of the situation as these affect and are affected by contexts and settings (above) and subjective dispositions of individuals (below).
SELF	*Self-identity and individual's social experience* As these are influenced by the above sectors and as they interact with the unique psycho-biography of the individual. Focus on the life-career.

(The elements CONTEXT, SETTING, SITUATED ACTIVITY, SELF are bracketed together under HISTORY)

Figure 7 Research map
Source: Layder 1993: 72

In practice, however, it can sometimes be an insurmountable undertaking to include in a single study everything the map encompasses. By nature all research is partial in relation to the real world. So in practice one focuses on one or a few of the elements of the research map. Such focusing should be done in those areas of the map that comprise the mechanisms you want to single out. It is only a question of focus, though, and one must keep in mind that the social world has an open and complex nature. In Chapter 3 we discussed a form of 'economizing' work: conceptual abstraction meaning, among other things, to isolate in thought certain aspects of reality. It is important, however, to distinguish this working method from what Giddens calls methodological bracketing. Giddens (1984) obviously means that in the type of analysis he calls strategic conduct analysis, one can put the structural level 'within brackets' – i.e. the researcher is aware that it is important but she omits it from the analysis and concentrates on the individual level. In the same way, according to Giddens, one can leave individuals out of account when doing institutional analysis. Even if such an approach can be fruitful, it is not quite in line with the perspective we present here – which will be made clear in Chapter 7, where we discuss the relation between agency and structure and where we emphasize the necessity of an analytical dualism.

Sampling

It is characteristic of most sampling techniques in the extensive approach that the aim is to provide information about the total population. (Sometimes the aim can be a different one, e.g. to develop a measuring instrument, but we leave such cases aside.) Therefore it is imperative to do the sampling in a careful and correct manner. The base can be a random sample or a systematic sample, a probability sample or a non-probability sample. Subjective sampling, for instance, is considered to belong to the latter category. In such cases the researcher herself decides who shall be included in the investigation. Sampling by self-selection also belongs to this category. These types of sampling can be problematic, since it is difficult to say anything about the larger population of which the sample is but a part. Based upon experience or on theoretical arguments, the question may sometimes arise as to whether it is judicious to accept inferences drawn from such sampling as valid in regard to the larger population. Such arguments, however, are rather doubtful. Random sampling can be of various forms. Independent random sampling, stratified sampling, quota sampling and cluster sampling are the most common. The point of these techniques is that they allow the researcher, with a recognized degree of uncertainty, to draw conclusions regarding the total population and not just the sample. Several techniques have been developed, so-called significance tests.

Unlike the sampling principle in the extensive approach, where the samples are usually statistically representative, the sampling principle in the intensive design is strategic. The empirical basis of the intensive design is 'cases'. We shall point out four types of 'case' and comment a little on how they are selected. First, we have pathological or extreme cases, which we discussed at greater length in Chapter 4. The designations imply that they are odd phenomena, although they need not be uncommon. These types of case often supply considerably more relevant information than a representative or average case. Second, there are some extremely varied cases. The purpose of selecting this type of case is to attain information about the importance of various conditions for producing the particular phenomenon under investigation. Here we select some cases that are very different from each other with regard to some of the dimensions of importance for the study. We analyse how mechanisms operate under different conditions. There are also so-called critical cases. Selecting such cases provide us with information about deviations from the least or the most probable circumstances – if, for instance, a person with strong social support is still seriously affected by stressful life experiences, or, alternatively, if a person without any social support is not at all affected by such experiences.

How then does one identify a critical case? It is difficult to say anything in general about this, but one way is to select a case where one particular symptom has appeared that should not have done so. Or the opposite: one selects a case where the property of interest should in all likelihood be found but is not. In other words: the question is not why does Jeppe drink, but why doesn't his brother drink?[5] A common example of the last category is the strategy used in research into problem children. Some thirty years ago the so-called 'superkids' attracted attention, children growing up in poverty-stricken environments abounding with criminality and all kinds of abuse, and yet getting on all right. The idea was that one would in this case be able to expose what the counteractive forces are that, despite the numerous mechanisms working in a destructive direction, still enable the children to flourish.

A fourth and last type of case is what we call the normal case. To an observant researcher, interested in analysis, reality is full of normal phenomena, from which one can learn a lot about current prevailing generative mechanisms. An illustrative example of such a 'case' is Asplund's (1987) analysis of greeting ceremonies. In a study of one of our most common everyday occurrences he tries to expose mechanisms directing our daily communication with other people. He is very descriptive in his account of how different mechanisms operate in different contexts, and how they counteract or reinforce each other so that the empirical outcome (to greet or not to greet) varies.

Some methodological restrictions

As we have mentioned earlier, precision is often highlighted as a valuable capacity of an extensive approach. It enables researchers to express in a very precise manner the existence of a phenomenon, changes, and the strength of a relation. Many of today's methodology books discuss this in detail. However, questions concerning the metatheoretical problems of measuring social realities are very seldom raised. What characteristics should an object have to make it meaningful to give it a mathematical representation? Can one, for instance, measure the purport of a social relationship, how much attention and consideration someone gets, etc.? The restrictions regarding which social phenomena can be transformed to measurable variables are apparently very few, judging by research practice and the methodology literature. On the other hand there are a number of restrictions and rules as regards the classification and treatment of variables.

We mentioned earlier that the use of mathematics – both statistics and mathematical models – is often criticized. The idea behind one critique is that social life is so complex that it cannot be grasped by simple mathematical models. Such models are unsophisticated and often very inexact from the epistemological perspective, in spite of their mathematical precision. This precision cannot be translated to a concrete social reality, according to the critics, and is consequently illusory. In reality advanced mathematical calculations demand considerable simplifications, hence they depart from the complex social reality and the theoretical conception. The method becomes crude and approximate. 'The language of natural science is irreducible, metaphorical and inexact, and formalized only at the cost of distortion of the historical dynamics of science development and of

the imaginative constructions in terms of which nature is interpreted by science',
writes Hesse (1980, cited in Bernstein 1986) when she summarizes the postem-
piricist critique of natural science. The counter-argument from the defendants,
though, is that simplicity is the strong point. Just as the physical world is
extremely complex but can be seized in some fundamental traits, the same goes
for the social world. 'That social behaviour is complex cannot be denied, but the
principles governing this behaviour need not be complex', says *The Social Science
Encyclopedia* (Doreian 1985: 504). An example of this is rational choice theory, the
basic idea of which is that 'when faced with several courses of action, people
usually do what they believe is likely to have the best overall outcome' (Elster
1989: 22).

In this connection we would like to point out some circumstances which are
seldom explicitly discussed. First, probably nobody would deny the fact that
social reality is so complex that some form of simplification is necessary to
enable scientific studies. It is therefore misleading to criticize simplification as
such, arguing that social reality cannot be simplified but that the complexity
must be maintained if one is to understand the phenomenon. People inspired by
postmodernism often take such a view. They are extremely sceptical about such
theories of which we gave examples above, i.e. rational choice theory. In particular they are critical of the grand philosophies like Marxism. However, we
argued in Chapters 2 and 3 that simplifications are both necessary and fruitful,
and in Chapter 4 we discussed in great detail modes of procedure for this, by
means of abstraction.

Second, the question of complexity is linked to questions of open and closed
systems. An analysis of open systems calls for alertness to constant changes in the
analysed phenomenon, and to the development of new emergent powers and
mechanisms.

Third, the question must be asked: Where do we take the foundation for our
models from and what are their components? Are they made up of empirical
data alone, or of structures in the sense that we described in Chapter 2? Models
exclusively based on the empirical level do not have the capacity to take into
account the underlying generative structures. This can be illustrated with an
example taken from Manicas (1987: 286–7). Kerlinger has developed a 'small'
theoretical model in the spirit of Merton (see Chapter 5 on middle-range theory)
to explain school achievement. The model contains four variables: social class,
motivation, intelligence and – what is to be explained – school achievement.
Data for the four variables are collected and then processed by means of various
quantitative methods. The result is then expressed in terms of this or these variables explaining this or that degree of school achievement. Such an analysis,
however, says very little about what the generative mechanisms may be. The
theory Kerlinger presents does not enable us to understand what these mechanisms are and how they operate. A full understanding requires knowledge of the
implicit assumptions behind his analysis. Manicas writes, '*It is the real theory in the
background of such analysis*, a real, but unstated theory, which fools us into believing
that the theory which is up front, the "partial relationships" among "dependent"

and "independent variables", is in any way explanatory' (Manicas 1987: 287, original emphasis). We can express this in another way by saying that what we actually do here is a form of abduction, i.e. we interpret observed empirical phenomena from an assumed pattern or context without, however, making this explicit.

One must, however, ask oneself what one actually does when studying the variance of the variables included in a model. Let us return to Manicas (1987: 291) for another example. He gives an account of a study which shows the relations between verbal ability and social environment and ethnicity. Here it is claimed that

> the correlation between verbal ability, a measure of mental development, and the combination of environment and ethnicity ..., R, was 0.78, and thus R^2 was 0.61. This means that 61 per cent of the variance of verbal ability was accounted for by environment and ethnicity in combination. Separate regressions between verbal ability and environment, and between verbal ability and ethnicity, yielded 0.50 and 0.45 respectively. By subtracting these from 0.61 we get the separate effects of environment and ethnicity; we get 0.16, thus 16 per cent of the variance in verbal ability is accounted for by environment alone.

Such reasoning – which is the foundation of multivariate analyses – presupposes that causes must be additive. Manicas is critical of this assumption, and consequently also of the benefit of such analyses. He finds them 'almost totally *meaningless*' (291).

Lawson (1997) has presented another general critique of mathematical modelling. He holds that 'the deductivist method ... is a precondition of mathematical modelling' (1997: 226). In Chapter 4 we discussed the deductive model at greater length, and shall not dwell upon it here. Suffice it to point out that the deductive way of explaining an occurrence is based on regularities as they appear at the empirical level. As has been shown in previous chapters, we are sceptical of such a view.

The use of mathematics in social science analysis has also been criticized from a more general perspective. It has been seriously called into question whether mathematical language is at all suited to represent the social world. Data given variable values and arranged on a line with real numbers can never be sociological variables in the strict sense of the word, i.e. there are no sociological quota and interval-level scale variables. On the other hand there may be variables of interest for sociological analysis (e.g. income), but variables covering social action and interaction cannot be measured in this way. Even variables which we generally perceive as belonging to this measurement level are often ambiguous. For instance, when we measure age in the traditional way, we put down the physical age as a variable value. But from a social science perspective that is not always the interesting feature; we would rather focus on an age which involves maturity – an age which cannot be expressed in figures indicating a certain number of calendar years. We may also be interested in a social or socio-cultural age, periods in a lifetime when a particular behaviour is to be expected. Neither is this suitable for marking on an axis with defined intervals. And the same goes for many other variables. IQ and numerical scores, for example, only provide an illusory precision, which sometimes leads away from a real understanding.

Considering ordinal scale measurement, where data are arranged in a certain order but nothing is said about the 'distance' between the observations, the use of this scale in social science has also been criticized. A frequent social interaction, for instance, differs in quality from a less frequent one. You cannot talk about more or less interaction, but about different types of interaction. Another example, taken from philosopher Henri Bergson, tells us that a great joy is not more than a little joy; it is a different kind of joy.

Not even nominal-level measurement is without its problems. Variables classified as nominal are in fact relational – they are defined in relation to each other, e.g. gender, nationality, civil status and/or class. We exemplified this earlier when we discussed gender as a biological or a social property and discussed the landlord/tenant relationship. The names do not convey the relationship and are consequently not grasped by the kind of sorting and classification carried out in the nominal scaling procedure.

It is hard to find in the literature any good answer to this kind of criticism that is firmly established in theory. What one could say is of a rather more pragmatic character – for example that it is difficult denying the fact that a frequent social interaction may differ in quality from a less frequent one, but taken that it has been proved analytically productive and meaningful to give these phenomena numerical values, researchers may very well do so.

Two comments may be appropriate here. First, it is important to point out that less rigid proponents of positivism do not maintain that a mathematical language is the only correct or even the best one – it is simply one of many languages. Second, not all critics think that social science should abandon measurement and the use of different scales, but the conclusion is that one should use them with more discrimination.

In spite of the criticism we relate here, we maintain that quantitative analytical models can be fruitful and are undoubtedly valuable – provided that their field of application is confined to what is suitable. It is of great value, for instance, to be able to measure and register changes in welfare development, so-called social statistics – measurements often calling for sophisticated mathematical methods. We have emphasized before that quantitative descriptions are often indispensable in the research process. The limitations are revealed mainly when it comes to explanatory ambitions. It is vital to be very observant of what kind of data one uses in the analysis. Since it is generally formal relations of similarities and taxonomic groups that are involved in the extensive approach, one can hardly draw any conclusions of a causal nature from such analyses. One must be careful not to overrate the method, and be aware of its limitations.

Types of result

Several times already we have commented on the different types of result which are the outcome of the two approaches, and it should have become clear that the crucial difference is that it is via the intensive approach that one is able to expose generative mechanisms. In an intensive design one can (at best) explain a particular occurrence or a particular object, as well as a larger social phenomenon. The extensive approach alone cannot answer questions of causation; on the other hand it can point out important empirical manifestations of mechanisms. Thus it can provide vital descriptive information, which may be useful as support in a discussion about causal powers, and it can contribute to generating questions of causality. In the fundamental issue of the relationship between the specific and the general, both intensive and extensive designs are indispensable features of the research process.

Conclusion

In this chapter we have discussed the issue of combining different methods. By way of introduction we described the growing insight that the traditional dichotomy of quantitative and qualitative methods is unproductive. There can be a number of objectives in the combination of methods. Quantitative methods are often characterized by statistical-causal analysis, variable analysis, aggregates of units where mathematics is given a central role, and by the fact that what is empirically observable is given priority. The qualitative method is more subtle, and we restricted ourselves to the discussion of the hermeneutic and phenomenological foundations respectively, on which it is based. The hermeneutic method is characterized by its case study design, the study of cases in their natural environment, and by its concentration on understanding, its 'closeness' and ability to generate theories. One of the distinctive features of phenomenology is that it is close to empiricism as well as being rationalistic. It takes its starting point in simple sense data, and obtains true knowledge by means of rationalist thinking.

Since the quantitative and qualitative methods are by tradition linked to different metatheoretical perspectives of which critical realism is sceptical, we choose to designate the two methodological approaches we have discussed in this chapter as extensive and intensive method. A mixed-model design combines intensive and extensive practices.

We criticized the circumstance in which, when there is a combination of the two methods, it very seldom involves a deeper reflection on the metatheoretical starting points. Metatheory, in our opinion, defines the limits of how to use the different methods. If a consistent connection between a conception of ontology and a methodological application is missing, then the methods will be employed in a less fruitful – and sometimes even totally wrong – manner.

The alternative we suggest to the traditional dichotomy of quantitative and qualitative method versus a pragmatic combination of methods is a model we call critical methodological pluralism. It implies the utilization of an intensive and an extensive research design, where the different approaches complement each other. It is important to emphasize that we do not advocate any new method; in the various approaches traditional social science methods are used, but in a critical realist inspired practice they correspond to different issues and needs. Critical methodological pluralism is critical, first in the sense that it opposes an unreflecting employment of methods; the choice must be grounded in metatheoretical consideration. Second, the label alludes to the methodological approach which is founded on the critical realist conception of ontology.

7 Social science and practice

What is the point of social science? Outside the academic sphere people sometimes refer to the 'ivory tower' of scientists, implying that what we occupy ourselves with is something divorced from reality and not very relevant to life in the rest of society. Even scientists sometimes talk about what happens 'in real life', thereby accepting this sheltered image of themselves. Then again, there is the opposite view where one maintains that knowledge with high demands on veracity is power, and that power entails oppression (perhaps no one has expressed this view more clearly than Foucault). Here science – as one of many forms of knowledge – becomes an instrument of oppression and nothing else.

However, we would like to argue that the social sciences are of great relevance to social life, and that the knowledge they provide can be emancipatory. Sayer even claims that this is the rationale behind social science as such:

> [T]he point of all science, indeed all learning and reflection, is to change and develop our understandings and reduce illusion. This is not just an external and contingent sociological condition of learning but its constitutive force, which not only drives it but shapes its form. Without this universal necessary condition, none of the particular methodological and ethical norms of science and learning in general has any point. Learning, as the reduction of illusion and ignorance, can help to free us from domination by hitherto unacknowledged constraints, dogmas and falsehoods.
>
> (Sayer 1992: 252)

Now, in this respect we can distinguish between different types of social science. There are apparently at least three different types:

(a) research motivated by social scientific theory, trying to identify what the social world comprises, its structures, mechanisms and tendencies;
(b) a social statistic mapping, in which data are collected about the extension of different phenomena – unemployment, number of three-room flats, suicide, etc.; and
(c) applied social science aiming at solving social problems.

In this book we focus on methodology of the first type. Yet we are far from regarding such theory as the only legitimate form of social science – on the contrary, we have all been engaged in social statistic mapping as well as in applied science. In the following, however, we wish to emphasize the relevance of theoretically motivated research for social practice. We shall discuss two aspects. The first one involves social planning in a broad perspective, where we believe that knowledge of structures, mechanisms and tendencies is highly constructive for good planning. We argue that in order to make better use of social scientific knowledge than that which at present seems to be the case, there must be a change in the division of labour between scientists and practitioners. The second aspect involves the relationship between research and a critique of society. We draw attention to the fact that in social science there is an internal questioning of the object of investigation, and so we will discuss an explanatory criticism. This also leads us to some moral issues. It is beyond the scope of this book to enter deeper into political and moral discourses, but from a methodological viewpoint we may at least stress their importance for the relationship between the social sciences and their practical application.

A precondition: the distinction of agency and structure

If social science is to contribute to social planning and actual practice, it is necessary to know what basically shapes social life. Society consists of two separate phenomena, which are nevertheless related to each other: acting people and social structures. For the development of social scientific theory and the importance of social science for practice, the manner in which the relationship between them is conceptualized and treated is crucial. This subject has been discussed at greater length elsewhere (e.g. Archer 1995; Bhaskar 1989a; Collier 1994; Lawson 1997), and we will therefore just briefly repeat a few arguments.

A structure is made up of a set of internally related objects; a certain structure may in its turn also be part of a greater structure – this has been discussed earlier (Chapter 3). The labour market, marriage, a language and a working team are all examples of social structures. And social structures have emerged from human agency and have received novel properties of their own, different from the properties of people. When we analyse a structure we do so by mapping, through abstraction, the relationships of which it is made up; the foundation of a structural explanation is made up of the mechanisms it possesses and the positions it contains.

When we talk of 'agents' we do so because we wish to highlight the particular property of a person that she can set up goals and try to reach them. The classical agency explanation is something like this: I wish something to happen, for instance that somebody gives me an ice-cream, that I become an MTV presenter, or that all wars come to an end. Further, I believe that if I take certain action, what I wish for will come true; it may involve paying a pound at the ice-cream stall, writing a letter to MTV enclosing photos, or joining a political party. For that reason, I do what I think will result in my wishes coming true. If we arrange the argument in the form of logical propositions it may look like this (Callinicos 1989: 36ff):

1 Person A wishes that p
2 A believes that q, that is to say that by doing x she will achieve p
3 Therefore A does x

This analysis builds on the presumption that an agent has an intention. To fulfil a wish, that is to obtain a goal, the agent uses a means to that end. This is obviously the most important difference between social structures and agents: social structures cannot set up goals and they cannot act; only humans can – agents are the only effective causes of society.

What are the relations, then, between social structures and agents? Let us examine this by taking our starting point in three paradigms or theories about this relationship in social science. According to what is sometimes called the social fact paradigm, all influence moves from structures to agents. Social structures have a real existence comparable to that of material things – and it is these structures that are the object of study in social science. Even the actions of individuals can be traced back to their positions in different structures. What we may call the agency paradigm builds upon the opposite standpoint. Here the individuals are agents acting for their own objectives and goals, in the light of the meaning they convey to their social environment and the interpretation they make of the phenomena of their context. Consequently, the starting point is not the social institutions and structures but a meaningful and intentional behaviour – what the individual does, because he or she wants to achieve a goal. These actions taken together are what make up social structures, but the latter have no real influence on what people think or do.

In both paradigms there is a 'conflation' of structure and agent, but they take place in opposite directions, so to speak (Archer 1995): in the social fact paradigm there is a 'downwards conflation', in that the agency will merge with the structure – people become epiphenomena of the social structure; they cannot be distinguished as independently operating individuals possessing autonomous powers. In the agency paradigm a corresponding conflation takes place 'upwards', in that the structures only become the result of the actions of agents – structures become epiphenomena of social agents; they cannot be distinguished as independent phenomena with autonomous and independent powers.

The so-called structuration theory, of which Anthony Giddens (see in particular 1984) is the most important proponent, is an influential attempt to unite these two theories. Instead of regarding agency and structure as separate entities, we should – according to this theory – talk of a structuration process and of duality. Structures do not exist separately from individuals; they are always the medium as well as the outcome of social action. However, this implies that agent and structure constitute one another in such a way that the one cannot be separated from the other; they can be conceptualized only in relation to each other. The structures are instantiated by the actions of the agents and beyond that they only have a 'virtual' existence; when they are not employed in social practices they only exist as 'memory traces' in people. It also involves a denial of emergence in social contexts, since agency and structure cannot be analysed as phenomena possessing powers and mechanisms. As a consequence of this, Giddens has to work with a totally different concept of structure than that of the earlier theories, namely that social structures consist of 'rules and resources'. Agency actions and social structures become different aspects of the same thing – social practices (Layder 1994: 141). An analysis of one 'side' of this unity demands ignoring the other, that is, what Giddens (1984) calls 'methodological bracketing'. He holds that in the analysis of social structures and institutions we must disregard agency and its properties; likewise, when we analyse agency we must disregard social structures.

This solution of the conflict between the social fact and action paradigms represented by the structuration theory will result in what Archer (1995) calls a 'central conflation'. While in the social fact model there are social structures but no actions and in the agency model there are actions but no social structures, no distinction is made between them in the model of the structuration theory. Instead it is a question of a central conflation, in which structure and agent can only exist by virtue of each other. (It should be noted that we are discussing explanatory models. No social scientist is likely to believe that society in practice works completely in line with any of the models.)

We will proceed by starting with the fact that agency and structure are not two elements of the same process; instead we have to deal with two different phenomena. The social structures already exist for every agent – they are simply there. This does not mean that society could not exist without human action or that this action could take place even if the individual had no comprehension of her action. On the other hand, one cannot say that individuals create society out of nothing – we may instead regard them as reproducing or transforming it. If social structures already exist, actions can only modify them – and the whole set of actions maintains or changes them. While social structures cannot be reduced to individuals, the former are a prerequisite for any human action – social structures enable actions but they also set limits to what actions are possible. From this line of reasoning we may form a transformation model of human activity, the foundation of which has been developed by Bhaskar (Figure 8).

Figure 8 The transformational model of the connection between social structure and
       agency

Source: Bhaskar 1993: 155

Collier (1994: 141, 151) finds the realist transformation model consistent with each one of the three models mentioned above, and with the arguments they refer to in their defence. None of this, however, is relevant to the models themselves. That does not mean that this is the Model with a capital M, and the ultimate truth about agency and structure (since it is a transitive object in social science trying to capture intransitive objects), but it indicates that it is the best model we have at present. The accent here is put on emergence, as social structure and agency are regarded as two separate phenomena with different powers and properties. This is also the starting point for yet another model, which is consistent with the transformation model and can be regarded as a development of it (Archer 1995; see also 1989). Here, too, the emphasis is on the fact that the social structures are always the context in which action and social interaction take place, at the same time as social interaction constitutes the environment in which the structures are reproduced or transformed. Structure and agency are separate strata, that is, they possess completely different properties and powers, but the one is essential for how the other will be moulded. When we conduct social scientific inquiries we should therefore not be content with merely studying one side or the other – for example by putting either of them within the 'Giddens brackets'; instead we ought to study the interplay between them.

In this connection Archer (1995) strongly points out that the consideration of emergence introduces a time dimension to the analysis. The interplay between social structure and agency takes place over time; emergence is a process. The properties and powers within a particular stratum precede another stratum, precisely because the latter emerges from the former. But as soon as an emergence has taken place, the powers within these strata have a relative autonomy with respect to one another. Having taken emergence as her starting point, Archer formulates a procedure she calls *analytical dualism*. 'Dualism' refers to the fact that social structures and human agency are different strata, 'analytical' to the fact that these strata and the interaction between them cannot be detected in the flow of social action and human experiences, but only by means of social scientific analysis. Analytical dualism places the fundamental model of structure and agency into a time dimension. The model thus says that structure and agency are two different strata with separate powers and properties, that structures constrain and enable the actions of the agents, and that agents reproduce and transform structures (Archer's term for the latter is 'structural elaboration').

Against this background, analytical dualism builds on two propositions: first, that the social structure in time precedes the actions, which lead to its reproduction or transformation; one cannot change or maintain something that does not exist, and so structure must come first. Second, that structural elaboration in time comes after the actions which create it; reproduction or transformation are results of the actions of agents, and so they must come before the elaboration. We thus have a string as in Figure 9: At the beginning (T^1) a social structure lays down conditions (in the form of constraints and enablements) for the actions of agents. In the next phase (T^2-T^3) the action and social interaction of agents takes place within these conditions. And finally (T^4) the interaction results in the

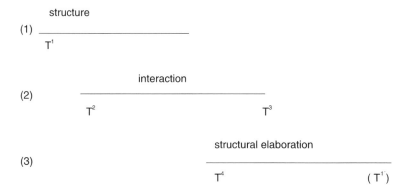

Figure 9 Analytical cycles in the interplay between social structure and agency
Source: Archer 1995: 76

structure in question being reproduced or transformed – the elaboration. In fact this is rather a cycle than a string, as the elaborated structure in the next instant becomes the condition for the next interaction (a new T^1), and so on.

Now, these phases cannot be directly detected in real life, but they represent analytical distinctions. However, without strictly distinguishing between structure and agency it is not possible to see the interplay in these phases. For analysis in social science we must be able to link structure and agency to one another, Archer (1995: 65) maintains, rather than sinking one into the other – as would be the result of a conflation. And such a linking can be done through examination of the interplay between structure and agency over time. The most productive contribution to social practice that social science can make, we conclude, is the examination of social structures, their powers and liabilities, mechanisms and tendencies, so that people, groups and organizations may consider them in their interaction and so – if they wish – strive to change or eliminate existing social structures and to establish new ones. Another contribution may be predictions of how interplay and structural elaboration will appear in the future. The whole matter, however, is more complicated.

Social science and social planning

In an article in the journal *Scientific American* from 1899 (cited in Etzioni-Halevy 1985) there is an estimation of future changes in the environment of big cities as a consequence of the advent of the motor car. When there are more cars, the writer suggests, we shall have a quieter environment and the cities will no doubt also be cleaner, dustless and odour-free. On the whole, claims the article, much of the frustration, irritation and stress of modern city life will disappear with the coming of the automobile. Today, with hindsight, we may smile at the professor's prediction. But subsequent predictions have actually not been much more successful.

We are now in the position when we can compare a great number of predictions about the future over the past thirty years with what has actually happened. We live at a point of time with which many of these predictions were concerned. If we were to make a survey of how even very qualified predictions and plans of different kinds have turned out in reality, we would have reason to be pessimistic. Let us take a few tangible examples, beginning with a relatively confined world – that of offices. During the 1970s and even the beginning of the 1980s, those who studied offices talked about the 'paper-free office' – with the help of electronic mail and the computer culture, paper would become outdated as a medium. All texts would be passed from monitor to monitor. But today offices consume more paper than ever – instead of the paper-free office we have the paper-waste office and desktop publishing. Nor did many computer experts predict the revolution that personal computers would bring about. Something similar could be said about the automation of offices. Offices simply do not look at all like they should according to the predictions.

In a larger, social perspective the deficiencies are just as obvious. In the 1960s there were several extensive studies looking to the year 2000. A central aspect of these was the notion that there would be an unlimited amount of energy at virtually no cost at all. The big question was: How will society adapt to this situation, never experienced before in history? Then the oil crisis arrived ...

One final example: one of the great social occurrences of recent decades is the fall of the Soviet Union and the political developments in Eastern Europe – German reunification, among other things. There was in fact a prediction of the collapse of the Soviet Union a couple of years before it took place – although it was assumed to be set to happen much later than was actually the case (Collins 1986; for a debate on this and other social scientific predictions in general, see *American Journal of Sociology*, 1995). But on the whole, this development seems to have come as a surprise to social scientists, experts on political matters, and the Soviet Union.

For a more solid discussion of the possibilities and the problems of making social scientific predictions, let us start with a theory that is fundamental to a positivist-inspired methodology. The criterion of a good explanation is that it results in a prediction; a phenomenon explained should also be possible to predict. We find an oft-cited formulation in Hempel and Oppenheim (1948: 138): 'An explanation is not fully adequate unless its explanans, if taken account of in time, could have served as a basis for predicting the phenomenon under consideration'. Let us start with these two elements – explanation and prediction – and relate them to one another (Table 7; see also Sayer 1992: 130–8).

Table 7 Prediction and explanation in the social sciences

		Explanation	
		Yes	No
Prediction	Yes	Explanatory prediction	Non-explanatory prediction
	No	Explanatory non-prediction	Non-explanatory non-prediction

In the present context we may leave the non-explanatory non-prediction open. Statements which neither explain nor predict anything certainly belong in social science – for example in the form of descriptions – but they do not fit in with what we are discussing at the moment.

The explanatory non-prediction is just what we argued for earlier (Chapter 3) as the position of critical realism. An explanation of an event involves a retro-duction of the mechanism or (usually) mechanisms producing the event in question. This means that we have attained knowledge of the mechanisms and their tendencies as well as of the conditions that have triggered them. But a prediction would require that we could beforehand make a detailed description of future social conditions. And we cannot, because social conditions are open.

There are, however, those who claim that this makes social scientific explana-tions incomplete (for instance in Kaplan 1964: 348, an almost classic account of 'methodology for behavioural science'), but this is of course misleading. It is not the explanation that is incomplete, but the possibility of describing conjunctions of contingent social conditions which have not yet occurred. However complete the explanations of currently existing social phenomena are, it does not follow that we can describe them empirically. That would require a closed system – something no society can offer. This leads to the conclusion that social scientific research cannot provide planners and other practitioners with explanatory predictions (for an analysis of the problems connected with prediction in the social science that has perhaps most frequently devoted itself to predictions – economics – see Lawson 1997: chs 7, 20).

What about non-explanatory predictions? It might be just as interesting to know beforehand *that* something is going to happen, as afterwards to know *why* it happened. In many cases this might be true. But – as we have shown in examples above – the fate of social scientific predictions, even without explanations, is not very inspiring. This concerns especially the extrapolation of some existing trend, that is to say assuming that what is relevant now will continue developing along some statistical curve. But even in such cases a prediction would require a closed system.

So, conditions for both explanatory predictions and non-explanatory predic-tions are not only unrealistic in terms of being at odds with a critical realist methodology – they are also unrealistic in the sense that they are unreliable as long as they involve social phenomena. Nevertheless, the potential of social science for social practices is not exhausted. We just have to regard it differently.

Social planning is a very frequent activity in politics, business and in everyday life – and it seems more than anything else to presuppose that some courses of events can be anticipated and controlled. This in turn requires two things: on the one hand that events are controlled by a direct conformity to a law of cause and effect, and on the other hand that we can have reliable knowledge about these conditions. In daily practice it is tempting to imagine that these conditions are fulfilled. It is true that all of us have experienced that things go wrong despite careful preparation, that things turn out otherwise than we expected – that not everything goes 'according to plan' – but we tend to see those instances as exceptions, accidental, instances of bad luck. Our faith in rational planning in effect usually remains unshaken. With more thorough and better-prepared planning – often including 'better knowledge' – things will certainly go right.

Is this faith really justified, in the light of the disappointing results of previous predictions? Are there any conclusions we could reasonably draw from past experiences? Have researchers been incompetent? Or are the social sciences as such still not sufficiently developed? Such questions immediately present themselves. However, we maintain that social scientific knowledge does have relevance for social planning, but that it is important to define what its contribution can be. For a realistic opinion of the relevance of social scientific knowledge, there must be a change in the approach to knowledge in this context, a new understanding, both among theorists and practitioners, of the nature of knowledge – and thus another approach to the application of knowledge. The view of knowledge we suggest is, needless to say, the one connected with a realist methodology, and in the continued discussion we shall return to some themes from previous chapters.

In some methodological perspectives – as in much of everyday understanding – there is a conception of scientific laws as being eternal, unchangeable and universal. Such a conception of laws, however, is applicable only to the extent that reality is one and the same always and everywhere. There are indeed some aspects of reality that seem to correspond to such demands, namely those we have defined as operating in closed systems. In the field of natural science there are phenomena approaching naturally closed systems, for instance in the solar system. It is also possible to create artificially closed systems, as in machines or laboratory experiments, where one can ensure that nothing irrelevant influences the processes aimed at. It is under such conditions that the prospect of exact predictions is most likely to succeed. But it entails hard and meticulous work to prevent conditions from becoming open again; extensive schooling is necessary to become a designer of machinery or an experimental researcher.

Reality functions in both more and less closed or open systems, respectively. The objects of study with which social and human sciences are concerned, however, always operate in open systems. Very often the result is that where we are seeking general knowledge, 'disturbances' and changes are an integral and essential part of just the reality and the processes we are trying to attain knowledge of. Thus the prospect of prediction, in the traditional sense of the word, decreases.

We have emphasized that reality is stratified and differentiated. A rough description would state that physical phenomena exist in one stratum, chemical ones in a second, biological ones in a third, psychological ones in a fourth, and social ones in a fifth stratum. Moving upwards through these strata, we find each new stratum built with powers and properties from the underlying strata – while at the same time obtaining completely new mechanisms. This new and different thing cannot be explained simply with the elements included from the underlying layers. It must have emerged as a result of distinct relations existing between these elements, and when the elements are brought together these relations give rise to qualitative changes, new phenomena with autonomous powers and properties. Human beings' ability to think, for instance, cannot be explained by reference to the cells that form us – the cells in themselves do not possess that ability. And social reality is something else than the total of the individuals included therein.

It is because of this emergence that reality contains a number of open systems. And since the potential for combinations among all the elements of reality increases the higher up we get among these strata, the more we must expect of emergence and the harder it becomes to make predictions – that is, close the systems. In the light of these facts the main question concerning the relation between social scientific knowledge and social planning is this: Does this difficulty of predicting what is going to happen in an open system compel us to renounce the idea that there exists valuable knowledge, which might be useful for planning, organizing or acting in any way? Our answer is: No, far from it.

The emergent properties of individuals and of social structures certainly present a problem, but at the same time their consequences indicate a way out of the difficulty. The great capacity for change, which is characteristic of the higher layers of reality, among other things provides a unique ability to affect other layers. One such form of repercussion is the creation of *pseudo-closed* systems. Any human organization – from a family household to a public administration, a department store or a factory – is an example of such a pseudo-closed system. They may be understood as the result of intervention by the higher strata both in other strata and in themselves, with the aim of creating some degree of regularity and predictability – thereby increasing the possibility of dealing with existence in a controlled manner.

This limited and conditioned closure in parts of society is attained by the condition that people are internally related to each other. Some of these relations and regulations are more central than others, and may result in regularities that are reflected in many areas of social life. For example, the organization of wage labour affects large parts of the organization of the rest of society, like school, leisure time, public transportation and business hours. While this social organization is indeed neither eternal nor universal, it has considerable stability over time. It also opens up chances for us to obtain tenable knowledge of social life.

To be sure, it is people who hold structural positions, play roles, support institutions, and so on. And it is powers and liabilities specific to people that enable us – on the one hand – to be influenced and shaped by society so lastingly that we actually manage to form an integral part, with other people, of society. It is also specific to us – on the other hand – that we can interpret phenomena in different ways, learn different ways to react in social situations and so become a new kind of people. Because of this ability we can also change the social systems of which we are a part (and these characteristics of ours, in their turn, depend on a certain biological constitution, specific combinations of chemicals, and so on, down through the layers).

It is individuals who reproduce as well as change society, and we do so by virtue of conscious and intentional action. As for the actual effects at the social level, these are seldom deliberate or intended. We do not go to work in order to maintain the social structure of wage labour, or marry in order to sustain the marital institution, but that is actually what happens when we perform these actions. And at the same time it is the structures that lay down the conditions for the actions of the agents in each case. Conversely, conscious efforts to change social structures do not *necessarily* result in any fundamental change. Still, societies change.

Societies exist and are what they are – among other things open, changeable systems – because we are humans and are what *we* are. And we as humans are what we are because societies exist and are what *they* are. But a society and a human being are not two sides of the same coin. On the contrary, they are two entirely different phenomena, each with its own relative autonomy. (That is why one should not mix up, for example, sociology and psychology, or reduce one to the other, even though most problems we come across in real life are such that we need both types of report.)

However, the relative autonomy of society does not usually allow it to change randomly or by chance, and never unconditionally. This circumstance provides a possibility for knowledge of social processes. In any science that deals with human beings and society, such concepts as 'universality', 'cause as a regularity' and the positivist meaning of 'generality' must be exchanged for the concept of 'necessity'. This concept indicates the existence of internal relations between objects in reality, internal relations which are the cause of emergence or, we might also say, which determine *what* it is that exists. There are also external relations between the social objects – relations that do not determine what exists, but do determine *whether* and *how* that which exists will manifest itself.

With regard to methodology, this implies – we have emphasized it before but it is worth repeating – that the fundamental question to be asked when studying a social phenomenon is this: What are the fundamental social relations without which this phenomenon would cease to exist? And further: What can this object achieve? The answers will point out causal mechanisms and thereby also tendencies behind the social courses of events we can observe. However, we will never be able to predict what the real effect will be. Causal mechanisms are a matter of powers and liabilities in the objects, which build up social phenomena. When these mechanisms are activated they give rise to particular effects – but whether they are activated, and in that case what the effects are, depends on the contingent relations which are constantly modifying the outcome. (That is why we talk of a mechanism in motion precisely as a tendency.)

Every social phenomenon is thus determined by a number of social relations, whereby both the necessary and the contingent ones determine what actually happens in the concrete event. The necessary relation is fundamental for the understanding of the phenomenon, but the contingent relations have an effect on the very pattern of events (what, where, when, how). It is almost impossible to attain complete knowledge of all these relations, and in addition many of them change rapidly.

Thus we will never be able to predict accurately concrete social events, for example exactly how people are going to act in a particular situation – and neither can we anticipate situations. This does not mean, however, that social scientific knowledge is useless for social planning. If we have knowledge of the mechanisms of social structures, we can identify the driving forces behind the events we are observing. Doing so we can also in a more qualified manner estimate the possibilities, deficiencies and limitations of the actions we plan. Without this kind of knowledge, the analysis of a phenomenon will always be superficial or even incorrect – particularly, as we have seen, if we make predictions. The knowledge we are discussing has a quality other than the knowledge on which social planning too often builds.

As a consequence of the arguments we have presented, we suggest a new distribution of work between scientists and practitioners or planners. The current division of labour often appears as if scientists impart facts and predictions and on the basis of these suggest appropriate actions. It seems to us that the scientist in doing so goes beyond what social science allows us to do. Our suggestion implies a more limited role for the social scientist and an extended role for the practitioner.

There is a widespread belief that theory and practice are two completely different things. To put it simply, it has to do with the notion that scientists have access to special and theoretical knowledge of an exclusive nature, which is hard to obtain and which cannot be of any immediate use to an uninitiated practitioner. The practitioners, on the other hand, have tangible and material problems to solve; when necessary they may consult scientists, who from their stock of knowledge put together a proposal for a solution to the problem, or alternatively start a new research project or investigation to arrive at some practical recommendations. Be that as it may, practitioners generally expect scientific knowledge to be delivered to them in the form of plain and indisputable facts, as something once and for all given and complete – a thing or a product, ready to use without further treatment. Sometimes this may work. But, just as we observed regarding predictions, it usually does not work at all. So there must be something wrong with the knowledge. Often it is blamed for being too abstract and theoretical and not sufficiently adapted for practical use.

However, we believe that the fault has more often been the opposite – and we take the opportunity of recalling the old saying that 'when it comes to practicality, nothing beats a good theory'. There is no contradiction between theory and practice, or between the abstract and the concrete. Theory is nothing else but the concepts we have of reality – no matter who has such concepts, scientists or practitioners; and the abstract element represents an extract of reality, an extract containing the fundamental or essential part or the core of a phenomenon. The difference between the theories is that social scientific ones identify in a systematic way social objects and their mechanisms.

Those of us who are sometimes engaged in 'applied' science tend to remove as many abstractions and theoretical concepts as possible when 'handing over' knowledge. And we do so in favour of what could be described as lectures, prescriptions and instructions for use. If we were but a little self-critical we would realize, from a realist perspective, that knowledge does not become more 'practical' in this way; more likely it becomes of very little use in practice.

Now, there are many reasons why research results so often are handed over in as non-theoretical a form as possible. An essential reason, we believe, is to be found in what we have been at pains to point out: an oversight of the fact that reality to a great extent is an open system. Uncomplicated instructions or prescriptions, prescribing step by step how to proceed without raising the more demanding question 'why', might work if one deals with closed systems; but since even the most mechanical knowledge is ultimately used by people in a social context, we must always take into account that human action takes place in open systems.

When the requisite knowledge is to be applied to people and societies, we must be aware of the fact that detailed tangible prescriptions of how to do things once and for all will prove untenable. If social scientists, despite this, start formulating prescriptions they use the authority of science in a basically unfounded way. The nature of social phenomena entails that it is a realistic understanding of the driving powers behind all the different, ever-changing social occurrences – the understanding of causes – rather than more mechanical knowledge, that determines whether different actions will have the expected effects. This also means that practitioners themselves must have access to the tools consisting of theoretical and analytical concepts, that is, what are commonly regarded as the specific tools of scientists. What social scientists should provide practitioners with is not prescriptions but social scientific theories. This is the only foundation for planning that we *can* provide. (In addition, social mapping and applied social science can provide descriptions of empirical conditions.) From our position as social scientists we do not have – nor can we have – the continuous contact with the particular field that the planning concerns. We do not have the insight and the expert knowledge required to enable us to distinguish the necessary from the contingent elements in changeable courses of events, and to estimate the scope of action in particular cases. This is exactly the reason why it would be extremely impractical to deliver knowledge in a form which requires all that.

An example: elderly people and relocation

Let us illustrate the argument of research and practice by looking at a research project on the consequences of forced relocation of elderly people (see Danermark and Ekström 1990; Ekström and Danermark 1991; Ekström 1994). The background of the inquiry is both the responsibility that Swedish municipalities have, confirmed by law, to increase the well-being of people through active social planning, and the situation that house building has more and more turned from the construction of new houses to the restoration of existing buildings. A large number of the elderly have become affected by such restoration of their flats, in that they have been forced to relocate – in some cases just for the time that the restoration work takes, but to many it means a permanent relocation. During one period there were reports from different authorities that elderly people do not manage very well when forced to move away from their usual environment. How can social scientific research contribute in terms of knowledge about relocation and the health of elderly people?

A survey of previous research turned up this result: it appeared that there had been many studies of the problem. The first one was conducted in 1945 (Camargo and Preston 1945) and was soon followed by others (Josephy 1949; Whittier and Williams 1956). These three studies indicate that relocation to an institution brought about an increased mortality rate among the elderly. Since then, several hundred studies have been reported. Most of them have focused on removals between and within various institutions, while others have dealt with removal from someone's own home to an institution, and others again with removal from one house to another. Among the studies there are some confirming the hypothesis that relocation has affected people's health in a negative way, while others find no such connection.

Despite the large volume of empirical material, researchers have not been able to arrive at a clear answer to the question of whether relocation causes an increase in mortality. This is particularly obvious in inquiries about relocation within and between institutions. Borup *et al.* (1979: 139, our emphasis) report that 'the data overwhelmingly support the premise that *relocation does not influence mortality*'. While Lawton's (1977: 291; our emphasis) conclusion is quite the opposite: 'There have been enough studies documenting the unfavorable effects of mass relocation on vulnerable institutionalized elderly people *to enable us to accept the relocation mortality hypothesis as being generally upheld*, especially for those who have significant physical and mental impairments'. The first type of inquiry, then, could result in a guideline of the following kind to social planners and other practitioners: 'There is no risk – relocations do not influence mortality. Just relocate!' While the second type of inquiry might produce advice such as: 'There is great risk – relocations bring about an increase in mortality. Avoid relocation!' The studies we are referring to are trying to find correlations between empirical patterns and to generalize from these. This research procedure makes it impossible to capture the contextual situation determining how the elderly experience the relocation – nor does it help practitioners do this. To this end, a deeper knowledge is required of the mechanisms behind the observed correlations. And such knowledge exists. This is true, above all, about the relations between, on the one hand, the physiological changes in connection with a psychosomatic illness – for instance loss of weight, headache, vitamin deficiency, palpitation, breathing problems, dizziness, ulcers, changes in hormone production, and reduced immune defence – and on the other hand, stress, anxiety and depression. Such knowledge will come from examination of the causal powers in different emotional circumstances, entailing physiological change.

The knowledge it would be reasonable to impart to practitioners in social planning and in preventive health care, therefore, rests on the question of what are the social mechanisms behind these emotions (that is, the results of a research aiming at developing social theory in line with the classification we outlined at the beginning of this chapter). Research has in this case primarily focused on stress, which can be defined thus (Lazarus and Folkman 1984: 19):

'Psychological stress is a particular relationship between the person and the environment that is appraised by the person as taxing or exceeding his or her resources and endangering his or her well-being'. At the centre of the mechanisms behind stress we find that the person cannot control and handle difficult and problematic situations.

In social science there are several theories about the mechanisms of emotions – abstract theories, which have evolved from data from many different empirical fields of examination, defining important powers in these situations. Let us mention three such theories. First, the social mechanisms of the theory of alienation: self-estrangement and meaninglessness. The formulation of these mechanisms is based on the assumption that our power of action – our ability and potential for a creative and self-manifesting action – is fundamental for our emotional lives. Creative action nourishes the sense of purpose, of belonging somewhere, and of happiness. The opposite of such action – submission, enforced and alienated action – is assumed to be devastating to the emotional life of human beings.

The second theory concerns the mechanisms generating trust and security on the one hand, and distrust and insecurity on the other. Our well-being depends basically on our trust in others, our feeling of security and of continuity in life. This foundation is laid in early childhood but also depends on the social conditions which mould our daily lives. These conditions may be marked by continuity, stability and relative independence, but also by sudden and critical changes, or by being forced to depend on anonymous forces one cannot influence in any way.

The third type of mechanism of importance to well-being is that which produces such emotions as guilt and shame on the one hand, and pride and dignity on the other. These emotions are closely related to people's sensitivity to others, that is, sociality. We are constantly assessing and re-assessing our identity and self-identity by trying to see ourselves through the eyes of others; and we reflect upon ourselves in the light of what we believe others expect from us.

Common to these mechanisms is that they are in one way or another related to people's control of their own lives. It is this theoretical insight we can pass on to practitioners. A relocation of elderly people in connection with the renovation of flats causes stress when it is seen as inevitable and at the same time practically impossible to control. This applies not only to cases where someone has been forced to move, but also when they move back not to their old flat but – as they experience it – to a new home. Feelings of self-estrangement and meaninglessness may arise as these people are forced to submit to changes they do not feel they are participating in; they have to move to a location they themselves have not been able to choose or influence in any way. Changes may jeopardize their basic feeling of security in life, as these threaten what could earlier be taken for granted; the continuity of daily life is broken by processes these people cannot influence – and perhaps not even understand. Feelings of shame and loss of dignity are created by such relationships of subjection, and when people are not taken seriously or are ignored.

In this act of passing on knowledge, we do not give any prescriptions. We may emphasize that social planning and preventive health care should be based on knowledge of the social mechanisms that affect people's control of their own daily life. But we cannot say 'Relocate!' Nor can we say 'Avoid relocation!' Only someone who has insight into the real circumstances and the daily life of the people concerned may estimate how these mechanisms may manifest themselves in specific cases. And to be able to do this, practitioners must make use of social scientific theories which specify the structures and mechanisms that are relevant to the field.

Another aspect of this example, is that the specification of mechanisms at the same time involves a criticism of the social structures and actions which may influence mortality among the elderly. In the concluding part of this chapter we shall take a closer look into the critical aspects of social science.

Social science as social criticism

Science parks are being set up in more and more countries. With the help of advanced technical efforts and pedagogical skill, old and young can learn the basics of how nature works: what the mechanisms of nature are, how they can cooperate to bring about an event, how they can be counter-active, how ecological systems can be affected by the actions of people, and how nature can be explored. When one of the writers of this book (Karlsson 1992) participated in an international conference about lifelong learning, there was a presentation during one of the sessions of the ideas behind and the creation of such a park.

In the presentation and the discussion that followed, special attention was drawn to the fact that many people still have a superstitious world-view, and that the parks have an important mission in communicating a more scientific perspective. The ambition is thus emancipatory – in this case getting rid of superstition, illusions and mysticism as far as natural phenomena are concerned. (One may observe that nowhere – to our knowledge – has a social scientific park been set up. The rather interesting question 'Why not?' conflicts between different social scientific theories, aspects of power in the various interpretations of society, and other reasons, and is anyway beyond the scope of our current subject.) What, then, can we learn in a park providing us with scientifically based knowledge about nature? First of all that which we call natural laws, that is, statements about forces and mechanisms in objects of nature (cf. Soper 1995). One example is the law of gravity, identifying a mechanism whose existence can be demonstrated in nature – a force attracting bodies towards the centre of the earth. But we also learn that the mechanisms are there, even when they are not operative, or when their effects are modified by the activity of other mechanisms. When we see a bird fly we cannot conclude that gravity has ceased to work, but instead we must assume that the bird possesses mechanisms which modify gravity.

The mechanisms of nature are used as an explanation of the phenomena we experience – that an apple falls down, that a bird flies. It is these explanations, where the causes are in the mechanisms of natural objects, which are the focus of interest in natural science parks. The aim is to counteract superstitious notions and false beliefs about the operations of nature. And it is with the help of such knowledge that we can employ natural laws to serve our purposes. To continue with the same example, it is through such knowledge that we can build machines counter-acting gravity – aeroplanes.

The basis for the emancipatory ambition of natural science parks is thus to use the mechanisms of natural objects to explain what happens in nature, as well as to demonstrate the results – for better and for worse – of our manipulations of nature. Knowledge of the mechanisms of nature is emancipatory insofar as it gives us the chance to employ these powers technically. Moreover, in natural science parks a foundation of emancipatory pedagogy is laid in order to replace false beliefs with knowledge.

Humanities and social science study objects are different from those of natural science in many ways (which we discussed above all in Chapter 2). For one thing they are socially produced, and people are intentional. We are, Bhaskar says,

> in the intentional domain, and so on the site of the human sciences, insofar as organisms – agents – possess beliefs that their actions manifest a certain property. The belief may be unconscious, unformulated or tacit, and it may be wrong; but it must be there or we are dealing with purely natural phenomena.
>
> (Bhaskar 1986: 163)

Unlike human beings, social structures are not intentional. However, they cannot be regarded as belonging to the natural sphere, since they are social products and dependent upon human action for their existence. And it is social structures that lay down the conditions for what we can do and not do by placing us in various social situations. That is why a *socially* emancipatory objective should be directed against structures. Emancipation here involves replacing undesired social structures with desired ones. And even in this context there are false beliefs to be considered.

We have been discussing a basic model by which researchers can detect structures and mechanisms (see Chapters 4 and 6), and this – we would like to add – also involves emancipatory objectives. The model we have presented includes these steps:

- a description of the event that is the object of investigation;
- an analytical division of the event into its components;
- a redescription of these components as seen through theories of structures and relations (abduction);
- through redescription finding the operative mechanisms behind the event;
- an evaluation of the explanatory power of these mechanisms, compared with those postulated by other theories;

- concretization in order to record how the mechanisms involved produced the event in question.

Should the event imply that people have suffered, that their needs have been thwarted, or that false beliefs have emerged, then there is reason to criticize the structures whose mechanisms have caused this.

Let us illustrate this by means of an example, which we take from Corson (1991: 237), even though the model he puts forward is somewhat simplified in comparison with the one we have presented:

1   An event is identified: the socio-cultural status of parents tends to influence their children's achievement in the education system.
2   A model of the mechanisms explaining the event: a theory of socio-cultural reproduction within education; the model may contain strategies of choice that the parents can follow to influence their children, and the strategies mediate between social structures and the activities for which these structures lay down the foundations.
3   Two types of inquiry, the first one involving isolation of the mechanism: empirical studies of the strategies (including conceptions about them) that parents apply in different social structures. The second type aims at eliminating alternative hypotheses: empirical studies in order to examine if other models are wrong, for example the notion that differences in quality between schools are merely accidental.
4   A positive recognition of actions taken to replace this structure with a more favourable one: The results encourage a policy that emancipates us from structures which generate these unequal conditions concerning education – or at least reduce the influence of parents' sociocultural status on the children's education.

The fourth point thus implies that the explanation comprises a critique of the social structure behind the problem under investigation – this also refers to false beliefs. Here a conclusion about emancipation is also to be found. Let us take a closer look. Social structures are reproduced or transformed by agents – and people act intentionally. In explaining social phenomena we must always consider what people think and believe – consider their ideas. This particularly applies to the beliefs about different social phenomena.

Let us, for instance, assume that many people believe that the divergences between what men and women do – at home, at school, at work – have biological causes: the biology of the sexes should be the reason why women do more household work than men, and choose other types of schooling and professions. If we want to explain this gender distribution, or segregation, of tasks, these beliefs must be taken into account. But the argument must also comprise a scientifically examined explanation of these conditions (concerning modern patriarchy, see Jónasdóttir 1994) – and we are of course interested in what mechanisms have produced these false beliefs about gender segregation. The explanation thus becomes a critique of these causes, as everyday thinking and social scientific explanation do not agree with each other:

> To say that some institution causes false beliefs is to criticize it. Given that (other things being equal) it is better to believe what is true than what is false, it is also better (other things being equal) that institutions that cause false beliefs should be replaced by, or transformed into, those that cause true ones. Further still, particular institutions and false beliefs about them may be in a *functional* relation, such that the false beliefs serve to preserve the institutions that they are about. Where institutions oppress a substantial number of people, they will only be stable if protected by such false beliefs.
>
> (Collier 1994: 172)

Fundamental to the critical side of social science is the standpoint that explanations of social phenomena require being subject to critique. Since social practice is concept-dependent, practice may build on false beliefs. Insofar as false beliefs have social effects, we must examine them and see what caused them – thereby criticizing the false beliefs in themselves, as well as the structures that cause them and are legitimated by them. In this way social science obtains an intrinsic critical dimension, and the explanations are an explanatory critique. We can hardly explain racist actions without considering conceptions about races and their characteristics – and in the explanation there is a critique of these conceptions. The same thing applies, for instance, to 'ethnic cleansing' and men's oppression of women. The critique arises when social scientists not only show that some beliefs are false, but also explain why people believe as they do, and how these ideas have developed. Social criticism is intrinsic in social science.

However, philosophers and social scientists within critical realism do not always agree on this issue. Some social scientists do not recognize themselves in the philosophers' reconstruction of their critical practice. This problem has been thoroughly examined by Andrew Sayer (1992, 1997, 2000), so let us follow some of his arguments. The starting point is that critical social science can reveal the mechanisms that create illusion and suffering. Having seen this, the way is open to immediate critique of these mechanisms, helping people in practice to strive to replace these structures with others, which will produce a good life instead. As we said, the idea is that unwanted social structures and sources of determination should be replaced by wanted social structures and sources of determination. (One structure of course must be replaced by another; there is no such thing as structure-free human life – or a life outside society.) In philosophy of science reconstructions (for example Bhaskar 1989b) one usually distinguishes between four steps in critical social science: the first step is to identify a problem, such as unfulfilled needs, suffering or false beliefs; the second step is to identify the source of these problems, such as some form of oppression or segregation; the third step is to give a negative judgement of this cause of the problem; the fourth is – *ceteris paribus* – to judge positively such actions as remove this cause.

If we return to Corson's (1991) previously mentioned inquiry and apply this model on that study, it might run along these lines: in the first step one identifies the problem – that the social status of parents tends to influence children's achievement in the education system. The second step in Corson's inquiry consists of a model of sociocultural reproduction and empirical investigation of its relevance in relation to other possible explanations. The third step is implicit in the argument – a critique of the social structures generating the influence that social status has on children's school achievement. And the fourth is his positive judgement of actions that can replace these unwanted structures with others that do not have these negative effects or at least reduce them.

Sayer focuses on the first and last step of the model, but the argument leads to a questioning of the third step, too. Regarding the first step – to identify a problem – Sayer claims that it calls for normative considerations: What are wanted and unwanted structures? What are good and bad social situations? But those questions are seldom discussed in the reconstructions of critical social science, and so he argues for the importance of examining normative issues systematically, and connecting social science descriptions and explanations with the discourses of moral philosophy. It is difficult to find self-evident and unproblematic normative grounds in existing social scientific practice. It seems instead to be marked by 'uncertainty and frequent inconsistencies in the implicit or explicit critiques made of social practices, and fundamental disagreements where alternatives are considered' (Sayer 2000: 165).

Proceeding to the fourth step – to support actions that can remove that which creates the problem – it comprises a *ceteris paribus* clause, that is, the positive judgement is valid, provided that everything else is the same. It is introduced to cover cases where the fulfilment of a certain need clashes with that of another and more important need. Collier (1994: 183) gives an example of a famine-stricken society. Children's need to play must be set aside, as they have to work to help procure food. To make the argument clear and simple, one often starts from a single mechanism in discussions about explanatory critique. But, Sayer reminds us, concrete social scientific inquiries usually have to consider several structures and mechanisms simultaneously (which we discussed in Chapter 3). And our theories often concern structures having both wanted and unwanted mechanisms, as well as mechanisms tending to produce both wanted and unwanted social situations. In our research we often have to face more complicated problems than what is seen in a philosophical reconstruction of critical social science. The whole complex of problems in social scientific practice tends to disappear into the *ceteris paribus* clause. The circumstance that we remove one problem does not automatically bring about an improvement – to accomplish that, the situation with which the problem is replaced needs to be more favourable.

Sayer's picture of critical social science in relation to the philosophical reconstruction of it – a judgement that we share from our experiences as social scientists – may be summarized thus: the definition of a problem comprises a normative component, which is seldom sufficiently examined; the *ceteris paribus* clause conceals conditions constantly present in social scientific inquiries, and which we as scientists must handle; by saying this it is not self-evident how to take the step to a negative judgement of the source of the problem; it may even involve us having to go back to the first step and revise the problem's original formulation.

Conclusion

In this chapter we have discussed the relation of social science to its object. In doing so, we have argued for two things. One line of argument is that practitioners within different fields can make use of results not only from so-called applied research, even if this seems to be the predominant opinion among researchers and practitioners alike. With a changed distribution of work, researchers may pass on knowledge of the social structures, mechanisms and tendencies identified by social scientific theories. The application of such knowledge on concrete social problems thus becomes the responsibility of practitioners, too.

The second line of argument is connected with the first one and is about the critical side of social science. Our explanations of social phenomena in themselves comprise a critique of them. However, this is a more complicated issue than the view that the only thing this critique would bring about would be a demand for the replacement of structures that generate suffering and false beliefs with other structures. Most social forms have both good and bad effects – at any rate by being good for some groups and bad for others. What is characteristic of society, that it exists in an open system, makes it impossible for us to predict social occurrences, but it does not mean that we can evade the analysis of possible consequences of mechanisms in alternative social forms.

8   Conclusion

In this concluding chapter we will start by summing up the underlying perspective of our book – that of critical realism, which we examined in Part I of the book. Then we shall sum up Part II, which is more oriented towards methodology.

Critical realism can be described in many ways. We will briefly outline what we consider to be the essence of the book's theme, methodological issues. We will concentrate the account on the following features: the idea of causality and mechanisms, the assumption that reality is stratified, the issue of closed and open systems, the transitive and the intransitive dimensions of reality, and finally the hermeneutic conditions of social science. We will also address the question of what the term 'critical' in critical realism signifies. But first, let us call to mind that critical realism has two analytical elements which we have linked in this book. One is a general ontology, originally called transcendental realism. The other is an attempt to apply this to the social scientific field, originally called critical naturalism. By and by, however, these two elements have been brought together in reports of the perspective, and the concept of 'critical realism' has only been established afterwards.

Causality and mechanisms

Things do not happen by chance or without a reason. Behind events and courses of events there are powers generating them. If you manage to produce a specific reaction in an experiment, it is because there are intrinsic properties in the object of study – properties which are capable of generating something, of producing a result. This also demonstrates the most fundamental enterprise in science, in natural as well as in social science: to find the inherent mechanisms that generate events. It is these inherent properties we call the 'causal powers'. The physical world abounds with such causal powers, and they exist whether they are being exercised or not. A person is capable, for example, of lifting a particular weight, remembering things or loving somebody. Sometimes this power is exercised and generates events, sometimes it is not exercised. Critical realism consequently takes its entry point on the basic assumption that objects in reality possess causal powers, that is, generative mechanisms.

The differentiation and stratification of reality

Reality is seen as differentiated. In critical realism three different domains of reality can be distinguished. The basic one is the so-called domain of real. Here we find the mechanisms. They exist irrespectively of whether they produce an event or not. When the mechanisms produce a factual event, it comes under the domain of actual, whether we observe it or not. When such an event is experienced, it becomes an empirical fact and comes under the domain of empirical. That means the critical realist perspective of the world is that the reality scientists study is larger than the domain of empirical.

Reality is also seen as stratified, in that mechanisms, so to speak, belong to different strata of reality. There are, for example, chemical, biological, psychological and social strata. What exactly these strata are and how they interrelate is a subject of debate. What is important is the idea that new mechanisms are continually created in their respective strata, so-called emergent powers. In social scientific analysis one should search for causal powers at the social level. However, it is not uncommon that social phenomena are inferred from other levels. For instance, there are often attempts to explain social phenomena by referring them to psychological mechanisms. Critical realism does not deny the fact that mechanisms from different strata are involved; what is maintained is that social phenomena are produced by social powers.

Closed and open systems

Closed systems exist when the generative mechanisms are operating in isolation and independent of other mechanisms. Performing an experiment involves producing certain events by creating closed systems and by keeping generative mechanisms under control, while at the same time manipulating them. This is how experiments are often carried out in the natural sciences. Social reality, however, is different and one cannot perform experiments like those in natural science. Although there have been some attempts, they have certainly not yet been performed in genuine experimental situations. Social events are the products of a range of interacting mechanisms. In practice we cannot just isolate some of them in order to manipulate a situation, with the purpose of studying what happens. Researchers in social science always work in an open system, that is to say, the generative mechanisms we study operate in a complex interaction with other mechanisms, which either cooperate with or work against the mechanism in question. Our alternative is instead to reduce in thought the complex empirical reality, by means of abstraction. In addition to the fact that there are always cooperative factors, we must also take into account that a mechanism is sometimes active, sometimes dormant, and that there may sometimes be counteractive mechanisms preventing an empirical manifestation of an active mechanism. The important conclusion social science can draw is that empirical testing of the kind that is common within the positivist tradition is usually not the best way of testing a hypothesis concerning causal powers.

The transitive and intransitive dimensions of reality

The realist element in critical realism indicates that it assumes that an external reality exists, independently of our conceptions of it. Consequently there exists a reality that can be subjected to analysis. This is the intransitive object of science. The purpose of science is to come as 'close' to this reality as possible. It is our theories and notions of reality that constitute our knowledge of it; they make up our transitive object, that is, what connects us as cognitive subjects with the objective reality. The transitive dimension is socially determined and changeable. This goes for all knowledge. What makes social science special, compared to natural science, is that social scientists seek knowledge about a socially produced reality, not just a socially defined one. This understanding is different from that of a naive realism – objectivism – holding that it is in principle possible to attain a correct and objective picture of reality. It also differs from perspectives which overemphasize the transitive side – constructivism and relativism – which argue that it is meaningless to claim that one statement about reality is more truthful than another statement, since all knowledge is socially defined.

The hermeneutic conditions of social science

As we have seen, there is a decisive difference between social and natural science in that their respective objects are essentially different. First, society is made up of thinking and reflective human beings. They are capable of continually changing the social reality. Therefore one might say that the reality social scientists study is socially produced. Second – and what is more decisive for methodological issues – we study other people's interpretations of the social world. Our object of study is thus socially defined. We interpret the interpretations of other people. An understanding of significance and meanings is absolutely decisive for our ability to explain the social world. In order to understand and explain the social world, as social scientists we try to understand and explain what meaning actions and events have to people, but we also endeavour to produce concepts, which make it possible to transcend common sense and attain a deeper understanding and explanation of a more abstract character. This has been called the double hermeneutics of social science. As researchers we are also a product of social interpretations.

The critical element of critical realism

The word 'critical' in the term 'critical realism' can have many meanings. First, there is the original word 'transcendental', which was later replaced by 'critical'. 'Transcendental realism' signifies an ontology transcending the empirical level; we described this ontology earlier using the concept of domains. In this sense, 'critical' can be seen as expressing a critique of 'flat' empiricism.

The second meaning of 'critical' – and this is how Bhaskar originally used the concept – is when common philosophy is applied to social science. Critical realism is critical of the conflation of structure and agency – a conflation that it tries to transcend by means of a transformational model, described in Chapter 7 (the TMSA model). Further, it criticizes a tendency to either individualize explanations – methodological individualism – or sociologize explanations – that is, to reduce or totally obliterate the individual for the benefit of the collective or the structure.

The third meaning of 'critical' stresses the limited possibilities of science. Critical realism is critical to universalist claims to truth, which are often made in positivist social science. By stressing the transitive dimension, these emphasize the social character of science.

Fourth, 'critical' can be associated with the original term for the application of transcendental realism to social science: 'critical naturalism'. When we lay bare the generative mechanisms at the social level, we thereby also explain social phenomena in terms of social causes. These are produced by people and can thus be changed by people. Relations of dominance and power can easily be seen. There is a great potential for social criticism here. Thus social problems do not originate in, for instance, biological or psychological factors, but in social ones. From this perspective sexual oppression as a phenomenon in society cannot be explained by reference to, for example, biological nature, but by social conditions, like patriarchal structure. Another current example is unemployment. The causes of this phenomenon are to be found at the social level, not at the individual psychological level. The emancipatory traits of critical realism are strongly emphasized.

Fifth and finally, we may point to another, similar meaning for 'critical'. Reasoning on the lines of critical realism, we often surpass everyday thinking. Such reasoning is often rational and understandable from an individual perspective, but nevertheless it is often mixed up with myths, illusions and pure ignorance. When this is revealed or removed through scientific practice, and when what was earlier taken for granted now appears to be produced by social processes and conventions, opportunities for critical reflection are created.

Critical realism and methodology

Before we proceed to sum up the principal methodological points of the book, we would like briefly to comment on the discussion concerning whether there exists one or two fundamental methodological approaches in science. The dualism between an explanatory and an interpretative methodological approach, which we have highlighted in this book, has long been questioned. The division between natural and social scientific method has not been self-evident to everybody. Advocates of the so-called Vienna Circle argued for the concept of scientific universalism. They started partly from the foundational positivist belief that all meaningful statements about reality, social reality as well as the natural world, must build on sense data. The principles for the study thereof are the same. They wanted to replace methodological dualism with the principle of a universal method for all science. Many theorists oppose this stance, Habermas for one. However, he did not defend traditional dualism. In his book *Knowledge and Human Interests* (1972, German original 1968) he sharply criticizes the positivist traits in social science as well as hermeneutic idealism. He holds that the latter too one-sidedly focuses on an attempt to reconstruct contextual meaning. Distinguishing between natural, social and human sciences, Habermas further believes that natural science has its (quantitative) methodology and human science its (qualitative) methodology, and that they co-exist without too much controversy, albeit not in total peace. The situation in social science is different. Here we must incorporate traits from both methodological approaches, and this requires a deeper analysis of the relation between an analytical and a hermeneutic approach. Habermas' answer is a synthesis, inspired by Weber, of interpretative understanding and causal explanation.

There was a fresh angle of approach during the 1970s to the issue of choice of method, through writings by, among others, Kuhn (1970) and Feyerabend (1993). Their critiques of positivism had many affinities, but Feyerabend was more radical in his criticism. He suggested that different paradigms are not comparable – the concept of incommensurability. Paradigms contain concepts which do not instantly permit translation into other paradigms, and there is no such thing as a neutral language of observation. The conclusion Feyerabend draws is that there cannot exist just one set of methods which can satisfy all demands for universal validity, but different methods must be allowed to exist side by side. There are no tools for deciding which methods are more relevant than others.

Critical realism, however, is sceptical of the idea of incommensurability, and therefore also about methodological relativism. It accepts the idea of relativism in the sense that all knowledge is socially produced, but all knowledge is not therefore equally valuable. In this context critical realism distinguishes between epistemic relativism and judgemental relativism. The former concept refers to the fact that our knowledge is 'contingent'; it is historically determined. Judgemental relativism implies that there are no grounds for deciding when one kind of knowledge should be preferred to another – and this assumption is refuted within critical realism. However, we can find criteria by which the convincing force of a theory can be measured, at many levels: historical, emancipatory, critical, and instrumental. In this book we have mainly reflected on the explanatory power of the critical ideas (see further Bhaskar 1991: 157).

We shall now proceed by drawing attention, in a somewhat compressed form, to the main methodological points: critical realism constitutes a 'third way' in the scientific debate between, on the one hand empiricism/objectivism, and on the other hand relativism/idealism. However, it is not a conflation of, or a compromise between, these perspectives; it represents a standpoint in its own right.

Critical realism concurs with the criticism of the empiricist/objectivist ideal of science concerning neutral empirical observations: all knowledge is conceptually mediated and consequently concept-dependent. Unlike relativism/idealism, however, critical realism contends, first, that there is a real world independent of our knowledge about it, and second, that it is possible to gain knowledge about this real world: facts are certainly theory-laden, but they are not theory-determined. However, knowledge is always fallible and more or less truthlike, and its usability varies in various social situations, since there are many different levels and forms of social practice.

Against empiricism and objectivism, critical realism further claims that the method of obtaining knowledge cannot be reduced to observation of events. Reality is not a series of events, where one thing follows on another with empirically observable regularity. The relation between reality and our knowledge about it comprises, as we have seen, three distinct ontological domains: the empirical (our experiences), the actual (events), and the real, where the mechanisms are what produce the events in the world. Empirical research comprises only a limited set of experiences out of all the events actually occurring. But not even events comprise all there is – even if there existed a method enabling us to experience all the events of the world, it would not provide the knowledge we are trying to obtain. Still, we would not know what it is that 'makes things happen', or alternatively not happen, when we expect it, and such restricted knowledge would be both impractical and sometimes dangerous. In the search for these mechanisms we must resort not only to induction and deduction, but above all to abduction and retroduction. In Chapter 4 we argued for this. To be able to discover meanings, relations and consistency, to be able to obtain knowledge of social structures and transfactual conditions, abduction and retroduction are necessary.

Where empirical research finds a 'flat' reality, reducible to events that can be observed, critical realism sees a deep dimension, comprising the mechanisms that produce events in the world. This is the first of the specifically critical realist contributions to the philosophy of science. The second one is the insight that reality is made up of many different objects, which, due to their distinct constitutive structures, also possess different powers and mechanisms. This means that many different mechanisms are operating at the same time, and that the relation between the generative mechanisms and their effects is contingent: the outcome of the activity of the mechanisms – the events we can observe – is a complex combination of the influences from different mechanisms, some mechanisms reinforcing each other while others counteract each other's manifestations. This also means that causal laws must be analysed as *tendencies*, not as universal empirical regularities. Furthermore, reality is stratified and comprises emergent powers and mechanisms. The higher a stratum is, the more mechanisms and possibilities for combinations between mechanisms there are. The consequence of this is that 'high strata sciences', like the social sciences, are practised in open systems.

Thus there are decisive differences in the nature of the objects studied by different sciences, and this deeply affects methodology in the social sciences. The natural sciences, studying lower strata, can to a large extent develop knowledge of the mechanisms of nature by isolating them in experiments, that is, they can create more or less closed systems for observation. This is impossible in the social sciences; social strata have emergent properties and powers in the form of human intentionality, reflection, language and a capacity for self-change, which means that the study of social phenomena is always pursued in an open system. If we want to transcend purely empirical observations of social phenomena and also explain what produces them, we must instead avail ourselves of 'thought experiments'. We must seek the generative social mechanisms with the help of conceptual abstraction via structural analysis. Obviously this abstraction must be grounded in empirical conditions. One empirical starting point could be the demi-regularities, discussed in Chapter 6. Under the heading 'Retroduction' in Chapter 5, we described the empirical methods that are particularly suitable when seeking the causal mechanisms of such demi-regularities. So we try to explain the fundamental preconditions for social relationships, human activity, reasoning and knowledge, the key issue being 'what internal relations make X what X is?' To be able to carry out retroduction successfully we are dependent on theories. Theorizing becomes an integral part of the research process.

As the social sciences deal with open systems, causal conditions in particular must be analysed as tendencies. Consequently the social sciences cannot make predictions in the proper sense of the word. Social science is often concerned with very complex matters, in the sense that a very large number of mechanisms are active. Time and again social science is criticized for not being able to explain what it does. Such criticism reveals a perspective which reduces the complexity of social reality. The view we argue for indicates that the task of social science first and foremost is to look for the causal mechanisms of the events we study. We cannot predict occurrences or anticipate situations; reality is too complex for that. But we can provide insight into the mechanisms and tendencies that make things happen in society. Today there are many social scientific theories drawing attention to social mechanisms; their explanatory power is huge even if they cannot predict concrete events.

As Outhwaite (1987: 34) writes, critical realism is ontologically bold but methodologically cautious. It is permeated with the notion of reality as having ontological depth and the consequences thereof, while at the same time showing a humble spirit in the face of the task of arriving at knowledge about a specific phenomenon, defined in time and space. It does not therefore exclude any method *a priori*, but the choice of method should be governed, on the one hand by what we want to know, and on the other by what we can learn with the help of different methods. The key issue is that we possess the ability to judge the strength and the weakness, respectively, of a method. Such judging is best done from well-grounded metatheoretical assumptions. This often leads us to require a combination of several different methods. This mode of combining must, however, be based on ontological considerations. It cannot, as has been maintained by certain method pragmatists, be based on practical considerations and on empirical conditions. In this book we have tried to demonstrate, first, what basic ontological conditions should inform the choice and use of method; second, what tools in terms of, for instance, retroduction and theory we need in concrete research work; and finally, how different empirical procedures (intensive and extensive) meet different demands in this work. We have labelled this working procedure 'critical methodological pluralism' – a pluralism informed by critical realism – and it is for such a pluralism that we have argued in this book.

Glossary

Abduction Inference or thought operation, implying that a particular phenomenon or event is interpreted from a set of general ideas or concepts.

Abstraction The outcome of a thought operation whereby a certain aspect of a concrete object is isolated.

Analytical dualism A development of the transformation model for agency/structure, to which a time dimension has been added. Thereby three phases can be defined: (1) social structure, laying down the conditions (constraining and enabling) the actions of agents; (2) actions, happening in a social interaction between agents; (3) elaboration, as a result thereof, that is, reproduction or transformation of the structure.

Causality Causes and effects. In critical realism this is a question of the nature of the object, which determines what a certain object can and cannot do = cause.

Closed system When generative mechanisms can operate under conditions where they are isolated and independent of other mechanisms; the outcome can be predicted.

Concretization Examining how structures that have been described in an abstract, isolated form, manifest themselves in concrete cases, in historical, social and cultural contexts.

Emergence The appearance of something new; objects composed of other objects so that new structures, powers and mechanisms have appeared.

Empirical generalization Describing properties as generally existing in an entire population of empirical phenomena. Empirical generalizations build on inductive inference, which means that from the knowledge about a limited number of empirical phenomena one draws the conclusion that what is true of these phenomena is also true of a larger population.

The epistemic fallacy Reducing reality to empirical observation, that is, apprehending and defining reality as identical with empirically grounded conceptions.

Epistemology From the Greek *episteme*, meaning certain knowledge as opposed to *doxa*, which indicates assumption or belief. Epistemology is one part of the theory of science. Epistemology is examination of the conditions, possibilities, nature and limits of knowledge.

Generative mechanisms   What makes something happen in the world.

Intensive and extensive research design   The plan of an intensive research design is to study one particular or just a few cases. The agents involved make up a causal group and they are studied in context. In the extensive design one studies a larger population and tries to find regularities and patterns. The group under observation is usually taxonomic, and the result is analysed by statistical methods.

Internal relations   Such a relation between objects, without which at least one of them would not be what it is in essence, if the relation did not exist.

Intransitive/transitive dimension   The intransitive dimension is that which primarily is the object of scientific knowledge, but it can be extended to comprising all that exists, that is, the ontological side. The transitive dimension is our conceptions of that which exists, that is, the epistemological side.

Merging models of agency and structure   Models in which agency has been reduced to structure, and structure to agency, or where it is impossible to discriminate between them.

Ontology   Notions about the nature of the world. Indicates the necessary features of that which exists. Bhaskar uses the word to designate what the nature of reality must be like for science to be possible.

Open system   When generative mechanisms operate in combination with each other; the more mechanisms involved, the more difficult to anticipate the outcome.

Retroduction   A thought operation involving a reconstruction of the basic conditions for anything to be what it is, or, to put it differently, it is by reasoning we can obtain knowledge of what properties are required for a phenomenon to exist. Transfactual or transcendental argument is a form of retroduction implying that one seeks these qualities beyond what is immediately given.

Stratum   The world is stratified, that is, divided into separate strata possessing their own mechanisms. They can roughly be divided into physical, chemical, biological, psychological and social strata, but the identification of strata is an ongoing process.

Structure   A set of internally related objects.

Transcendental   Circumstances beyond the concrete, immediately evident, which constitute necessary and fundamental preconditions for human activity. Critical realism is based on a transcendental realism implying that the basic preconditions for our knowledge of reality are to be found in this reality, which is independent of our seeking knowledge.

Transfactual (transcendental) argument   See **retroduction**.

Transformation model of agency/structure   Structure and agency are specifically distinct objects, but they are related to each other insofar as a structure limits and enables the actions of agents, at the same time as these actions reproduce or transform the structure.

Notes

1 Introduction

1 We are grateful to our colleagues Björn Johansson and Martin Lind for drawing our attention to the similarities between Bunge and Bhaskar.
2 The notion that language is of vital importance has led to something called the linguistic turn. The expression 'the linguistic turn' originated in Bergman's *Logic and Reality* (1964), see Bryant (1995).

2 Science, reality and concepts

1 This perspective on scientific activity bears a strong resemblance to Althusser's analyses of 'theoretical practice', at the same time as there are important differences. For a discussion, see for example Collier (1994: 52–4).
2 This 'something' can be a discourse, a social practice or the physical world.

3 Conceptual abstraction and causality

1 Sometimes the criticism against abstractions claims that 'ordinary' people do not recognize their reality in the abstract concepts used. This is, however, another complex problem we dealt with in the previous chapter under the heading 'The conditions of conceptualization within social science'.
2 It does happen, however, that ideal types do just that. In those cases it is perhaps quite possible that the researcher, guided by good scientific intuition, quite simply has struck the core. It is a distinctive feature of critical realism that as a scientific theory it in many ways represents clarification and systematization of obvious principles for the search of knowledge, principles often used in practice whether or not they are brought up in the literature on method.

4 Generalization, scientific inference and models for an explanatory social science

1 This is true about both the social science with its roots in positivism and that with its roots in hermeneutics. To Wilhelm Dilthey, one of the founders of hermeneutics, the relation between the universal and the particular was a fundamental methodological issue. Hermeneutic understanding entails an

application of *general* categories in order to understand *individual* meanings (see e.g. Habermas 1972).

2 Regarding the relation between Peirce's development of the concept of abduction and his development of semiotics and pragmatics, see e.g. Jensen (1995) and Habermas (1972).

3 Anyone familiar with hermeneutics can see that abduction is very similar to the so-called hermeneutic circle (see Ödman 1979: 78). According to the hermeneutic circle we always interpret and understand individual parts in relation to ideas of a whole. A method of switching between the parts and the whole is advocated; this enables a consecutive revising of interpretations, both of the parts and of the whole (see Chapter 6). The two concepts of abduction and hermeneutic circle both describe how reasoning and interpretation are developed in a process that focuses on the relationship between the individual and the general, or the parts and the whole.

4 In deductive logic, the concept of necessity is used in the sense of logical necessity regarding the binding relation between premises and conclusions. In retroductive inference we speak of necessity in another sense, namely the necessary (transfactual) conditions for anything to exist and to be what it is.

5 By 'traditional experiment' we refer to methods where one is concerned with examining causal relationships between variables, by excluding or controlling other variables which might affect this relationship. These experiments are usually performed in some kind of customized laboratory situation, where the researcher can expose the objects of study to influencing factors while at the same time trying to control other factors, which might affect the outcome. This method is based on two fundamental assumptions (which we have problematized in Part I). First, that it is possible to study causal relationships in a closed system; second, that the causal mechanisms themselves are not changed by the experimental situation created by the researcher. When we speak of 'social experiments' below, we refer to something different to that, which we have decided to call 'traditional experiments', which should be evident from the text.

5 Theory in the methodology of social science

1 Morrow and Brown use the term 'empirical theory', which we consider a somewhat misleading term, since theory is something qualitatively different from empirical research. In our view, what they are referring to is better captured by the term 'descriptive theory'.

2 The essay from Merton's book that we will discuss here, however, had been published ten years earlier in his book *Social Theory and Social Structure*. The book by Glaser and Strauss can partly be seen as a reaction to the viewpoint argued for by Merton among others.

3 Merton's methodological argument is permeated with a notion that science expands cumulatively. If only we have a sufficient number of tested theories at a middle range, we may consecutively build up a more general knowledge of society. Merton also seems to mean that the disagreements, which are often pointed out when different all-inclusive theoretical perspectives are compared, are of little or no significance in a science devoted to developing and testing *middle-range* theories. This idea of cumulativity through empirical

decidability has been strongly questioned in the philosophy of science for some decades now. An important work in this respect was presented in 1970, three years after Merton's *On Theoretical Sociology*, when Thomas Kuhn's *The Structure of Scientific Revolutions* was published.

4 To Durkheim this is related to his conviction that sociology should study social facts. However, suicide only becomes a social fact when we define it not as an individual action but as a collective phenomenon – e.g. a certain suicidal frequency as being characteristic of a certain society. If we study Durkheim's way of reasoning about suicide and the mechanisms behind it, it seems doubtful that he sticks to what he defines as social facts.

5 In grounded theory, there is often talk about coding, conceptualizing and categorizing in turn, without clarifying the difference between these concepts. In many cases the terms seem to be used about the same thing. This is a problem, since in connection with method, coding often implies putting rather arbitrary labels (often figures) on different empirical categories (e.g. woman = 1, man = 2) to be able to bring together and work on data in an efficient way (usually with the help of computer programs). However, as we have shown before, conceptualizing is quite another matter. In some instances one may even see a tendency within GT to reduce conceptualizing to trivial coding and sorting of data.

6 Critical methodological pluralism

1 The terms 'intensive' and 'extensive' have been used to denote different methodological approaches in social science. The first discussion about such a division that we know of was conducted by Stevens (1946). However, Harré (1970) and Sayer (1992) are usually mentioned as those who have evolved this dichotomy. Van Meter (1994) suggests the terms 'ascending' and 'descending' methodology as alternatives to qualitative and quantitative. Those terms, however, lead one to think about induction and deduction, i.e. a traditional view of different types of method. We think the terms extensive and intensive better characterize the two approaches.

2 Popper, as well as the logical positivists, stresses the importance of keeping these two fields of the research process apart. Glaser and Strauss (1967) also emphasize this division and maintain that focus should lie on 'discovery'. This position is criticized by Kuhn and Feyerabend, who argue that it is impossible to separate them in practice; they are different components of one and the same research process.

3 This might give the impression of logical positivism as being a unitary current of theory, which is not the case. It encompasses many incompatible positions, e.g. the standpoint that observations can be made independently of theory versus that of theory dependency.

4 The person who coined the term 'covering-law model' was the American philosopher W. Dray, who was very critical of Hempel's argument.

5 This example alludes to the comedy by the Danish playwright Ludvig Holberg about the unhappy Jeppe, where we find this line: 'Everybody says that Jeppe drinks, but nobody asks why Jeppe drinks'.

Bibliography

Ahrne, Göran, Roman, Christine and Franzén, Mats (1996) *Det sociala landskapet. En sociologisk beskrivning av Sverige från 50-tal till 90-tal*, Göteborg: Korpen.
American Journal of Sociology (1995) vol. 100, no. 6.
Ang, Ien (1991) *Desperately Seeking the Audience*, London: Routledge.
Archer, Margaret (1989) *Culture and Agency*, Cambridge: Cambridge University Press.
——(1995) *Realist Social Theory: The Morphogenetic Approach*, Cambridge: Cambridge University Press.
Archer, Margaret, Bhaskar, Roy, Collier, Andrew, Lawson, Tony and Norrie, Alan (eds) (1998) *Critical Realism: Essential Readings*, London: Routledge.
Ariès, Philippe (1973) *Centuries of Childhood*, Harmondsworth: Penguin.
Asplund, Johan (1987) *Om hälsningsceremonier, mikromakt och asocial pratsamhet*, Göteborg: Korpen.
Bauman, Zygmunt (1989) *Modernity and the Holocaust*, Cambridge: Polity Press.
——(1993) *Postmodern Ethics*, Cambridge, MA: Blackwell.
Beck, Ulrich (1992) *Risk Society: Towards a New Modernity*, London: Sage.
Benhabib, Seyla (1992) *Situating the Self: Gender, Community and Postmodernism in Contemporary Society*, Cambridge: Polity Press.
Berger, Asa Arthur (1982) *Media Analysis Techniques*, London: Sage.
Bernstein, Richard J. (1986) *Philosophical Profiles: Essays in Pragmatic Mode*, Oxford: Blackwell.
Bertilsson, Margareta and Christiansen, Peder V. (1990) 'Introduktion', in M. Bertilsson, P. V. Christiansen and R. Mattz (eds) *Charles Sanders Peirce: Pragmatism och Kosmologi*, Göteborg: Daidalos.
Bhaskar, Roy (1978) *A Realist Theory of Science*, Hassocks: Harvester Press.
——(1986) *Scientific Realism and Human Emancipation*, London: Verso.
——(1989a) *The Possibility of Naturalism: A Philosophical Critique of the Contemporary Human Sciences*, Hassocks: Harvester Press.
——(1989b) *Reclaiming Reality: A Critical Introduction to Contemporary Philosophy*, London: Verso.
——(1991) *Philosophy and the Idea of Freedom*, Oxford: Blackwell.
——(1993) *Dialectic: The Pulse of Freedom*, London: Verso.
——(1994) *Plato etc.: The Problems of Philosophy and Their Resolution*, London: Verso.

Blalock, Hubert (1984) *Social Statistics*, London: McGraw-Hill.

Borup, Jerry H., Callego, Daniel T. and Heffernan, Pamela G. (1979) 'Relocation and its effect on mortality', *The Gerontologist*, 20: 468–79.

Brownmiller, Susan (1975) *Against Our Will: Men, Women and Rape*, New York: Simon and Schuster.

Bryant, Christopher (1995) *Practical Sociology: Post-empiricism and the Reconstruction of Theory and Application*, Cambridge MA: Blackwell.

Bunge, Mario (1993) 'Realism and antirealism in social science', *Theory and Decision*, 35: 207–35.

——(1979) *Causality and Modern Science*, New York: Dover.

Callinicos, Alex (1989) *Making History: Agency, Structure and Change in Social Theory*, Cambridge: Polity Press.

Camargo, O. and Preston, G. H. (1945) 'What happens to patients who are hospitalized for the first time over sixty-five years of age?', *American Journal of Psychiatry*, 102: 168–73.

Carleheden, Mikael (1996) *Det andra moderna. Om Jürgen Habermas och den samhällsteoretiska diskursen om det moderna*, Göteborg: Daidalos.

Collier, Andrew (1989) *Scientific Realism and Socialist Thought*, Hemel Hempstead: Harvester Wheatsheaf.

——(1994) *Critical Realism: An Introduction to Roy Bhaskar's Philosophy*, London: Verso.

Collins, Randall (1985) *Three Sociological Traditions*, New York: Oxford University Press.

——(1986) *Weberian Sociology*, Cambridge MA: Harvard University Press.

——(1988) *Theoretical Sociology*, Orlando: Harcourt Brace Jovanovich.

——(1990) 'Stratifications, emotional energy, and the transient emotions', in T. Kemper (ed.) *Research Agendas in the Sociology of Emotions*, New York: State University of New York Press.

Coniavitis, Thomas (1984) 'Metodologisk pluralism. Till kritiken av den existerande sociologin' (*Acta Universitatis Upsaliensis*, Studia Sociologica Upsaliensia 22), Uppsala: Uppsala Universitet.

Connell, Robert William (1987) *Gender and Power*, Cambridge: Polity Press.

Corson, David (1991) 'Bhaskar's critical realism and educational knowledge', *British Journal of Sociology of Education*, vol. 12, no 2.

Creswell, L.W. (1995) *Research Design: Qualitative and Quantitative Approaches*, Thousand Oaks: Sage.

Danermark, Berth and Ekström, Mats (1990) 'Relocation and health effects on the elderly: a commented research review', *Journal of Sociology and Social Welfare*, 1: 25–49.

Denzin, Norman (1989) *The Research Act: A Theoretical Introduction to Sociological Methods*, New Jersey: Prentice Hall.

——(1993) *Images of Postmodern Society: Social Theory and Contemporary Cinema*, London: Sage.

van Dijk, Teum (ed.) (1997) *Discourse as Social Interaction*, London: Sage.

Doreian, Patrick (1985) 'Mathematical models', in A. Kuper and J. Kuper (eds) *The Social Science Encyclopedia*, London: Routledge and Kegan Paul.

Durkheim, Emile (1979) *Suicide: A Study in Sociology*, London: Routledge and Kegan Paul.

Eco, Umberto (1984) *Semiotics and the Philosophy of Language*, London: Macmillan.

Ekecrantz, Jan and Olsson, Tom (1994) *Det redigerade samhället*, Stockholm: Carlssons.

Ekström, Mats (1992) 'Causal explanation of social action: the contribution of Max Weber and of critical realism to a generative view of causal explanation in social science', *Acta Sociologica*, 35: 107–22.

——(1993) 'Sociologiska förklaringar och variabelanalysens gränser: en kritisk analys med exempel från medicinsk sociologi', *Sociologisk Forskning*, no. 2.

——(1994) 'Residential relocation, urban renewal and the well-being of elderly people: towards a realist approach', thesis (*Acta Universitatis Upsaliensis*, Comprehensive Summaries of Uppsala Dissertations from the Faculty of Social Sciences 42), Uppsala: Uppsala Universitet.

Ekström, Mats and Danermark, Berth (1991) 'The study of power mechanisms: an interactive and generative approach to a case study of Swedish urban renewal', *Scandinavian Housing and Planning Research*, 8: 153–70.

Ekström, Mats and Nohrstedt, Stig Arne (1996) *Journalistikens etiska problem*, Stockholm: Rabén Prisma.

Elster, Jon (1989) *Nuts and Bolts for the Social Sciences*, Cambridge: Cambridge University Press.

Etzioni-Halevy, Eva (1985) *The Knowedge Elite and the Failure of Prophecy*, New York: Allen and Unwin.

Fairclough, Norman (1995) *Media Discourse*, New York: Edward Arnold.

Feyerabend, Paul (1993) *Against Method: Outline of an Anarchistic Theory of Knowledge*, London: Verso.

Flax, Jane (1990) *Thinking Fragments: Psychoanalysis, Feminism and Postmodernism in the Contemporary West*, Berkeley: University of California Press.

Føllesdal, Dagfinn, Walløe, Lars and Elster, Jon (1990) *Argumentationsteori, språk och vetenskapsfilosofi*, Stockholm: Thales.

Garfinkel, Harold (1967) *Studies in Ethnomethodology*, New Jersey: Prentice Hall.

Giddens, Anthony (1976) *New Rules in Sociological Methods*, London: Hutchinson.

——(1984) *The Constitution of Society: Outline of the Theory of Structuration*, Cambridge: Polity Press.

——(1990) *Consequences of Modernity*, Cambridge: Polity Press.

——(1991) *Modernity and Self-identity: Self and Society in the Late Modern Age*, Cambridge: Polity Press.

Gilje, Nils and Grimen, Harald (1992) *Samhällsvetenskapernas förutsättningar*, Göteborg: Daidalos.

Glaser, Barney (1978) *Theoretical Sensitivity*, Mill Valley: The Sociology Press.

Glaser, Barney and Strauss, Anselm (1967) *The Discovery of Grounded Theory: Strategies for Qualitative Research*, New York: Aldine.

Goffman, Erving (1990) *The Presentation of Self in Everyday Life*, London: Penguin.

Habermas, Jürgen (1972) *Knowledge and Human Interests*, Boston MA: Beacon Press.
——(1984) *The Theory of Communicative Action: Volume I*, Cambridge: Polity Press.
Harré, Rom (1970) *The Principles of Scientific Thinking*, London: Macmillan.
——(1979) *Social Being*, Oxford: Blackwell.
Hellevik, Ottar (1984) *Forskningsmetoder i sociologi och statsvetenskap*, Stockholm: Natur och Kultur.
Hempel, Carl Gustav (1965) *Aspects of Scientific Explanation*, New York: The Free Press/Macmillan.
Hempel, Carl Gustav and Oppenheim, Paul (1948) 'The logic of explanation', *Philosophy of Science*, 15: 135–75.
Heritage, John and Greatbatch, David (1991) 'On the institutional character of institutional talk: the case of news interviews', in D. Boden and D. H. Zimmerman (eds) *Talk and Social Structure*, Cambridge: Polity Press.
Hesse, Mary (1980) *Revolutions and Reconstructions in Philosophy of Science*, Brighton: Harvester Press.
Hindess, Barry and Hirst, Paul (1977) *Modes of Production and Social Formation*, London: Macmillan.
Howe, K. R. (1988) 'Against the qualitative–quantitative incompatibility thesis or dogmas die hard', *Educational Researcher*, 17: 10–16.
Hume, David (1966) [1748] *Philosophical Essays Concerning Human Understanding*, Oxford: Clarendon Press.
Jakobsen, Liselotte and Karlsson, Jan Ch. (1993) *Arbete och kärlek. En utveckling av livsformsanalys*, Lund: Arkiv.
——(1999) *Vardagsliv och risk: En livsformsanalys*, Karlstad: Räddningsverket.
Jensen, Klaus Bruhn (1991) 'Introduction: the qualitative turn', in K. B. Jensen and N. Jankowski (eds) *A Handbook of Qualitative Methodologies for Mass Communication Research*, London: Routledge.
——(1995) *The Social Semiotics of Mass Communication*, London: Sage.
Jensen, Klaus Bruhn and Jankowski, Nicholas (eds) (1991) *A Handbook of Qualitative Methodologies for Mass Communication Research*, London: Routledge.
Johansson, Ingvar (1984) 'Är Newtons mekanik ännu inte filosofiskt förstådd?', in S. Wellin (ed.) *Att förstå världen. Vetenskapsteoretiska essäer*, Lund: Doxa.
Jónasdóttir, Anna G. (1994) *Why Women Are Oppressed*, Philadelphia: Temple University Press.
Josephy, H. (1949) 'Analysis of mortality and causes of death in a mental hospital', *American Journal of Psychiatry*, 106: 185–9.
Kaplan, Abraham (1964) *The Conduct of Inquiry: Methodology for Behavioral Science*, San Francisco: Chandler.
Karlsson, Jan Ch. (1992) 'What can be learned in a humanities park?', in T. Stockfelt (ed.) *Lifelong Learning in Educating Cities*, Göteborg: 2nd International Congress of Educating Cities.
Keat, Russell and Urry, John (1978) *Social Theory as Science*, London: Routledge and Kegan Paul.
Kellner, Douglas (1995) *Media Culture*, London: Routledge.

Koestler, Arthur (1975) *The Act of Creation*, London: Picador.

Kuhn, Thomas (1970) *The Structure of Scientific Revolutions*, Chicago: University of Chicago Press.

Lawson, Tony (1997) *Economics and Reality*, London: Routledge.

Lawton, M. Powell (1977) 'The impact of the environment on aging and behavior', in J. E. Birren and W. K. Schaie (eds) *Handbook of the Psychology of Ageing*, New York: Van Nostrand Reinhold.

Layder, Derek (1993) *New Strategies in Social Research: An Introduction and Guide*, Cambridge: Polity Press.

——(1994) *Understanding Social Theory*, London: Sage.

——(1998) *Sociological Practice: Linking Theory and Social Research*, London: Sage.

Lazarus, Richard S. and Folkman, Susan (1984) *Stress, Appraisal, and Coping*, New York: Springer.

Liedman, Sven-Eric (1994) *Arbetsfördelning, självmord och nytta. Några blad ur samhällsvetenskapernas historia från Adam Smith till Milton Friedman* (Högskolan i Örebro, Skriftserie nr 8) Örebro University.

Lindqvist, Kent (1990) 'Vägen från socialismen', *Bokbox*, nr 101.

Livingstone, Sonia and Lunt, Peter (1994) *Talk on Television: Audience Participation and Public Debate*, London: Routledge.

Manicas, Peter T. (1987) *A History and Philosophy of the Social Sciences*, Oxford: Blackwell.

McCarthy, Thomas (1988) *The Critical Theory of Jürgen Habermas*, Cambridge MA: MIT Press.

Merriam, Sharan B. (1988) *Case Study Research in Education: A Qualitative Approach*, San Francisco: Jossey-Bass.

Merton, Robert (1957) *Social Theory and Social Structure*, New York: The Free Press.

——(1967) *On Theoretical Sociology: Five Essays, Old and New*, New York: The Free Press.

van Meter, Karl M. (1994) 'Sociological methodology', *International Social Science Journal*, 139: 15–25.

Morgan, Gareth (1986) *Images of Organization*, London: Sage.

Morris, Desmond (1994) *The Naked Ape: A Zoologist's Study of the Human Animal*, London: Vintage.

Morrow, Raymond and Brown, David (1994) *Critical Theory and Methodology*, London: Sage.

Mouzelis, Nicos (1995) *Sociological Theory: What Went Wrong? Diagnosis and Remedies*, London: Routledge.

Outhwaite, William (1987) *New Philosophies of the Social Sciences: Realism, Hermeneutics and Critical Theory*, London: Macmillan.

——(1994) *Habermas: A Critical Introduction*, Cambridge: Polity Press.

Owen, David (1995) *Nietzsche, Politics and Modernity: A Critique of Liberal Reason*, London: Sage.

Peirce, Charles (1932) *Collected Papers of Charles Sanders Peirce vol. 2*, eds C. Hartshorne and P. Weiss, Cambridge MA: Belknap Press.

——(1990) *Pragmatism och kosmologi*, Göteborg: Daidalos.

Popper, Karl (1959) [1935] *The Logic of Scientific Discovery*, London: Hutchinson.

——(1963) *Conjectures and Refutations: The Growth of Scientific Knowledge*, London: Routledge and Kegan Paul.

Potter, John (1996) *Representing Reality: Discourse, Rhetoric, and Social Construction*, London: Sage.

Prawitz, Dag (1991) *ABC i symbolisk logik. Logikens språk och grundbegrepp*, Stockholm: Thales.

Roman, Christine (1994) *Lika på olika villkor. Könssegregering i kunskapsföretag*, Stockholm: Symposion Graduale.

Rorty, Richard (1980) *Philosophy and the Mirror of Nature*, Princeton: Princeton University Press.

——(1989) *Contingency, Irony and Solidarity*, Cambridge: Cambridge University Press.

Rose, David and Sullivan, Oriel (1996) *Introducing Data Analysis for Social Scientists*, Buckingham: Open University Press.

Saussure, Ferdinand de (1966) *Course in General Linguistics*, New York: McGraw-Hill.

Sayer, Andrew (1989) 'The "new" regional geography and problems of narrative', *Society and Space*, 7: 253–76.

——(1992) *Method in Social Science: A Realist Approach*, London: Routledge.

——(1994) 'Alternatives and counterfactuals in critical social science', contribution to the thirteenth World Congress of Sociology, Bielefeld, July.

——(1997) 'Critical realism and the limits to social science', *Journal for the Theory of Social Behaviour*, 27: 473–88.

——(2000) *Realism and Social Science*, London: Sage.

Schlick, Moritz (1930) *Fragen der Ethik*, Vienna: Julius Springer.

Sève, Lucien (1975) *Marxism and the Theory of Human Personality*, London: Lawrence and Wishart.

Silverman, David (1993) *Interpreting Qualitative Data: Methods for Analysing Talk, Text and Interaction*, London: Sage

Smith, Dorothy (1987) *The Everyday World as Problematic: A Feminist Sociology*, Boston MA: Northwestern University Press.

Soper, Kate (1995) *What Is Nature?* Oxford: Blackwell.

Strauss, Anselm and Corbin, Juliet (1990) *Basics of Qualitative Research: Grounded Theory Procedures and Techniques*, London: Sage.

Tashakkori, Abbas and Teddlie, Charles (1998) *Mixed Methodology. Combining Qualitative and Quantitative Approaches*, Applied Social Research Methods Series, vol. 46, Thousand Oaks: Sage.

Therborn, Göran (1995) *European Modernity and Beyond: The Trajectory of European Societies 1945–2000*, London: Sage.

Toulmin, Stephen (1992) *Cosmopolis: The Hidden Agenda of Modernity*, Chicago: University of Chicago Press.

Tuchman, Gaye (1980) *Making News: A Study in the Construction of Reality*, New York: The Free Press.

Uggla, Bengt Kristensson (1994) *Kommunikation på bristningsgränsen*, Stockholm: Symposion.

Wallace, W. (1971) *The Logic of Science in Sociology*, New York: Aldine.

Weber, Max (1977) [1904] *Vetenskap och politik*, Göteborg: Korpen.

Whittier, J. R. and Williams, D. (1956) 'The coincidence and constancy of mortality figures for aged psychotic patients admitted to state hospital', *Journal of Nervous and Mental Disease*, 124: 618–20.

Zimmerman, Don H. and Boden, Deirdre (1991) 'Structure in action: an introduction', in D. Boden and D. H. Zimmerman (eds) *Talk and Social Structure*, Cambridge: Polity Press.

Ödman, Per-Johan (1979) *Tolkning, förståelse, vetande*, Stockholm: AWE/Gebers.

Index